Richard Koch is the author of *The 80/20 Principle*, which has sold more than a million copies, and been published in approximately forty languages. He is also a successful entrepreneur and investor whose ventures have included Filofax, Plymouth Gin, Belgo restaurants and Betfair, the world's largest betting exchange. He was formerly a partner of Bain & Company, and co-founder of LEK Consulting. He has written more than twenty acclaimed books on business and ideas.

Unreasonable Success

And How To Achieve It

Unlocking the Nine Secrets of
People Who Changed the World

RICHARD KOCH

PIATKUS

PIATKUS

First published in Great Britain in 2020 by Piatkus

9 10

Copyright © Richard Koch 2020
Illustrations © David Andrassy 2020

A CIP catalogue record for this book
is available from the British Library.

ISBN 978-0-349-42292-3

Typeset in Bembo by M Rules
Printed and bound in Great Britain by
Clays Ltd, Elcograf S.p.A.

Papers used by Piatkus are from well-managed forests
and other responsible sources.

Piatkus
An imprint of
Little, Brown Book Group
Carmelite House
50 Victoria Embankment
London EC4Y 0DZ

An Hachette UK Company
www.hachette.co.uk

*For Jamie R, Jamie S, John, Marx, Matthew, Nicholas
and Pedro, friends and principal co-conspirators on this book*

Contents

PART THREE:
LESSONS LEARNED – MY JOURNEY AND HOW YOU TOO CAN REACH UNREASONABLE SUCCESS

The future is a land of which there are no maps.

—A. J. P. TAYLOR

Man cannot create the current of events. He can only float with it and steer.

—OTTO VON BISMARCK

The people who are crazy enough to think they can change the world are the ones who do.

—Apple 'Think Different' commercial, 1997

unreasonable success n.

1. such success in changing the world, that it might seem unreasonable for any individual to have so much impact

2. success that is unexpected, and was not predicted when the individual was young or early in their career

3. success that goes well beyond what the individual's skills and performance seem to warrant

4. success based on leaps of intuition rather than on logic and reason

PART ONE

The Map of
Unreasonable Success

1

Can We Map Success?

In his dazzling book *Outliers*, Malcolm Gladwell presents a theory of outstanding success based around the early accumulation of skills – the famous '10,000 hours' – in developing new areas of expertise. This is how Bill Gates happened to gain vast experience of computer programming long before almost anyone else. He was able to do this not just because he was obsessed with the new field, but also because privileged access to computers at school gave him a head start over his peers. The Beatles were just a mediocre high-school band in 1960 – what transformed them was playing eight hours a day, seven days a week, in the strip clubs of Hamburg. 'We got better and got more confidence,' said John Lennon. 'We couldn't help it, with all the experience playing all night long.'[1]

And so on. Raw talent is one thing, but circumstances enable rapid accumulation of experience; without these particular circumstances we might never have heard of The Beatles.

The trouble with this theory is not that it is wrong for the people that Gladwell cites, but that there are many more cases of extraordinary success which don't fit the template of 'early accumulation of experience'. While I was rereading his book recently, the thought struck me – what if we *could* map success in a way that isolates the causes of their remarkable success for almost any high achiever?

Would it be possible to construct a map of success that works for almost any eminent person in any field, at any time? Something that applies to Leonardo da Vinci, Marie Curie and Albert Einstein, Bob Dylan and Madonna, Helena Rubinstein and Steve Jobs, Paul of Tarsus and Otto von Bismarck, John Maynard Keynes and Jeff Bezos, J. K. Rowling and Walt Disney, and even to Vladimir Lenin, Winston Churchill, Margaret Thatcher and Nelson Mandela?

Preposterous.

But this is where the idea of a map comes in. Any individual's life contains countless unique particularities. Everyone's story is different. But underneath the blur of local circumstances and personal idiosyncrasies, is there a common map that successful people followed which shows the way forward? It took me a long time to find it, but I think it exists.

I started with around fifty possible 'landmarks' – experiences or reasons for success – for the map, and then tried them out one by one on a small number of cases of high achievers whose life stories I knew intimately. If the explanation didn't work in nearly all cases, I discarded it.

I was surprised to find – although in retrospect I should have expected this – that there were a few landmarks which were so powerful that they were almost universally present. But they were not all present from the start, nor were they mainly to do with the inherent personal characteristics of the successful people. Anyone who has studied history knows well that the way individuals react to the strange, unexpected crosscurrents of events in their life greatly affects success or failure.

Successful people typically don't plan their success. Instead they develop a unique philosophy or attitude that works for them. They stumble across strategies which are short-cuts to success, and latch onto them. Events hand them opportunities they could not have anticipated. Often their peers with equal or greater talent fail while they succeed. It is too easy to attribute success to inherent, unstoppable genius. Usually this is an illusion; sometimes, a travesty of the truth.

So what excites me is this: if we can construct a useful map of success – one that is based on a theory and structure and can be tested historically – it becomes possible for *anyone* to see the processes and events they need to go through if they want unreasonable success. If we wish to emulate such success, we should try to acquire the few indispensable conditions for it, and become aware of the experiences or circumstances which can propel us to high fortune. Some of these experiences can be deliberately acquired, but others are a matter of reacting the right – but entirely specific and predictable – way to events, taking charge of them as they unfold.

What is success? What is unreasonable success?

The dimensions of success are legion – for example, creating great art or music or a revolutionary new business, changing the course of local or world history, discovering and demonstrating an important scientific or spiritual truth, relieving poverty or suffering – and perhaps the least important of all, unless used for a great philanthropic purpose: making a fortune.

Success is also a continuum – you don't have to become rich or a household name to be successful, and there are degrees of success. I define success as achieving something you regard as worthwhile – as getting to a destination which makes you feel proud and fulfilled. By this criterion, everyone can set out on the hike towards success and navigate intelligently to stand the best chance of reaching it.

But what is *unreasonable success*? I define it by four characteristics:

- It is a very high degree of success in changing the world the way an individual wants to, so that it might seem remarkable or even unreasonable for one person to have such impact.
- It goes well beyond what their skills and performance seem to warrant.
- It is unreasonable in the sense that the person's success appears to stem not so much from the use of logic and reason as from inexplicable leaps of intuition. What unreasonably successful people do happens to mesh well with the strange ways the world works – the people in this book were successful not so much because they were fabulously talented or productive, but because their approach produced astounding results. Their extraordinary success is not entirely 'deserved' in a conventional sense; they win by a fortuitous combination of experiences, personal characteristics and judgement which leverages their actions enormously, giving enormous impact for a mere mortal.
- Unreasonable success has an element of surprise, out of all proportion to what would have been predicted from the person when they were young, or, sometimes, well into their career. Failure, whether early or late, is often the precursor to unreasonable success.

Though unreasonable success can seem arbitrary, it means that there is hope for us all. Who could have predicted that Nelson Mandela, a once-obscure lawyer, could have averted the feared bloodbath in South Africa and reconciled South Africans of all heritages to each other while establishing a viable democracy? Or that Helena Rubinstein, a young woman growing up in the grotty ghetto of Kraków, Poland, could have changed the face of beauty throughout the world? Or that the illegitimate son of a notary would become one of the world's greatest painters, known universally by his first name, Leonardo? I could go on and on, because nearly all the famous people in this book came from nowhere, and they are coming still – there are many people around us who are still unknown and who will make their mark on the world's richness and diversity, to the astonishment and delight of those who knew them when they were apparently insignificant or down on their luck.

Yet, if success is a continuum, it is also 'fractal'. Fractal means that the pattern is endlessly varied but endlessly similar; the small scale is a miniature version of the big scale. Coastlines are fractal – every coastline in the world has similarities, with bays, inlets, and twists and turns which are unpredictable unless you know the terrain or have a map. But so are careers – they all have squiggly lines up and down, periods of success and failure, of wrong turns and unexpected paths to glory, of alternating euphoria and exhaustion. Every girl or boy in the playground or the classroom experiences the same kind of snakes and ladders as the greatest musicians, artists, scientists or world leaders; but while the scale of the map is different, the landmarks and the process of putting one foot in front of the other are the same.

Human nature, too, is the same. The way the universe treats you can be terrific or terrible but is always subject to reversals of fortune. This book exists to reveal the few universal landmarks we can look out for to help us on the way.

It's now time to unfurl the map of success. Soon you can start your journey towards a new, unreasonably successful future.

2

The Map Unfurled

The map has nine landmarks, places to be visited. Each landmark is either an attribute of the players – my word for the twenty individuals who are central to this book – or one or more life-changing experiences they had, a platform they created or chanced upon to propel them forward, or a state of mind which enabled them to make progress even in tough terrain.

As we will see in Part Two, the heart of this book, our players 'visited' most or all nine landmarks. This was not because of genius, calculation or sure-footedness on their part. Rather, they turned out to be successful because they were fortunate enough to have the attitudes, experiences and strategies that lead to success. They visited the landmarks without knowing that they were situated on the map to fame or fortune. In some cases, they were just plain lucky to run into the landmarks. In others, they had the character or inclination that led them to do the right thing. And, of course, they did not have the advantage you'll soon possess of having access to this map!

In the nineteenth century, the historian-philosopher Thomas

Carlyle claimed that there are certain 'great men' who would have stamped their greatness on history regardless of circumstances. I see the evidence differently. Accidents of history and tiny localised incidents decide who will be elevated to greatness. For example, Steve Jobs only glimpsed the future of computing through a chance visit to the Xerox PARC research lab in 1979. As we shall see, Margaret Thatcher owed her success largely to the fascist dictator of Argentina, General Leopoldo Galtieri, and her response to his invasion of the Falkland Islands on 2 April 1982.

Life's caprice limits our ability to plan the future. This may sound discouraging, but there's another way of looking at it. If we understand how success and failure are meted out, and if we adjust our minds to be alert to impending failure or absent opportunities, we can greatly improve our chances.

The landmarks fall into two broad categories – 'attitude' and 'strategy'. 'Attitude' encompasses the main psychological characteristics likely to facilitate unreasonable success. These characteristics are not immutable. The players can and did adjust some of their attitudes in the quest for great results.

'Strategy' comprises the experiences, personal philosophies and objectives pursued by the players, as well as the assistance they contrived to garner from their own organisations and collaborators.

One of the most exciting and encouraging findings of this book is that the way we position ourselves for success is far more important than our talent or competence. Improving our performance is far less likely to produce the results we want than having the appropriate attitudes and strategies.

Here are three quick examples of the power of the landmarks.

The first landmark is **self-belief**. If we don't have strong self-belief, it's almost impossible to become unreasonably successful. But by tracing how self-belief developed for our players, we can work out how to acquire it. Remember that Steve Jobs only fully believed in himself and his team when they had cracked the problem the Xerox boffins failed to solve: how to build a really simple and cheap personal computer. Margaret Thatcher only became confident that she could 'save' Britain and able to do so after her dicey triumph in the Falklands. There are multiple sources of ineradicable self-belief, but you must realise how vital it is for your success, and look out for events which will fully create or cement that self-belief.

Another landmark is **transforming experiences**. Our players typically had one or two such experiences, and without them would not have achieved success and notoriety. If you know this, and have not had such an experience, it becomes important to engineer one.

One breakthrough achievement is another landmark. Our players mostly had *one* achievement which changed the world around them, propelling them to high fortune. Not several achievements; just one. If you know that, you must decide what your breakthrough achievement is, or could be, and how to hone it. Knowing you only need one such achievement – and the type of achievement that can work wonders – saves a lot of time, effort and frustration.

In Part Three, to make the journey come alive, I'll relate how I encountered each landmark, and the lessons I learned en route. I'll then invite you to draw your own map.

A word of warning: nobody can guarantee high achievement. The odds are always against huge success. Only a fool would dare to say how it might happen.

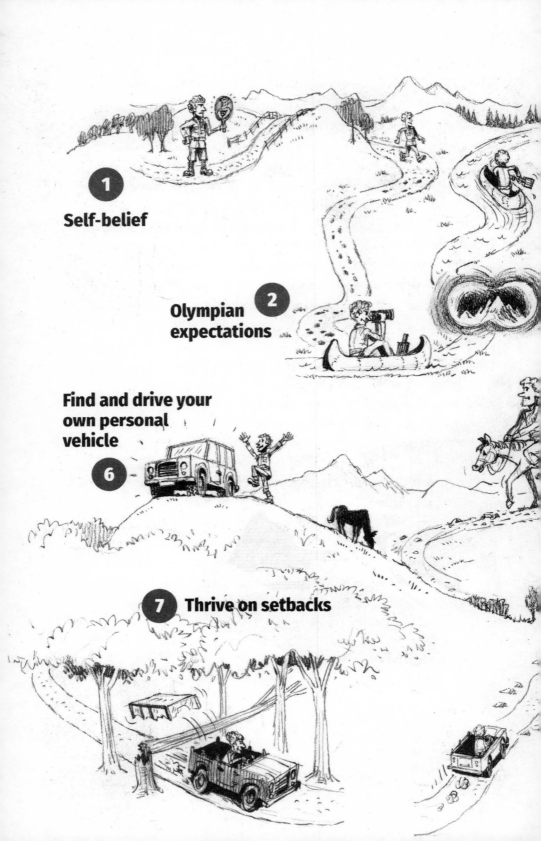

3

The Players

We are about to go through the landmarks, one by one. But before that I'll list the players central to the book. They will crop up intermittently in the landmark chapters in Part Two, to illustrate how the landmarks can be 'visited' and so set us on the right path for quite unreasonable success.

Bill Bain (30 July 1937–16 January 2018)

You may not have heard of Bill Bain, so why is he here? Simple: he was one of my two great mentors and, along with Bruce Henderson, changed the way global business is conducted. He founded Bain & Company in 1973, now one of the top three consulting firms in the world, with fifty-six offices worldwide and revenues of $4.5bn, and Bain Capital in 1984, one of the most successful alternative investment firms in the world with assets

under management of $90bn. Through the example of these and then of other private equity firms, business leaders were strongly influenced by the 'strategy paradigm' – the virtues of dominant market share, global scale, continually lower costs and prices, and product innovation.

Jeff Bezos (b. 12 January 1964)

Adopted son of a circus performer, Bezos has been fiercely competitive since he was a young man. He wanted to make a pile of money, and he is now the richest person in the world, with a net worth of $111 billion at the time of writing.[1] He realised the potential of the internet very early and developed a plan for an electronic 'everything store' marked by unbeatable prices and aiming to become 'Earth's most customer-centric company'. Uncompromising, nerdish and dictatorial, the high priest of Amazon has always done what he set out to do. He also has the supreme virtue of unreasonable luck.

Otto von Bismarck (1 April 1815– 30 July 1898)

He was the most successful European statesman of the nineteenth century. As Chancellor of Prussia, he defeated Austria and France, and founded the German Empire. He was a remarkable politician who remained supremely powerful for twenty-seven years. He combined iron strategic objectives with extreme tactical flexibility.

His strategy – which I have copied – was to wait patiently until events played into his hands, and then pounce decisively. A great person to mimic for unreasonable success in any field.

Winston Churchill (30 November 1874–24 January 1965)

Statesman, army adventurer in his youth, the most unlikely British prime minister to emerge in the desperate days of 1940, champion alcohol consumer ('I have taken more out of alcohol than it has taken out of me'), but famous above all for one thing – being the only person on the planet able to take on Adolf Hitler, rallying the British through incomparably confident defiance and uplifting words. He was a dreadful failure through almost all his career, but his example provides the best evidence that ludicrous belief in destiny, the ability to inspire followers and the adoption of a bold strategy can matter more than competence – or anything else.

Marie Curie (7 November 1867– 4 July 1934)

Born in Warsaw, Poland, under oppressive Russian rule, Curie overcame poverty, discrimination and repeated misfortunes to become the first woman to win a Nobel prize, and the only woman to win two Nobel prizes, one for physics and one for chemistry. Barred from university in Poland, she worked for three years as a governess to save money, before going to

Paris and studying physics at the Sorbonne. She graduated first in her class in 1893. The following year she fell in love with Pierre Curie, a professor at the School of Physics and Chemistry, and they married in 1895. She conducted original research in the hot new area of x-rays and radioactivity, a word she coined. In July 1898 Marie and Pierre announced the existence of a new element, polonium, which was 330 times more radioactive than uranium, previously thought to be the only mineral to generate radiation. In December 1898 they announced the discovery of a second new element, radium, which was 900 times more active than uranium. In 1903 Pierre Curie demonstrated that radium could cure growths, tumours and certain types of cancer. In 1914, Marie Curie set up the Radium Institute, and during the First World War she operated a fleet of mobile units to x-ray wounded soldiers, helping to save an estimated million lives. She died in 1934 as a result of prolonged exposure to radiation.

Leonardo da Vinci (15 April 1452–2 May 1519)

The epitome of a Renaissance man – thinker, artist, sculptor, scientist and engineer, most noted for his incomparable paintings, anatomical sketches and drawings of imaginary devices such as the helicopter, parachute and tank. The illegitimate son of a notary, he had virtually no formal education. At the age of fourteen he became apprenticed to the artist and engineer Andrea del Verrocchio, who ran one of the foremost workshops in Florence: a hub of the arts, crafts, technology and commerce. Friendly and gentle, beautiful, graceful and strong as a young man, and homosexual, da

Vinci was said to be good company but also dark and troubled at times with hints of a manic-depressive streak, when he would retreat into introspection in his notebooks. A perfectionist who painted relatively few paintings, he constantly revised them, leaving many unfinished. He was an acute observer of nature, but he also, as he said, imagined 'infinite things that nature never created'.[2]

Walt Disney (5 December 1901–15 December 1966)

A pioneer of anthropomorphic cartoons, and the creator of Mickey Mouse, Donald Duck, Dumbo, Bambi and many other characters that have entered the world's psyche. He was the most successful movie producer ever by number of Academy Awards, and the creator of Disneyland and its successors: a type of perfect, sanitised, controlled and wholesome amusement park which appealed to all ages and struck deep into the consciousness of what American community life could be at its best. He was also the only film magnate to make a seamless transition to television. Disney has been hailed as an incredibly imaginative, fun-seeking, and, in later years, avuncular figure.

Bob Dylan (b. 24 May 1941)

Legendary singer-songwriter and poet Bob Dylan arrived in New York City as an unknown and unaccountably self-confident teenage folk singer, started writing his own material, and obtained a recording contract with Colombia Records despite his inability to sing. He became 'the voice of a generation' with political songs such as *Blowin' in the Wind*, but refused to be pigeon-holed and explored many different genres of American music, confounding and confronting his fans. A supreme wordsmith, he pursued his own trail with enchanting arrogance over many decades, exerting influence well beyond his relatively modest record sales. A conservative in radical's clothing.

Albert Einstein (14 March 1879–18 April 1955)

German, Swiss, and later American physicist who, with little academic background or support, formulated the theory of relativity, which along with quantum mechanics (on which relativity was partly based) revolutionised physics and led to nuclear power, nuclear bombs and many other inventions. An amiable loner who made his breakthroughs from imagination and thought experiments, not from intensive data-mining or practical experiments, his academic record was mediocre and he was relatively weak in mathematics. It didn't matter – his intuition and insight into the nature of the universe were unparalleled. He believed in an impersonal deity who ordered a rational world and planted secrets for scientists to comprehend. In later life this belief could not explain the weird world he himself had helped uncover.

Viktor Frankl (26 March 1905–2 September 1997)

He was a doctor, psychotherapist and concentration camp survivor who developed the 'third wave' of psychology after Freud and Adler. He held that everyone is in search of personal meaning, and that mental health and a happy life were impossible without finding this. Frankl was immensely influential and the first of the existential philosophers who insisted on free will – even in a concentration camp.

Bruce Henderson (30 April 1915–20 July 1992)

 He was a brilliant thinker who shifted savvy corporate chiefs from short-term profit maximisation to dominating markets and therefore eventual cash maximisation. Fired for increasing cantankerousness at Westinghouse and then at Arthur D. Little, he started what became the Boston Consulting Group in 1963 with, as he often said, 'one room, a desk, no telephone, and no secretary'.[3] He invented the virgin territory of 'strategy consulting', a beautiful blend of marketing and financial theory, distilled into a simple, practical chart – the 'Boston box' of cows, dogs, question marks and, most valuable of all, stars. He insisted that having a higher market share and accumulated experience in a tightly defined market would lead to lower costs than competitors and to their discomfort – and also to long-term cash flow. He hired great young people, mainly from top business schools, and constantly challenged

them, motivating them with icy complaints based on irrefutable logic. 'Few people,' said *The Financial Times* of Henderson, 'have had as much impact on international business in the second half of the twentieth century.'[4]

Steve Jobs (24 February 1955–5 October 2011)

Perhaps the most important product creator of the late twentieth and early twenty-first centuries, Jobs was the inventor of the Mac personal computer, iTunes, iPad, iPhone and many other incredible digital devices. He was a romantic and self-obsessed drop-out whose self-belief and totally unreasonable demands on colleagues moved mountains. His technical skills were weak but his artistic flair, imagination and ability to mesmerise and inspire followers who were stronger than him in many respects was unparalleled. He bullied his brilliant teams and his drive for product perfection and simplicity inspired them to do the impossible.

John Maynard Keynes (5 June 1883–21 April 1946)

The high priest of twentieth-century economics, he provided a route to salvation during the Great Depression of the 1930s, avoiding the rock of unconstrained capitalism and the hard place of dictatorship. A voracious and predatory gay man who married and became devoted to a Russian ballerina, he managed to maintain a delicate balance between bohemian decadence and being a highly respected and fully paid-up member of the British ruling class. One of the greatest intellectual and practical influences on the twentieth century.

Vladimir Ilyich Lenin (22 April 1870–21 January 1924)

Born Vladimir Ilyich Ulyanov, he was the inventor of practical communism. He led the coup of 25 October 1917, crushing the incipient democracy in Russia and turning the old ramshackle tsarist tyranny into an efficient and more terrible one. He invented the one-party state and death camps for dissidents and 'enemies of the people', which Hitler emulated.

Madonna (b. 16 August 1958)

By the age of twenty-six, Madonna had sold a million records. Singer, songwriter, film star, video and record producer, model, fashion merchandiser, author and businesswoman, Madonna's career in her sixties continues unabated, buoyed up by a constant stream of publicity and controversy. Her talents may be ordinary, but she knows her audience, and the results she has achieved are quite extraordinary – unreasonable success indeed.

Nelson Mandela (18 July 1918–5 December 2013)

Influenced more by Methodism than Marxism, the saintly terrorist's greatest achievement emerged after he was imprisoned on Robben Island, off Cape Town. Mandela in jail became the *de facto* leader of the African National Congress (ANC), and the more intelligent leaders of the apartheid regime came to believe that Mandela could be trusted to deliver a deal – democracy in South Africa in return for ensuring no subsequent bloodbath of the former white oppressors. It worked under Mandela, the first black president, from 1994 to 1999.

J. K. Rowling (b. 31 July 1965)

Joanne Rowling is world-famous as the creator of the schoolboy wizard Harry Potter. Born in Gloucestershire, England, she studied French and classics at the University of Exeter, before moving to work as a secretary in London. In June 1990, stuck on a broken-down train for four hours, she saw in her mind's eye a scrawny, black-haired boy with round spectacles who didn't know he was a wizard until he travelled on a train to a school for wizards. She felt herself receiving a kind of 'download' of his character and story. She was tremendously excited and started writing the boy's story that evening, but it took her seven years of hardship and intermittent labour to write the first Harry Potter book and have it published. In 1991 she moved to Porto, Portugal, to teach English. She married a local man; they had a baby, Jessica, but soon separated acrimoniously. In 1993 she left Portugal for Edinburgh, where she lived on government benefits and a little secretarial work. She finished *Harry Potter and the Philosopher's Stone* in 1995, and after another two years it was published, the first of seven such books. Harry Potter fired the imagination of children throughout the world, making Rowling Britain's highest-earning woman. She has sold over 500 million books, and Hollywood film rights and other income have taken her lifetime earnings to an estimated £1.2 billion.[5] The image of J. K. Rowling struggling to write her story longhand in Edinburgh cafés, nursing both her infant daughter and a single coffee for hours, has become the stuff of legend, and an inspiration to aspiring authors everywhere.

Helena Rubinstein (25 December 1872–1 April 1965)

Born in the Jewish quarter of Kraków, Poland, Rubinstein left home when her mother wanted to marry her off. When she was twenty-four she emigrated to Australia. Five years later she became a waitress in Melbourne, where she made friends with four customers, and, under their guidance, opened a beauty salon to sell her proprietary face cream. She invented the modern female beauty industry, transforming herself into the rich 'Madame' she had always dreamed of becoming. An early and fanciful marketer, she was one of the most commercial and innovative entrepreneurs of the time, building a large, highly profitable global empire.

Paul of Tarsus, c.AD 5–67

Both a committed Jew and a Roman citizen, Paul appreciated Hellenic culture and wrote forceful and elegant Greek. Paul's life was turned upside down around AD 33 by a vision of the Living Christ, in which he heard 'unspeakable words', saw the mysteries of the universe, and was called, he believed, to spread the good news of Jesus to 'the Gentiles' (non-Jews) throughout the Roman world. After years of reflection, and fuelled by the power of Jesus within him, Paul emerged throughout Roman cities in Europe and the near East as a missionary-exorcist-healer-magician. Without Paul, what eventually emerged as Christianity would neither have achieved lift-off, nor transcended its Jewish roots. Paul's exotic yet sublimely romantic and liberating vision largely defined early Christianity – thrusting Jesus, God and mankind into a new light.

Margaret Thatcher (13 October 1925–8 April 2013)

Thatcher smashed the mould of British politics, as the first woman to challenge for the leadership of a major political party, and to win; the first to become prime minister; the longest-serving prime minister of the twentieth century; the first British leader since Churchill to seek to avert national decline and to win a war, and to be universally known by their first name (or a diminutive thereof); the first prime minister ever to take on the miners and win, and the first in the twentieth century to win three consecutive elections. She was also the first prime minister to be deposed by her party without losing an election. The so-called Iron Lady was in fact a mass of contradictions, and only became transformed, and started her breakthrough achievement, three years after she became premier. Were it not for this breakthrough, and for her extraordinary bravery and willingness to gamble at long odds, she would have gone down in history as one of the most inglorious, intellectually challenged, and weak prime ministers. Unreasonably successful? Almost the defining case.

PART TWO

The Secret Map

4

Landmark 1: Self-belief

Of course I am an egotist. What do you get if you aren't?

—WINSTON CHURCHILL

Magic is believing in yourself. If you can do that, you can make anything happen.

—JOHANN WOLFGANG VON GOETHE

What is self-belief?

The essential starting-point for success — the first landmark — is self-belief. All our case studies of great success manifested — sooner or later — a firm base of self-belief.

Self-belief is the courage to get going on your quest for unreasonable success. Self-belief means starting the journey, conjuring up the confidence that you will find your way to success, even if you don't yet know the route or the destination.

Self-belief can start — as it did in about half the people I studied — with a vague general belief in their 'star' or destiny. This sense was emotional and not rational – many of the people in this book felt it early in life, before they could have any reasonable basis for that belief.

Winston Churchill: Self-belief from heritage

Sometimes unthinking confidence in one's future seems to have been encouraged by the achievements of parents, or even distant forebears. It is most obvious in the case of Winston Churchill, who was always conscious of his lineage – not just aristocratic, but as a scion of the Duke of Marlborough, one of highest nobles in England. How important was this in the mind of young Winston? We cannot tell. His distinguished biographer Roy Jenkins assures us that Churchill's 'devotion to his career and his conviction that he was a man of destiny were far stronger than any class or tribal loyalty'.[1] Maybe so, but his provenance was probably not insignificant in incubating that sense of destiny.

Consider Churchill's upbringing. His father, Lord Randolph Churchill, was a prominent – if somewhat dissident – member of the late-Victorian Tory establishment, and Chancellor of the Exchequer. When he was 19, Winston met most of the leading statesmen of the day in the comfort of his home, where he was treated by them as an equal. Churchill's autobiography, *My Early Life*, is itself a testament to his belief in his own destiny. It was written in 1930, ten years before he became prime minister – very few people at that time wrote an autobiography before their life had matured. In it he wrote that when he was in his late teens, 'politics seemed very important and vivid to my eyes in those days'. In 1893 alone, he met three future prime ministers across the table at lunch or dinner.[2]

We can trace the gradual unfolding of Churchill's self-belief, which he reveals with great charm in his autobiography. In terms that could just as well apply to you or me, he tells how he was placed in the lowest class in his school, yet he saw this as an advantage. Unlike the brightest pupils, who were taught Latin and Greek, the rest were taught English. Churchill had an inspirational teacher, and, he said, 'thus I got into my bones the essential structure of the ordinary English sentence – which is a noble thing'.[3]

His early success with English at school seems to have given him enormous self-confidence for a 'dunce'. He won a prize for faultlessly reciting from memory twelve hundred lines of an epic poem. Later, his great speeches were delivered without notes, as Churchill had memorised every line.

When he was just sixteen, he told a friend that he foresaw a future world of war in which Churchill would come to the rescue when London was attacked – 'in the high position I shall occupy, it will fall to me to save the capital'.[4]

He did not go to university, and took three tries to pass into Sandhurst, the military academy. Afterwards, he enjoyed 'great fun' in the army. In the Boer War (1899–1902) he was captured by the Boers in South Africa. He escaped – a long saga which he turned into a massive money-spinner, recounting his adventures to full houses in England and America.

Churchill, however, is not the sole example of boundless inborn self-confidence. That of a British economist had huge results, helping to lift the world out of the worst economic trauma of the twentieth century.

John Maynard Keynes: The economist as priest and saviour

Today we think we live in a democracy, yet we have quasi-hereditary presidents, prime ministers, politicians, writers, broadcasters and even pop stars, whose self-belief often flows from familial osmosis. One interesting case is that of John

Maynard Keynes, the economist, whose father, Cambridge economics professor John Neville Keynes, clearly gave his son a head start. Maynard Keynes was one of the great figures of the twentieth century, whose unorthodox ideas provided an escape route from the Great Depression of the 1930s, showing how to ensure there was no repetition of that terrible event.

For whatever reason, the young Maynard Keynes was an exceptional believer in his own capabilities. His biographer, Robert Skidelsky, said: 'Keynes' life as it unfolded was continuing confirmation to him of his supreme talent . . . He had every reason to be colossally confident, and so he was.'[5]

Skidelsky also tells us that this self-belief was already evident when Keynes was a teenager. He thought of himself as a member of the ruling class, just as Churchill did. This class-based confidence, says Skidelsky, began to disintegrate after the First World War. In the age of democracy, self-belief, while now open to everyone, may paradoxically be more elusive for anyone. There is nothing more conducive to self-belief than belonging to a homogeneous elite. Yet self-belief can also arise from having a parent, as Keynes did, or another mentor, as an example of how to succeed.

Bob Dylan: The believer who selects his own mentor

For seventeen of our twenty players, heritage and background are irrelevant to their self-belief.* Instead, it comes randomly yet naturally, often as soon as the individual begins their career. Consider Bob Dylan. By all accounts, as soon as he arrived in New York in midwinter 1961 as an unknown but aspiring teenage folk singer, he oozed self-assurance. Later, in his brilliant but unreliable memoir, Dylan was categorical:

---

* The exceptions are Churchill, Keynes and Bismarck.

Outside of Mills Tavern the thermometer was creeping up to about ten below. My breath froze in the air, but I didn't feel the cold. I was heading for the fantastic lights. No doubt about it ... I'd come from a long ways off and had started from a long ways down. But destiny was about to manifest itself. I felt it was looking right at me and nobody else.[6]

Against all odds, including the limitations of his own voice, after being turned down by every folk label, Dylan managed to land a recording contract with blue-chip Colombia Records. His eponymous first album wasn't very good and it didn't sell, but Dylan's self-belief never faltered. As Ian Bell, Dylan's biographer, says:

His ambition is vast, amplifying what small talent he may seem to possess in 1961 and '62.[7]

What becomes obvious, through all the anecdotes, all the Dylan half-truths and misremembered facts, is that he began to live within his head at any early age. Something drew him and something spooked him. He was alienated from his parents ... for no reason that is obvious or clear. He was drawn to music with an intensity that spoke of need.[8]

Dylan was a romancer, a dreamer, a poet, someone who found his very soul deep inside the different musical traditions of America. This came through not so much in his singing but in his songwriting; his profound but ambiguous connections with American history, music, and politics; and above all through his *act*, where his personality was his performance and his performance was his personality – by turns wistful, truculent, and acidly perceptive.

Dylan knew all this from an early age. 'There were a lot of better singers and better musicians around these places,' he wrote in *Chronicles*, 'but there wasn't anybody close in nature to what I was doing. Folk songs were the way I explored the universe, they were pictures and the pictures were worth more than anything I could say. I knew the inner substance of the thing. I could easily connect the pieces.'[9]

Even with this degree of internal certainty, bordering on the Messianic and delusional, a role model was important. Dylan believed he should follow in the footsteps of the folk singer-songwriter Woody Guthrie – and had the *chutzpah* to seek him out in his bed in New Jersey's Greystone Park Hospital, where Guthrie was in the painful throes of Huntington's chorea, a terrible terminal disease. Dylan sang Guthrie's songs to Guthrie 'because he knew two hundred of them'. As if by the laying on of hands, Dylan assumed Guthrie's unique status as a singer–songwriter – at the time a very unusual combination, because most folk singers sang the traditional folk canon and did not presume to enlarge it – who created himself as a philosopher-cum-protest phenomenon.[10] Dylan's *Song to Woody* is one of only two original tracks on his debut album, but before long his recordings become almost exclusively his own compositions.

Whether Guthrie was aware that he was Dylan's mentor is unclear, but curiously irrelevant. Today we tend to think of a mentor relationship as something well-defined and almost contractual. This may be too precise. It may be better to define a mentor as someone who has a deep impact on one's life and served as either a role model or an instructor – whether the mentor was fully, partly or not at all aware of their influence on us. What we might call a 'fantasy mentor' can be more useful – and certainly easier to arrange – than a real one.

The legendary investor and currently the fourth-richest person in the world, Warren Buffett, had the British-born investor Benjamin Graham as his original mentor. Lenin had the writings of the late Karl Marx to inspire him to make revolution in Russia.

Bruce Henderson, the founder of the Boston Consulting Group, and Bill Bain, founder of Bain & Company, were my mentors, though neither spent much time with me, nor knew their importance to me. So, select a mentor much as Bob Dylan did, by conscious choice and without necessarily asking their permission. The most important thing a mentor can do is to galvanise and infuse us with their spirit, so that our self-belief is enhanced and focused on what similar or greater ends we can attain. A mentor can do all this without knowing us at all.

Albert Einstein: No scientific background, no mentors, just curiosity

In yet other cases – such as Paul of Tarsus, Marie Curie, Leonardo, Einstein, Bruce Henderson, Steve Jobs, Bill Bain, Bismarck, Walt Disney, J. K. Rowling and Helena Rubinstein – there seems to have been no important role model, whether familial or otherwise; and yet, a clear sense of self-belief emerged anyway, often when young.

The case of Albert Einstein is fascinating and encouraging. Neither his mother's nor his father's family histories boasted any academic or other worldly distinction – they were Jewish tradesmen and peddlers making a modest living in rural southwest Germany. His father and uncle were small businessmen.

Albert was slow to learn to talk; the family's maid called him 'the dopey one', and they thought he might be backward. His grades at school up to the age of sixteen were poor – he resented being told to learn by rote and was quietly rebellious. He failed to make it into the Zurich Polytechnic – which was not even the most prestigious school in the city – when he took the entrance exams at the age of sixteen. Although never boastful, even at this age Einstein had total belief in his future as a scientist. He was relentlessly curious about the universe, imagining what it would be like to ride along a light beam. A year later, after moving to a more progressive school, which encouraged students to learn independently, he retook the entrance exams. Asked his 'plans for the future', he wrote:

> If I am lucky and pass my exams, I will enrol in the Zurich Polytechnic. I will stay there four years to study mathematics and physics. I suppose I will become a teacher in these fields of science . . .
>
> Here are the reasons that have led me to this plan. They are, most of all, my personal talent for abstract and mathematical thinking . . . This is quite natural; everyone desires to do that for which he has a talent.[11]

Here we can see Einstein's self-belief shining through; he was admitted to the Polytechnic. Nevertheless, he graduated close to the bottom of his cohort.

Four years later, having failed to find a permanent teaching job, he became a substitute teacher, and then had to settle for a low-paid job evaluating inventions in the Swiss patent office at Bern. Still, he was able to complete his duties there in two or three hours each day, spending the rest of the day utterly engrossed in the new ideas in physics which would lead to the topsy-turvy revolution of quantum mechanics. He fell in love, and when he was told that Mileva Maric, his partner (who was also a student of physics) had become pregnant with his child, he wrote to her at once. Instead of starting with the news of the conception, he said how happy he was because:

> I have just read a wonderful paper by Lenard on the generation of cathode rays by ultra-violet light. Under the influence

of this beautiful piece I am filled with such happiness and joy that I must share some of it with you.

Only then did Einstein make a brief reference to their impending parenthood.[12]

Though Einstein was head-over-heels in love, it was the scientific partnership with Mileva Maric which he appears to have valued even more. She was a better mathematician than Einstein and checked the calculations in his scientific papers, as well as being a sounding board for his thought experiments. Their first child was a girl born out of wedlock. They then married and had two sons. Eventually they fell out of love, and Einstein asked her for a divorce, saying that one day he would win the Nobel prize, and she could then have the money from that as a settlement. She accepted the deal, and eventually collected.

Despite lack of academic success, the young Einstein had supreme faith in his own intuitive judgement. The partnership with Maric aside, he worked largely on his own, and once he had arrived at a breakthrough – such as the Special Theory of Relativity in 1905 – he held fast to his conclusion, even in the face of apparent contradictions. One of his Zurich Polytechnic professors told him, 'You're a very clever boy, Einstein. An extremely clever boy. But you have one great fault – you'll never let yourself be told anything.'[13]

Einstein's overwhelming self-assurance came from his faith that the universe was rational; its secrets could be discovered through mathematics and thought experiments, which only the most intuitive and unconventional scientists might uncover. He never doubted he was one of that elect. He read everything that might be relevant to his investigations, and he loved to debate concepts and throw around ideas with the very best brains in quantum mechanics; but he never needed their patronage or agreement to arrive at his insights.

Walt Disney: Generic self-belief
turns into a unique mission

There are two other categories in our case studies. One is where self-belief builds gradually, grounded in a general sense of being special, but becomes increasingly pronounced, as positive feedback accumulates in an increasingly focused way. Walt Disney's biographer, Neal Gabler, tells us that when he was eighteen, Walt 'landed in Kansas City during the fall of 1919 determined to be successful. Almost all his acquaintances then remarked on his resolve and absolute faith in himself, manifested ... in a sunny ebullience ... he brimmed with a self-confidence that was neither entirely justified nor particularly well directed, since he arrived without a plan. He was a go-getter who did not know where he was getting to, only that he would get somewhere.'[14]

Initially Disney had two different ambitions. His first notion was that he would become an actor or actor-comedian; he adored Charlie Chaplin. With his friend Walt Pfeiffer he did a double act – Disney as Chaplin and Pfeiffer as Chaplin's enemy the Count. Apparently, they garnered great applause, and Disney became addicted to it. But then in his final year of school, he flourished as an artist. He went to evening classes at the Chicago Academy of Fine Arts and again received praise, though more for his caricatures than his straight drawing. Disney's greatest delight was in taking a class in cartooning from a *Chicago Herald* artist. At the age of seventeen he became a professional artist and commercial illustrator, developing skills in the fast-expanding field of cartoon animation.

When barely nineteen, he set up his own art studio with a colleague, Ubbe Iwerks,* and gained some artwork business.

---

* Originally Iwwerks – he later simplified his name to Ub Iwerks. I use 'Iwerks' throughout.

Before long, however, work dried up and Disney dissolved the business and declared bankruptcy. When he was twenty-one, Disney decided to move to Hollywood – the 'most flourishing factory of popular mythology since the Greeks', according to Alistair Cooke, the iconic British commentator.

Neal Gabler says, 'Walt Disney was made for Hollywood. He loved dress-up and make-believe, was boisterous, outgoing, self-aggrandizing, and craved attention. Hollywood was his spiritual destination . . . He arrived early in August 1923 in his borrowed suit with nothing but pluck and his peculiar self-confidence . . . he had travelled first-class, because "he always wanted the best way".'[15] Before long, he set up a proper animation studio in partnership with his brother Roy and the faithful Iwerks.

After a sticky start the business prospered, setting new standards in cartoon animation. The breakthrough came in 1928 when Walt and Iwerks invented Mickey Mouse.

He is so ubiquitous that it is hard now to appreciate how innovative Mickey Mouse was, and what appreciation the rodent generated. When the first Mickey cartoon was shown to audiences around Los Angeles, it drew fantastic spontaneous applause, far more than the feature films that were meant to be the main attraction.

Mickey Mouse had a genuinely distinctive adult-like character based, Gabler says, on 'raw ingenuity and a sadistic determination'.[16]

The other thing that propelled Mickey and Disney to global fame was Walt's idea – to give a voice to the cartoon character, which had never been done before. One of Disney's young artists voiced a common question – 'Why should a *voice* come out of a cartoon character?' The artist answered his own objection by insisting that the voice had to reflect the action, 'as if the noise was coming right from what the character was doing'. Audiences went crazy, demanding encore after encore: 'The sound itself gave the illusion of something emanating directly from the screen,' said Iwerks. 'Walt was exultant,' his biographer tells us. 'He kept saying, "This is it! We've got it!"[17]

In a different field, at a different time, we can trace the same process – of general self-belief becoming increasingly targeted – with the young research scientist and barrister Margaret Thatcher. Switching to politics in 1959, she was one of the first women to become a UK cabinet minister, and then, in 1975, had the audacity to challenge the leader of her party, Ted Heath, and, against the odds, to replace him as leader of the opposition Conservative Party.

Thatcher was originally viewed as a second-rate leader and unlikely to become prime minister. Even when she became PM, she was at first tentative in ploughing her 'Thatcherite' furrow. It seems she only had the courage to do so after gambling everything on the expedition to recapture the Falkland Islands, eight thousand miles away, and winning the war and the subsequent general election in 1983. Self-belief flourished gradually and with ever-accelerating force over three decades, until its brilliant intensity overran the banks of common sense and brought her down.

By contrast, without his having spent three years in Hitler's concentration camps, we would probably never have heard of Viktor Frankl, one of the world's most influential psychotherapists. Frankl survived the camps by imagining a purpose in life beyond them – he pictured himself after the war lecturing, propounding his existential philosophy that a personal meaning in life is essential for mental health. For Frankl self-belief was a matter of life or death.

His moving book, *Man's Search for Meaning*, about his time in the camps and his philosophy, was voted by a Library of Congress study one of the top ten most influential books in the United States. It has sold tens of millions of copies. I reread it frequently; it refreshes me.

To sum up: self-belief is essential for unreasonable success. All the people in this book not only had, or came to have, self-belief; they also had a particularly potent dose of it. But, you ask, what options are open to someone who has a genuine thirst for success, yet currently lacks strong self-belief?

What do you do if your self-belief is not strong?

The stories in this book suggest three possible remedies:

- Search for transforming experiences (see Chapter 6).
- Attract well-deserved praise; develop a breakthrough achievement (Chapter 7).
- Narrow your focus until your work is unique and you've defined your destination (Chapter 8).

Search for transforming experiences

All our players had one or more 'transforming experiences' in their life – that is, an unusual and intense interlude, usually of a year or more, that changed them. They went into each experience as one person, and came out as another, better equipped to search out and travel the road to outstanding accomplishments.

Attract well-deserved praise

Positive feedback of some kind is nearly always essential for humans to thrive. If you doubt this, look at the way famous people from Churchill to Einstein remembered the few teachers who praised them. We are all far more brittle and dependent on approval than we realise or admit. Self-belief is hard if you get little applause. Today children get too much and adults too little.

We all deserve praise to quite different extents in quite different circumstances. Therefore you must find the field where you can excel. There is one for each of us. You must find it.

Experiment with a variety of surroundings – places, companies, teams, jobs, roles, projects, co-workers, and hubs with extensive links to the outside world – until you find the right one, where you receive great acclaim.

Plaudits feed self-belief, which itself leads on to success; but praise is also a form of market feedback, a signal that our self-belief is justified.

Acclaim *must* be genuine and merited. For a generation educators and parents have lavished praise on children indiscriminately, believing it would raise self-esteem and motivation. But children are not stupid. They know when praise is deserved and when it is not. And praise can create expectations that they know they are not always going to meet, which become a trap.

One father was extravagant with praise when his young daughter beat him at a board game she'd never played before – 'You're so talented,' he said. The next day they played the game again, and she lost. She burst into tears, saying 'Dad, did I just lose my talent?'[18] Inflated praise is demotivating, or else it leads to delusions which sooner or later will be demolished.

For adults as for children, only *genuine* positive feedback is useful. This does not mean, however, that someone who doesn't get much positive feedback and doesn't have much self-belief should accept that as permanent. Though it is probably apocryphal, Albert Einstein is alleged to have said: 'Everybody is a genius. But if you judge a fish by its ability to climb a tree, it will live its whole life believing that it is stupid.' Fish out of water must find the stream richest in results and appreciation.

Narrow your focus until your work is unique

A third key to unlocking self-belief is to realise that it is gener-ated within narrow corridors. As with Walt Disney or Margaret Thatcher, as with everyone who achieves marked success, they come to believe either that they can do specific things better than their rivals, or that they can do things that nobody else has thought of doing.

For unusual success, wide experimentation is followed sooner or later by extreme focus, and then by blazing a wholly original trail. Ultimately, self-belief needs to be specifically attached to achieving an unusual goal. You cannot reasonably believe in yourself except in the context of what you want to achieve; but if you can give yourself a unique worthwhile mission – one that plays to your strongest suit – it is much easier to come to believe in yourself. Even if there is no initial generic self-belief, it is never too late to define a bold target and come to believe it is attainable. Belief in the destination can become belief in the self.

The value of self-doubt

Self-doubt does not preclude self-belief; nor the other way round. Whereas some characters in this book do not appear to have suffered – or benefitted – from self-doubt, many others did. Self-doubt voices the question, 'Am I really on the right road to my destination? Will I find my way?' Self-doubt is typically constructive.

The most famous self-doubter in history

Perhaps the most dramatic instance was the (soon-to-be) Apostle Paul's experience of a 'revelation of Jesus Christ'. Although Tintoretto depicts Paul as being blinded and falling from his horse on the way to Damascus, and the author of the Acts of the Apostles says Paul was blinded for three days and heard a voice from heaven, Paul's own account is more straightforward – he realised that he was doing utterly the wrong thing. Paul writes to the followers of Jesus in Galatia:

> For I want you to know, brothers and sisters, that the gospel I proclaimed is not of human origin: for ... I received it through a revelation of Jesus Christ.
>
> You have heard, no doubt, of my earlier life in Judaism. I was violently persecuting the church of God and trying to destroy it ... But when God ... was pleased to reveal his Son to me, that I might proclaim him amongst the Gentiles [non-Jews], I did not confer with any human being ... but I went away into Arabia, and afterwards returned to Damascus.[19]

Paul had been a member of the Jerusalem Temple Police, employed by the Jewish high priest to eliminate the followers of Jesus, who were seen as Jewish zealots and hence a threat both to the Roman authorities and to the quisling Jewish priestly caste.[20]

Paul's vision of the Risen Christ changed all that. Not only did Paul turn one hundred and eighty degrees to eventually become the most powerful promoter of Jesus; he also shifted the message and the target market. Jesus commissioned Paul to save 'the Gentiles' – Romans and Greeks – and turn a movement which threatened the Roman authorities into a Rome-friendly one.

Self-doubt required years of reflection in Arabia. When Paul returned to urban civilisation, he had a wholly original perspective on life, the universe and everything, which gradually and wholly unexpectedly took the Roman world by storm. The most profound self-doubt led to one of the greatest intensities of belief and self-belief ever known.

Steve Jobs: Self-doubt propels singular ambition

For Paul, self-doubt was compressed into – or at least described as – a single event. A modern sense of self-doubt typically occurs not as an event, though it may be triggered or brought to the surface by one, but as a conspiracy of emotions related to earlier experiences or interpretations of them.

Steve Jobs is a case in point. One single cause – that he was a much-loved adopted child – fed both self-belief and self-doubt. Jobs always thought of the couple who adopted him simply as 'my parents' and remembered very specifically what they said:

> They were very serious and looked me straight in the eye. They said, 'we specifically picked you out.' Both of my parents said that and repeated it slowly for me. And they put an emphasis on every word in that sentence.[21]

Jobs' biographer, Walter Isaacson, comments: 'Abandoned. Chosen. Special. Those concepts became part of who Jobs was and how he regarded himself.'[22]

Isaacson also quotes a friend of Jobs:

> Steve talked a lot about being abandoned [by his biological parents] and the pain that caused. It made him independent. He followed the beat of a different drummer, and that came from being in a different world than he was born into.[23]

When Isaacson told Jobs of the comment, Steve denied the 'abandoned' part, but reiterated the 'special' comment: 'I have never felt abandoned. I've always felt special. My parents made me feel special.'[24]

That Jobs felt special – that he had a peculiarly acute sense of self-belief from childhood – is beyond dispute. A very close colleague of his, Andy Hertzfeld, said:

> He thinks there are a few people who are special – people like Einstein and Gandhi and the gurus he met in India – and he's one of them ... Once he even hinted to me that he was enlightened.[25]

In the 1980s, Jobs became very close to the former human relations director of Intel, Ann Bowers. She left Intel after she married its co-founder, the great Bob Noyce. Bowers joined Apple in 1980 and became one of the very few people who could calm down the famously fiery Jobs. Jobs became a friend of Noyce's too – he would often arrive unannounced for dinner at their home. Bowers said of Jobs: 'He was so bright and also so needy. He needed a grown-up, a father figure, which Bob became, and I became like a mother figure.'[26]

Another long-standing colleague said of Jobs:

> His desire for complete control of whatever he makes derives directly from his personality and the fact that he was abandoned at birth. He wants to control his environment and he sees the product as an extension of himself.[27]

It seems that for Jobs self-belief and self-doubt were twin cherries on a single stalk. His adoption made him believe in himself with passionate intensity, and also impelled him to make perfect products and seek to control colleagues and customers alike.*

---

* Jobs insisted that Apple products combine proprietary hardware and software, with which the customer could not meddle – quite different from the 'open source' philosophy behind most digital products. When taken to their extreme, both approaches work well.

Summary and conclusion

Self-belief is the foundation of success. This is an iron rule. Nobody ever became unreasonably successful without a strong belief in themselves.

Self-belief can start with a vague but deep sense of being special. This sense sometimes arises simply from being born into privilege or because of encouragement from role models around us, such as parents and relatives. Equally, however, conviction in one's destiny can arise from defiant vulnerability or isolation in childhood, when the self is thrown back on itself and creates an imaginary future to compensate for a barren present.

Early belief in one's star can take someone a long way. Yet our case studies also show that it is never too late to develop robust self-belief.

Self-belief must ultimately become specific to the field in which you will ultimately triumph. Belief in your destiny will fizzle and fade without a clear idea of the stage on which your success will be played out. Nobody reaches a target without defining it and believing — sometimes naively and to almost-universal ridicule — that it is attainable.

For example, during his time in the political wilderness during the 1930s, Winston Churchill, when he was out of office and isolated, not widely respected by his Conservative colleagues in the government, and with his career apparently washed up, scarcely wavered from his belief that he ought to become prime minister, not from personal aggrandisement but from his ability, he believed, to thwart Hitler.

By highlighting the need to stand up to the German dictator, and by arguing with great force that any accommodation with him was both immoral and self-defeating, Churchill positioned himself as the inevitable choice for leader should war with Germany eventuate.[28]

Self-doubt may or may not arise along the way – even Churchill had his times of depression, the 'black dog' which pursued him. Self-doubt is usually an asset – it does not cancel out self-belief, but rather purifies and distils it.

Self-doubt and self-belief comprise a rhythm of yin and yang, a dialectic where self-doubt crystallises, reinforces, refines or completely changes the doubter's mission, and para-doxically leads to high confidence that it can be achieved. Self-doubt is only damaging if it is repressed or permanently swamps the mind.

Consciously and unconsciously, with our reason and our emotions, strong and specific self-belief – the utter conviction that we can achieve something unique, which fuses our talents and our personality with good or bad openings provided by the universe – is the first and greatest of the landmarks. It is also the rarest. The reason most people do not achieve extraordinary results is that they do not believe that they can, or do not want to enough – which comes down to the same thing. The players in this book were, in this respect above all, quite different.

Self-belief

- Define self as special and important
- Sense of destiny and belief in star
- Can only flourish if tied to a specific goal

Self-doubt

- Complements, not opposites
- May come from sense of abandonment, isolation or neglect
- Useful to prompt drive for personal control

5

Landmark 2: Olympian Expectations

High standards are contagious. Bring a new person onto a high standards team, and they'll quickly adapt. The opposite is also true.

—JEFF BEZOS

The second common factor amongst our players is that they all had sky-high expectations of themselves and the people they chose to work with. Since we've just dealt with self-belief, you may be wondering how Olympian expectations are different.

Self-belief, we've seen, is the conviction a person has of being special, exceptional and destined to do great things, that is increasingly well defined and clear as their life unfolds. It is also the feeling, there from the start or burgeoning over a lifetime into near-certainty, that they are destined to succeed. Self-belief is essentially an emotion, a pulsing and energising sensation, which not only grips the individual but also communicates itself to other people and influences them, but in no way depends on them.

Olympian expectations are different. For sure, they are to do with the individual, but they are also to do with their subordinates and co-workers. Olympian expectations are more clearly defined than self-belief – they are to do with quite unusual and exceptional results expected by the person. Expectations explain *how and why* the individual is changing the nature of reality. There are five interlinked components of Olympian expectations:

- Expectations are set **much higher** than is normal.
- **Thinking big** – not concerned with details but with changing the big picture.
- Being **unreasonably demanding** of self and others – the standards had jolly well better be met, without exceptions or excuses.
- **Progressive escalation** of expectations over time – no resting on laurels; more like an ever-expanding sliver of razored ice[1] in the soul demanding ever-greater success.
- The expectations are **unique** to the individual and can be succinctly expressed. For instance, Leonardo – 'perfect paintings'; Churchill – 'stop Hitler'; Thatcher – 'reverse national decline'.

Expectations rig results

Of all the true stories in the book, this is the most shocking, yet also the most liberating.

Researchers Robert Rosenthal and Lenore Jackson tested eighteen classes of schoolchildren for their IQ. They then gave the results not to the pupils but to their teachers, identifying the children with outstanding intellectual potential. Notwithstanding the results, the teachers were instructed to treat the kids impartially.

Eight months later, they were retested. Amongst the children *not* identified as unusually gifted, about half performed better and half performed worse on the IQ test, as one would expect. But four-fifths of the 'outstandingly gifted' children scored significantly better the second time, gaining at least ten IQ points. And a fifth of them gained thirty more IQ points – a significant and surprising transformation.

The study is staggering because there was no real difference in performance the first time round between the 'outstandingly gifted' kids and the rest – the ones identified as gifted were selected by the researchers precisely because in truth they had *average* scores. The researchers had deceived the teachers. And yet, those false expectations of the pupils' potential had generated outstanding results the second time.[2]

The experiment – since replicated many times – shows the importance of expectations, and how they operate in our unconscious minds. Expectations of the children's performance became self-fulfilling, even without any conscious communication. The kids were not given their scores, and the teachers were told not to treat the 'gifted' pupils differently. Yet, unconsciously, the teachers must have communicated something of the potential of the children to them – they absorbed a message about their intelligence and potential.

So often in life, people see what they expect to see, and this compounds the expectation, making it real.

- Others' positive expectations of us can make us perform outstandingly well.
- Our expectations determine our performance as well. If we expect to succeed, we likely will.
- Our self-expectations also affect people around us. Unless

we have a reputation for bragging, people will be strongly influenced by our own expectations. They will take us at our own genuine, unconscious valuation.

- A small lead in performance will become larger and compounded over time. Even an incorrectly perceived aura of outperformance will lead over time to a large measure of real outperformance.
- Those who inherit the earth will be those who expect to.

The higher we set our expectations, the more likely we are to reach the top. There are limits, of course – we cannot become Napoleon or Jesus by imagining that we are. There is a fine balance between optimism and delusion. But if some students can gain thirty points of IQ through the operation of a teacher's expectations, we can make quite unexpected progress through lifting our own expectations a notch. And once this notch has been reached, we can continue this 'uplifting' process. One notch at a time, followed by success, can lead us on to another notch, and then another . . .

This is what seems to have happened to our players. Not only were they able to ratchet up their expectations of themselves, but they also became more powerful by ratcheting up the expectations of their followers: expectations of what both they, and their leader, could do. The cases of Lenin, Winston Churchill and Steve Jobs show that there is a very fine line between collective delusion and collective achievement through 'unrealistically' high expectations, and we could say the same about many other charismatic but sociopathic leaders, such as Adolf Hitler and Mao Zedong, who chose to act beyond the constraints and restrictions of civilised behaviour.

Let's start with someone else whose expectations were sky-high.

Paul of Tarsus: Save humanity

None of the players, and I doubt any individual anywhere at any time, had higher expectations than Paul.

Whether you regard Paul – as he did – as the embodiment of the Living Christ, who knew the Mind of God because it had been revealed to him, or whether you think he was plainly delusional or mad, there can be no better illustration of the power of Olympian expectations.

Paul's vision of Christ on his way to Damascus had an immeasurable impact on his expectations – we will touch on this again in later chapters. What matters here is the impact on Paul's expectations. 'Whatever the nature of the experience,' says A. N. Wilson, 'it left him forever altered. He writes not as a man who is searching but as one who has found: not as one who struggles for the truth but as one who has heard it. He has known Christ, and he is in Christ.'[3] After his vision, Paul had a high degree of certainty about his life and his purpose.

He believed that the death and resurrection of Jesus brought a new cosmic reality. Everyone could be saved and enjoy eternal life, but time was short; soon Christ would appear on the clouds and take his people off to heaven. Paul had to save as many people as possible before the world ended.

Paul absorbed the view held by the 'cognoscenti' (a group of believers known as the Gnostics) that humans comprised both body and spirit – the body was irretrievably flawed, and the spiritual, divine side of mankind was hopelessly compromised, imprisoned within evil flesh. 'For what the flesh [body] desires is opposed to the Spirit,' Paul wrote, 'and what the Spirit desires is opposed to the flesh: for these are opposed to each other, to prevent you doing what you want.'[4] The struggle of men and women to be good – the bromide of religion and philosophy throughout the ages – was entirely futile.

According to Paul, Christ offered the way out of this impasse – surrender of the human will to God, and the activation of Christ within the believer, could lead to an entirely new species of humankind, living within the love of God. People who are 'in Christ' experience the mystical presence of Christ in their daily lives, converting badness into goodness, hate into love. The believer with 'Christ inside' could reach standards of behaviour well beyond human potential.

Paul was wrong about many things. He did not see Christ arrive on the clouds, wind up the world, and take his followers to everlasting life. But Paul propelled his gospel throughout the Roman Empire, and a belief in Christ eventually supplanted all the gods the Romans had previously revered.

Paul is unique in history, and spiritual values are not directly comparable to those in the worlds of science, art, literature, business and entertainment. And yet these worlds, at their best, can also demonstrate incredibly high standards of truth and beauty, and the ability to inspire followers and feed our collective imagination. The higher the standards, the greater their ability to uplift our minds and to enrich the world. Could *cartoons* have these effects? One man thought so.

Walt Disney: Quasi-religious awe

Right from the start of his career, Disney had 'big dreams and outsize aspirations'.[5] Even when he was twenty, he was 'too independent-minded to think of himself as someone else's employee'.[6] A secretary who came across him said, 'He had the drive and ambition of ten million men.'[7] When he went to Hollywood, he fitted right in with the world's biggest and best dream factory; he was always a dreamer on a grand scale.

Like Steve Jobs, like Leonardo, Disney wanted perfect product quality. Although he loved having his own studio, Disney 'was never as interested in building an operation . . . as he was in improving the product . . . as a matter of personal pride and psychological need.'[8] Like Dylan and Jobs, Disney saw the product as an extension of himself; and however hard up he was – in the early years he was chronically short of cash – he demanded the highest quality even at the expense of profit. According to one biographer, 'he was adamant about not surrendering control, no matter how badly he needed revenue . . . He wanted to be the king of animation . . . As fervent as ever that quality was his only real advantage, Walt was determined to spend as much on his cartoons as producers were spending on their live comedies.'[9] In the Great Depression which started in October 1929, 'rather than cutting costs, he kept increasing them'.[10]

Disney believed in having the very best animators and inspiring them with his restless demands for the very best. They knew that Disney's studio was pre-eminent and felt like pioneers, 'as if we were members of the same class at West Point'.[11] On one occasion, he hired a highly sought-after animator, Ben Sharpsteen, at more than double Disney's own pay.[12]

Like Bruce Henderson, Walt was 'in the grip of his own obsession with excellence, which made him compulsively dissatisfied. Everyone seemed to recognize that Disney not only consistently produced the best animations but had begun to reinvent animation . . . Disney's animators appreciated that they were pioneers.'[13]

Disney reinvented animation in 1931 in a parallel way to Steve Jobs' reinvention of the personal computer in 1983. The essence of the Lisa, precursor to the Mac, was that it made using a computer intuitive and easy, an order of magnitude simpler and less intimidating than the previous 'gold standard' of IBM. One key aspect of Apple products' simplicity and ease of use was smooth scrolling – the way that you could move down between paragraphs and pages quickly and with no abrupt jumps. Before

1931, cartoons shunted from pose to pose. Disney's animators invented 'overlapping action', so that action flowed smoothly from scene to scene. Disney's cartoons looked different and elegant.[14]

Walt Disney was held in awe by the creative people working for him. Animators thought of themselves as gods, bringing their characters to life and determining their fortunes. But Disney was more like God Almighty – the animators spoke of him 'in quasi-religious terms'. One of his team said: 'When he'd come into a room, your hair would stand up on the back of your neck. He'd have that effect on you. You'd feel the presence. It was spooky.' Another said he had 'an overwhelming power over people and the voice of a prophet'. As biographer Neal Gabler summed up, 'By the mid-1930s the Disney studio operated like a cult, with a messianic figure inspiring a group of devoted, sometimes frenzied acolytes . . . disciples on a mission.'[15]

Disney and his team worshipped at the altar of product quality. And so, in a completely different field, yet in a remarkably similar way, did a more recent artistic-business hero, and those of his team who were strong enough to thrive on his extremely demanding leadership style.

Steve Jobs: Demanding, unreasonable, supremely ambitious

Jobs had incredibly high expectations of himself. We saw earlier that, like Keynes, he thought he was of similar calibre to some of the great people in history. Perhaps Jobs went even further. 'Throughout his career,' says Walter Isaacson, 'Jobs liked to see himself as an enlightened rebel, a Jedi warrior or Buddhist samurai fighting the forces of darkness' – such as IBM.[16]

It was for this reason that he craved perfection in his products; he would not settle for less. This also explains his very unusual policy of insisting Apple controlled the design and integration of both hardware and software, and so be a rival of both IBM and other computer manufacturers, *and* Microsoft and other software houses. This made it hard for Jobs to win his battles, but it was part and parcel of his vast ambition. Without a unified system, without end-to-end control of product design and execution, he would not have been able to create devices that were so intuitive and easy to use.[17]

It is a classic rule of strategy not to fight against powerful enemies on two different fronts. This was a rule Jobs disregarded – he fought both IBM and Microsoft, and later the major alternative smartphone hardware makers that were using the dominant Android software developed by Google. At times Jobs struggled, but his Olympian expectations, verging on megalomania, eventually won through. He ultimately succeeded in building (at times) the most valuable company on Earth, and some of the most magnificent products of our age.

Jobs inspired his followers, raising their eyes to the hills, despite being, in conventional terms, one of the worst people-managers in recent history. He demanded that their expectations match his own, so that he was able to do things that he alone could not. Unlike his great rival, Bill Gates, Jobs himself was a lousy programmer and product designer. Yet Apple managed to design better and simpler products. If your vision is perfection, demand and ye shall receive. As Ann Bowers, the motherly HR figure who had the personal authority to call out Jobs for his appalling treatment of other people, explained of her protégé, Jobs 'had these huge expectations, and if people couldn't deliver, he couldn't stand it'.[18]

Though some excellent people quit after Jobs' relentless personal onslaughts, most did not. As Joanna Hoffman, whose family were refugees from Eastern Europe and who had the temperament – and temper – to stand up to Jobs, said, 'His behaviour can be emotionally draining, but if you survive, it works.'[19] Now for another cantankerous and unreasonable person who also changed the world of business for the better, by inventing not products, but a superior model of strategy for any business. (He also provided a model for how I would spend my life.)

Bruce Henderson: Invent strategy, change the way business is run

Bruce Henderson, founder of the Boston Consulting Group (BCG), changed the way America and the world did business.

Bruce was a towering, impressive, intimidating figure. He rarely smiled, chose his words carefully, and, quite frankly, was a little scary. I first met him when I was working for BCG, at a conference in England's New Forest. He asked me a question about business strategy, which stumped me. Bruce then lectured me for a long time, which was enthralling, though I was so nervous that I instantly forgot everything he said.

At the conference, BCG showcased its theories to a grand collection of British and European business leaders. I thought we presented very well. Bruce sat quietly observing, saying nothing. The event certainly led to some new business. But after the guests had left, Bruce ripped us to shreds. 'I was saying all this *three years ago*,' he said, as if an ice age had since intervened. 'Haven't you learned anything new since then?'

He was massively demanding. I never heard him praise anyone or anything. He was always driving us on to the next big insight. You might imagine that this diet – a full plate of criticism, an unfulfilled expectation of something much better from us, and a complete absence of praise – would be demotivating.

But it wasn't. We were working right at the boundaries of received business concepts, and even the dunderheads who ran corporate America were starting to listen to us. We felt on the verge of a new discovery every day.

At the age of forty-eight, and with a chequered career behind him, his ambition and intent verged on the ridiculous. Starting with nobody but himself, he created one of the three best consulting firms in the world. From the outset, the firm's mission was to create a new way of thinking about 'business strategy' – a concept invented by Bruce.

BCG hired only the very brightest brains from top business schools. BCG was probably the first company in the world to place intellect above all other qualities. Since then, other firms have stolen this strategy and applied it effectively to different spheres, notably investment banking and venture capital.

Before Bruce, businesspeople wanted their company to be market leader so they could extract high prices and high profits from customers. Wrong, wrong, wrong, said Bruce. Market share was valuable because it lowered costs. To gain market share, therefore, leading firms should *lower* prices, thus further increasing market share, driving costs down further, and making life hard for competitors with smaller sales and higher costs. The eventual upshot of lowering costs and prices, Bruce promised, would be higher profits and market value. Pure heresy in Bruce's day, but it is what Amazon has done today with amazing effect, changing the global retail scene forever.

Jeff Bezos: Olympian standards – the final frontier

Jeff Bezos (pronounced 'Bay-zos') is notable for two simple ideas which he has applied with great dedication and purity. And because of his extraordinary success, perhaps we should take his ideas seriously.

One of these ideas – that pursuing sales and market share

is hugely more important than seeking profits in anything but the very long term – is why Bezos is the spiritual heir to Henderson. Indeed, Bezos has taken the idea even further, with astounding audacity and success. This formula for success will be explored later in the book – we'll see the white-knuckle ride of Amazon's history and Bezos' refusal to budge from his views – and how failing to grab easily available profits took the venture almost to the brink of bankruptcy. But here, I want to turn the spotlight on Bezos' other great principle – Olympian standards.

First, a little background on the man himself. His biological father was a circus performer, but Bezos last saw him as a three-year-old. At the age of ten he was told he had been adopted. Like Steve Jobs, Bezos grew up in a loving family – his film-star-handsome Cuban adoptive father had escaped from Castro's socialist paradise via a rescue programme of the Catholic church, and arrived in Miami alone when he was sixteen, speaking no English. Jeff Bezos was quickly seen as unusually gifted and fiercely competitive, a model, almost a caricature, of self-belief and capitalist aspiration. He had a penchant for *Star Trek*, and his desire to make money, his high-school girlfriend said, was due to his ambition 'to get to outer space'.[20]

From the outset, Bezos was gripped by one central tenet – the need to build 'Earth's most customer-centric company' – and by his conception of the main way to do it – through 'relentlessly high standards'. Many people, said Bezos, 'may think these standards are unreasonably high'. Too bad. In his 2018 report to shareholders, Bezos devotes the first four pages to Amazon's consistently high ranking – top for the last eight years – in the American Customer Satisfaction Index, and a lecture on the main way to 'stay ahead of ever-rising customer expectations', which is '*high standards* – widely deployed and at all levels of detail ... We've had some successes in our quest to meet the high expectations of customers. We've also had billions of dollars' worth of failures along the way.'

What does Bezos believe?

- High standards can be taught. If you start with a high-standards team, newcomers will quickly adapt.
- High standards are domain-specific. 'When I started Amazon,' Bezos says, 'I had high standards on inventing, customer care, and hiring. But I didn't have high standards on operational process ... I had to learn and develop high standards on all that (my colleagues were my tutors).'
- High standards result in better products and services for customers. But less obviously, 'people are drawn to high standards – they help with recruiting and retention'.
- 'And finally, high standards are fun! Once you've tasted high standards, there's no going back.'

So much for the theory. How does that work out in practice?

It's not all sweetness and light. There's a story from the Christmas holidays in 2000, when demand was exploding, and the customer-service department was increasingly stretched by customer calls. At a meeting of thirty senior executives, Bezos asked the head of customer service how long customers had to wait to get help.

'Well under a minute.'

'Really?' said Bezos. 'Let's see.' He punched in the Amazon service number on the speakerphone. Jolly seasonal music. Lots of it. Bezos went red in the face waiting. A vein in his forehead started to pulsate. Tense silence in the room. After four and a half minutes – which seemed an eternity – a cheerful voice trilled, 'Hello, Amazon.com!' Bezos then slammed down the phone and laid into the customer service boss.[21] He didn't last long.

*

All the players made great demands on their followers. Yet Olympian expectations do not *necessarily* require an effect on followers; the expectations may be so huge that the main or exclusive impact is on the players and not on any followers. Here are four examples – Einstein, Leonardo, Keynes and Dylan. It may not be coincidental that they were thinkers and artists rather than entrepreneurs or politicians. Perhaps people of action need their Olympian standards to be shared by the team who must execute the work – over five hundred and sixty thousand people in Amazon – whereas artists and thinkers set standards primarily or exclusively for themselves, as they are necessarily the great creators of their work.

Einstein: Quest for hidden harmony in the universe

In probing Einstein's expectations, we discover a very unusual player, the archetype, not of the normal workaday scientist or thinker, but of the man or woman who is perfectly cast to make monumental breakthroughs. The necessary ingredients are insatiable curiosity, quirky intelligence, the paradoxical combination of confidence and awe which I term 'modest arrogance', and a particular guiding philosophy.

While still a teenager, Einstein appears to have had two extraordinarily fertile expectations. We have touched on one of them earlier – that nature exhibits hidden harmonies which speak the language of mathematics and are precise, invariable and perfect; and secondly, that he had been put on the planet to lift the cloak of underlying reality. At a time of emotional stress when he was eighteen, Einstein found solace in his quest: 'Strenuous intellectual work and looking at God's nature are the reconciling, fortifying yet relentlessly strict angels that shall guide me through all of life's troubles.'[22]

Three years later, he wrote, 'I am more and more convinced that the electrodynamics of moving bodies as it is presented today does not correspond to reality and that it will be possible to present it in a simpler way.'[23] The following year, while unemployed, Einstein said, 'It is a glorious thing to discover the unity of a set of phenomena that seem at first to be completely separate' – something that far better qualified scientists had not seen.[24] And again in 1901, at the age of twenty-two, he wrote, 'I have been engrossed in Boltzmann's work on the kinetic theory of gases' – Boltzmann, professor at the University of Leipzig, was Europe's top statistical physicist – 'and these last few days I wrote a short paper that provides the missing keystone in the chain of proofs that he started.'[25]

These are extraordinary claims made in a matter-of-fact tone – Einstein is saying that he has gone beyond all the top brains in physics. This is what I mean by 'modest arrogance' – there is excitement but no crowing; there is certainty and absolute confidence. Without such presumption, what jobless polytechnic student, without any academic credentials, would have dared to play in this league of discovery? Without such outrageous expectations, Einstein would never have cracked the code of the microworld.

Leonardo: To know everything about the world

Walter Isaacson says, 'Leonardo had almost no schooling and could barely read Latin or do long division', and yet he expected 'to know everything there was to know about the world'.[26] Leonardo had a quality of 'modest arrogance' very similar to that of Einstein, driven by relentless curiosity.

Leonardo wrote in his notebook, 'The good painter has to paint two principal things – man, and the intention of his mind. The first is easy and the second is difficult, because it has to be represented through gestures and movements of the limbs.' As Isaacson says, 'By the end of his career, his pursuit of how the brain and nerves turned emotions into motions became almost obsessive. It was enough to make the *Mona Lisa* smile.'[27] Leonardo was also the first artist to capture fully the art of perspective, which marks the transition from medieval to modern art.

Leonardo expected painters not only to record nature, 'but also infinite things that nature never created'[28] – including cannons, armoured vehicles, flying machines (one of which resembled the modern helicopter), lizards that turned into dragons, and dozens of other fantasies.

Because of his enormous expectations and perfectionism, Leonardo left many of his masterpieces, such as the *Adoration of the Magi* and *Saint Jerome*, unfinished. Only fifteen paintings accredited to Leonardo now survive, but they establish him as one of the greatest painters of all time.

Now from great art to great economics, and an economist of a distinctly artistic and intellectual bent.

Maynard Keynes: Only interested in being great

Keynes' biographer Robert Skidelsky nails the point: 'Like many who aspire to it, Keynes thought a great deal about greatness – how it came about, what it consisted of.'[29] Keynes was not interested in being a good economist; he wanted to be a great one. In an essay on Alfred Marshall (1842–1924), the dominant English economist of his day, Keynes wrote that 'the master economist must possess a rare combination of gifts ... mathematician, historian, statesman, philosopher ... as aloof and incorruptible as an artist, yet sometimes as near the earth as a politician.'[30] Keynes clearly thought he embodied all these qualities, and given this expectation, he did.

Writing about an earlier genius, Isaac Newton, Keynes praised his 'divine intuition' and 'unusual powers of continuous concentrated introspection', as well as many other qualities – 'logical capacity, a feel for the salient facts, style, many-sidedness, theoretical and practical gifts in combination' – Keynes claimed were vital for a great economist.[31] According to Skidelsky, Keynes 'realized that beneath the knowledge in which he publicly dealt there lay an esoteric knowledge open only to a few initiates, the pursuit of which fascinated him as it did Newton'.[32]

Perhaps Newton was Keynes' 'fantasy mentor', an intuitive genius and a model for Keynes. 'The thought that he [Keynes] was saying something new seems to have been with him from the start,' Skidelsky tells us, 'coupled with the conviction that his elders were too stupid or conventional to understand it.'[33] Keynes refused to be constrained to the role of economist, writing as befitted a historian, philosopher, theologian and statesman. 'Keynes,' notes Skidelsky, 'always had intellectual ambitions, or tastes, surplus to the requirements' of any economic problem.[34]

Keynes' self-expectations were good for the world. Would anyone else have discovered a practical middle way between *laissez-faire* capitalism on the one hand and totalitarian government on the other – or solved the problem of mass unemployment without resorting to serfdom, slavery or war?

We turn now from one intellectual giant to another, a songwriter who could express the spirit of his age in unforgettable words.

Bob Dylan: Telescoping great ideas

'I was born in the spring of 1941,' Dylan tells us in his book *Chronicles*. 'If you were born around this time . . . you could feel the old world go and the new one beginning. It was like putting the clock back to when BC became AD. Everyone born around my time was a part of both. Hitler, Churchill, Mussolini, Stalin, Roosevelt – towering figures that the world would never see the likes of again, men who relied on their own resolve, for better or worse, every one of them prepared to act alone, indifferent to approval – indifferent to wealth or love, all presiding over the destiny of mankind and reducing the world to rubble.'[35]

Not content with the company of world rulers, Dylan also feels himself part of earlier history and its great thinkers. 'It was said that World War II spelled the end of the Age of Enlightenment, but I would not have known it. I was still in it ... I'd read that stuff. Voltaire, Rousseau, John Locke, Montesquieu, Martin Luther – visionaries, revolutionaries ... it was like I knew those guys, like they'd been living in my backyard.'[36]

When it came to music, well, Dylan was on intimate terms with the greats there too. Pop was pap. 'Folksingers, jazz artists and classical musicians' passed his test because they made long-playing records rather than singles. 'There was nothing easy-going about the folk songs I sang. They weren't friendly or ripe with mellowness. I guess you could say they weren't commercial ... They were my preceptor and guide into some altered consciousness of reality, some different republic, some liberated republic.'[37]

As for singers, Harry Belafonte made the grade with Dylan, not just for his music – 'the best balladeer in the land', 'a fantastic artist, sang about lovers and slaves: chain gang workers, saints and sinners', 'repertoire full of old folk songs' – but also because he was larger than life. 'He was a movie star also ... an authentic tough guy ... dramatic and intense on the screen, had a boyish smile and a hard-core hostility.' 'There never was a performer who crossed so many lines as Harry. He appealed to everyone ... steelworkers or symphony patrons or bobby-soxers, even children.' Harry 'said that all folksingers were interpreters ... He even said he hated pop songs, thought they were junk. I could identify with Harry in all kinds of ways ... Harry was that rare type of character that radiates greatness.'[38] 'In world news, Picasso at seventy-nine years old had just married his thirty-five-year-old model. Wow ... Life hadn't flowed past him yet. Picasso had fractured the art world and cracked it wide open. He was revolutionary. I wanted to be like that.'[39]

It's quite a pantheon Dylan felt adjacent to – the great dictators plus Churchill and Roosevelt; the great philosophers and Martin Luther; Harry Belafonte; Picasso. Dylan had no modesty stopping him from basking in great company such as that. Right from the start, he saw himself, not as a singer or entertainer, or, God forbid, as a pop star, but as a *prophet* endowed with great originality and attitude. 'Robert Shelton, the folk and jazz critic for the *New York Times*, would review one of my performances and say something like, "resembling a cross between a choirboy and a beatnik ... he breaks all the rules in song-writing, except that of having something to say". ... It wasn't like I ever meant to break them [the rules]. It was just that what I was trying to express was beyond the circle.'[40] 'My little shack in the universe was about to expand into some glorious cathedral, at least in song-writing terms.'[41]

Later, Dylan became a family man and for a time went into semi-retirement. 'What did I owe the rest of the world? Nothing. Not a damn thing,' he wrote defiantly. He was already sure of his place in the gallery of greatness. 'Sometime in the past I had written and performed songs that were most original and most influential, and I didn't know if I ever would again and I didn't care.'[42]

*

Einstein, Leonardo, Keynes, Dylan. The first couple are perhaps more likeable than the last two, but they all have this in common – the highest possible regard for what they could beget, and a sense of greatness. They were iconoclasts; bold and self-possessed; expecting and requiring nothing from themselves except that what was beyond the reach of ordinary mortals. They expected to produce work of the highest originality and importance. It's hard to imagine how anyone can be great without having similar reach and vision. In our own league, whether the premier division or something worthwhile but less grand, great expectations are still the midwife of great creation.

My emphasis on great leaps forward goes against the grain of current educational psychology, where the prevailing view is that the surest way to achievement is through a series of 'baby steps' – a small conquest is followed by greater confidence and another small step, and so all the way up. This works well enough, especially for people who initially lack confidence.

Yet a great truth can be compatible with its opposite. We are looking at people of *unreasonable attainment*, who start with the vision of their personal greatness and then work backwards to fill in the necessary intermediate steps. Because of their unusual self-confidence and aspiration to greatness, the higher the standards they set, the greater the possible achievement. This does not work for everyone; but conversely, I found no examples of unreasonable success which did not involve great leaps forward based on quite outsized expectations. If you can visualise yourself as a great achiever, this does not guarantee great success – far from it – but it makes it hugely more likely.

Summary and conclusion

Expectations – of others for us, of ourselves, and of our associates and followers – become self-fulfilling. This is one of the few magic tricks left in the world, perhaps the most important.

Therefore, set your expectations as high as you possibly can, consistent with believing they can be realised. If you want unreasonable success, you must have completely unreasonable expectations. The ceiling on your future is the most you can imagine and expect.

Although Olympian expectations are the property of a tiny minority, the funny thing is that the people holding these beliefs are often obscure and unnoticed until their presumptions come to fruition. This suggests that many more people – perhaps, dear reader, you included – could reach unsuspected heights.

Take heart. There are seven more landmarks on our journey, but if you have strong self-belief and genuinely Olympian expectations, you are halfway to victory already. The terrain is downhill from here. Next, we see the life-changing fillip that you can gain from having one or more transforming experiences.

Olympian expectations

- Experiment to generate instances of success
- Early experience of success
- Extreme ambition: Think big; think bigger
- Unreasonably demanding of self and others

6

Landmark 3: Transforming Experiences

The goal is ... the transformation of your mind and character ... choose places of work and positions that offer the greatest possibilities for learning.

—ROBERT GREENE, *Mastery* (2012)

One of my thrilling and important discoveries in writing this book was that nearly all my players had at least one unusual experience which prepared them for unreasonable success. They were transformed by an event or episode which made a deep impression on them and equipped them with unusual insight, knowledge or convictions. Without these experiences, we might never have heard of them. There are profound and hopeful implications for how to drive forward your own career.

The transforming experiences
of Nelson Mandela

Nelson Mandela was destined for a significant role where he grew up, in the Transkei – 'a beautiful country,' as he tells us in his autobiography, 'of rolling hills, fertile valleys, and a thousand rivers and streams'.[1] The Transkei was a nominally independent republic in the south-east of South Africa from 1976 to 1994, when it was incorporated into the Eastern Cape province. Mandela's homeland was a relatively prosperous rural backwater, the home of the Thembu people, where life continued as it had for centuries.

Mandela was connected to the Thembu royal house, and his father was a local chief, privileged to have several wives. 'Although I was a member of the royal household,' Nelson tells us, 'I was not trained for rule. Instead, I was groomed, like my father before me, to counsel the rulers of the tribe.'[2]

But it was not to be. Two transforming experiences removed the predictable path of his lineage, substituting instead a role on the world stage which would have been totally unimaginable in his early years.

The young Mandela was sent to school, the first in his family to go there. 'On the first day of school . . . Miss Mdingane told me that my new name was Nelson.'[3]

Other schools then moulded Mandela, broadening his horizons and transforming his view of the world. At sixteen, he was sent to the Clarkebury Institute, founded in 1825 as a Wesleyan mission. The college head was a white man, Reverend Harris, who, Mandela says, 'ran Clarkebury with an iron hand and an abiding sense of fairness. Clarkebury functioned more like a military school than a teacher-training college.'

Mandela was impressed by his African teacher, Ben Mahlasela. 'In those days,' he writes, 'a black man with a BA was expected to scrape before a white man with a primary-school education,' but Mahlasela was an exception, and would not be cowed even by the powerful head of the college. 'Mr Mahlasela would walk into the Reverend's office without fear ... he met him on equal terms, disagreeing with him where others simply assented.'4 Mandela was simultaneously becoming aware of the inequity facing black South Africans and of the fundamental equality which, once confidently asserted, could not be denied.

When he was nineteen, Mandela joined his great friend Justice, the son of the ruling regent of Thembu, at Healdtown, another Methodist college, with a beautiful campus – it was the largest African school south of the equator. Here he imbibed two conflicting yet complementary values which framed his life – his love and respect for the best of English-style education and customs on the one hand; and, on the other, his quest for equality regardless of race. The first was reflected in the prestige and rigour of life at Healdtown – 'the educated Englishman,' Mandela says, 'was our model; what we aspired to be were "black Englishmen" ... we were taught – and believed – that the best ideas were English ideas, the best government was English government and the best men were Englishmen'.5

Yet Mandela was deeply influenced by two incidents which begat what we might now call 'black pride'. First, his house-master faced down the pompous headmaster, who harped on about his descent from the great Duke of Wellington, victor of Waterloo. When the housemaster, Reverend Mokitimi, was dealing with a commotion amongst students, headmaster Wellington bustled over to take charge and demanded to know what was going on. 'Reverend Mokitimi stood his ground: "Dr Wellington, I am the housemaster and I have told you that I will report to you tomorrow, and that is what I will do." We were stunned. We had never seen anyone, much less a black man, stand up to Dr Wellington, and we waited for an explosion. But Dr Wellington simply said, "Very well," and left. I realized then that Dr Wellington was less than a god and Reverend Mokitimi more than a lackey, and that a black man did not have to defer automatically to a white, however senior he was.'[6]

Another event, Mandela recounts, 'for me was like a comet streaking across the night sky'. The school was assembled and gasped when Dr Wellington brought on to the stage 'a black man dressed in a leopard skin kaross and matching hat, carrying a spear in either hand'. The man spoke magnetically and heretically in Xhosa – the spear, he said, 'stands for what is glorious and true in African history; it is a symbol of the African as warrior and artist . . . the brutal clash between what is indigenous and good, and what is foreign and bad'.

For the first time, Mandela considered himself both a Xhosa and an African, and in an ambiguous relationship with his white teachers: 'I had many new and sometimes conflicting ideas floating in my head. I was beginning to see that Africans of all tribes had much in common . . . I saw that an African might stand his ground with a white man, yet I was still eagerly seeking benefits from whites, which often required subservience.'[7]

Two further transformations were critical. The first of these arose when the regent called together Justice and Nelson. 'My children,' he said sombrely, 'I am not long for this world, and before I return to my ancestors, it is my duty to see my two sons properly married.' He had arranged for Justice to marry the daughter of a nobleman and Nelson to wed a Thembu priest's daughter. Justice and Nelson resolved to avoid the unions; they escaped to Johannesburg via a complicated route fraught with danger, involving deception, lies, theft and comic episodes worthy of a cinematic sub-plot.[8]

For Mandela, Johannesburg was a totally new world – exhilarating, precarious, supremely testing. He was lucky to come across Lazar Sidelsky, a liberal Jew in his mid-thirties, partner in a successful law firm, who made the young Mandela an articled clerk, a very rare step. Mandela recalls that Sidelsky, a slim, courtly man who supported African education with his own money, treated him most kindly. Sidelsky advised him to avoid politics, and specifically the company of men such as Gaur Radebe and Walter Sisulu, who were members of the ANC (African National Congress) and the Communist Party. Nevertheless, Mandela was taken by Radebe's conviction that the ANC was the engine of change, the way for Africans to attain equality and civil rights; and even more impressed by Walter Sisulu, whom he found 'strong, reasonable, practical, and dedicated'.

In 1941 the regent died. Mandela returned to his childhood home for the funeral, spending a week there thinking about his life. 'There is nothing,' he wrote, 'like returning to a place that remains unchanged to find the ways in which you yourself have altered . . . I no longer saw my future bound up with Thembuland and the Transkei. My life in Johannesburg, my exposure to men like Gaur Radebe, my experiences at the law firm had radically altered my beliefs. I looked back on the young man who had left Mqheskezweni as a naïve and countrified fellow who had seen very little of the world. I now believed I was seeing things as they were. That too, of course, was an illusion.'[9]

Mandela spent more and more time with Walter Sisulu, living in his home for several months. He gradually became politicised – 'There was no particular day on which I said, Henceforth I will devote myself to the liberation of my people; instead, I simply found myself doing so, and could not do otherwise.'[10] The transformation from a life of service within the Thembu royal household to that of a freedom fighter was now complete.

There was one further, extremely unpleasant, transformation ahead of Mandela, which, terrible as it was, had to be endured before he could fulfil his destiny as the liberator of South Africa. We will examine the third and final transformation of Nelson Mandela in the next chapter – like all good thrillers, the story is impossibly bleak before the ending.

The transforming experience of Jeff Bezos

Before launching Amazon, Bezos had a transforming experience at another exceptionally unusual firm. If that firm had not existed and he had not had that transforming experience, there would have been no Amazon and you and I would never have heard of him.

Bezos joined the firm D. E. Shaw & Company ('DESCO') in 1990 when he was twenty-six. He had become disillusioned while working on Wall Street and was about to quit the financial field when a head–hunter persuaded him to see DESCO. It was a different type of financial firm – highly elitist and ambitious, valuing intelligence and quantitative skills above all; quirky, secretive, geeky, informal, yet intensely demanding of its employees.

DESCO had been founded just two years earlier by David E. Shaw, a former computer finance professor, and its style differentiated it sharply from your standard–issue Wall Street firm. For its first three years, DESCO was housed not in a glass tower, but atop a communist bookstore in the West Village; the dress code was jeans or shorts. Bezos loved working there, rapidly building a strong personal bond with Shaw. They were kindred spirits – off-the-scale bright, methodical, introspective, enthusiastic and unreasonably ambitious. Shaw wanted his firm to be as successful in its specialist field of quantitative investment management as Goldman Sachs was more generally, and he attained his goal. Today DESCO has $47 billion under management, and it has given its investors the third-highest returns of any hedge fund in the world since it was founded.[11]

DESCO's business bore no resemblance to that of the future Amazon, and yet DESCO gave Bezos the model for Amazon in four vital ways:

- The template for a firm with **incredibly high standards and brilliant people.**
- More specifically, **the early discovery of the internet and its amazing growth potential.**
- Even more specifically, the **vision for Amazon** originated at DESCO.
- Yet more precisely, the **ideal first product for Amazon** was identified at DESCO.

Template for a firm with incredibly high standards and brilliant people

For Shaw, Bezos and their colleagues at DESCO, it was a terrific experience – intense, impassioned and fun. Shaw thought the most important decision any new firm can make is the type of people it will hire. He hired computer scientists and mathematicians because quantitative analysis was the firm's power alley, but it wasn't this focus which mattered most. What mattered was the intellectual firepower of his people.[12]

Bezos imbibed the necessity of hiring only super-'A' people and of holding everyone to very high performance standards. 'A' people, he realised, wanted to work with other 'A' people; admitting any 'B' people was the slippery slope to mediocrity and oblivion.

The internet would change the world – the vision for Amazon

Computer technology was the future. The internet, Shaw in-
tuited, was going to be massive. He saw DESCO as 'a versatile
technology laboratory full of innovators'. He registered the
URL Deshaw.com in 1992, two years before Goldman Sachs
and three years before Morgan Stanley registered their URLs.
Shaw asked Bezos to work with him on how the internet might
open up new markets for DESCO.[13]

The idea they loved most they dubbed 'the everything store' –
selling a wide range of consumer goods over the internet. They
also had the idea of having customers write evaluations of the
products on the website.

Bezos decided that the everything store should start with just
one category to prove the concept. He made a list of twenty
possible products such as computer software, music and office
supplies. But the one he liked best was books. One advantage
was that every copy of any title was the same, so customers
could be sure they weren't getting an inferior product. Another
plus was that there were just two wholesalers who between them
held nearly all books in stock, so it would not be necessary for
the new internet retailer to develop relationships with hundreds
of publishers. With over three million books in stock, the internet retailer would be able to offer a hugely wider range of books
than any bookshop.[14]

The more he thought about it, the more Bezos wanted to
create the everything store. But he didn't want to do it within
DESCO; he needed to be a founder-entrepreneur, the absolute boss, not a second string, even to a soulmate like Shaw. In
spring 1994 he told Shaw he wanted to leave to start the online
bookstore himself.

Shaw took Bezos for a two-hour walk in Central Park, trying
to persuade him to build the new business within DESCO, but

leaving Bezos to decide. Jeff started Amazon in his garage on 5 July 1994. The rest you know.

The Jeff Bezos saga is the starkest example of the most frequent pattern of transforming experiences within business – an exciting and challenging job in a high-growth venture which leads the individual to acquire rare knowledge and think that they can change the future by starting their own company.

The transforming experience of Lenin as a young student

Once upon a time there was a sixteen-year-old boy called Volodya, jovial enough but somewhat cool and withdrawn, whose two main interests were his studies and chess – he excelled at both. He was a walking encyclopaedia, helping his schoolmates, now with a translation, now with other schoolwork, but he had no real friends and reserved his affection for his family – his father, mother, sisters and especially his elder brother Sacha. His childhood and early teenage years were idyllic, growing up in a close-knit, intellectual middle-class family in Simbirsk, Russia.

Sacha was adored by young Volodya and their other siblings. He attended St Petersburg University and was briefly taught by the distinguished chemist Dmitry Mendeleyev, famous for creating the periodic table of elements. Sacha was good-looking, romantic, well-behaved and absolutely devoted to his studies; he collected insect specimens and had a particular fascination, shared in faraway England by Charles Darwin, for earthworms.

Then tragedy struck. In 1886, Sacha's and Volodya's father, a conscientious and well-respected civil servant, suddenly had a stroke and died prematurely.

Sixteen months later, on 8 May 1887, when Volodya was seventeen and taking a geometry exam – for which he earned top marks – something happened which transformed his life. That morning, five young men were taken from the Shlisselburg Fort near St Petersburg and unceremoniously hanged. There were only three scaffolds, so the last two men had to wait and see three of their compatriots hang, before taking their turn. The last to die, six weeks after his twenty-first birthday, was Sacha. He calmly kissed the Cross before dying with great dignity.

The family were only told of Sacha's execution the following day. The five students had plotted to kill Tsar Alexander III, who read the entire record of the case and admired the transcript of Sacha's speech – 'this frankness and honesty, is even touching!' Nonetheless, he refused to commute the death sentence.

The effect on the family, and particularly Volodya, was dramatic. Grief was compounded by their rejection by the town – those who had respectfully attended the father's funeral now shunned this family tainted by subversion, even though none of them had had any idea of Sacha's involvement in rev-olutionary politics. Volodya in particular was overcome by a vitriolic hatred of 'middle-class do-gooders'. 'The bourgeois,' he declared endlessly from that day forward, 'will always be traitors and cowards.'

As his biographer, Victor Sebestyen, wrote, 'A young boy who rarely thought about politics became radicalised almost overnight.'[15] Vladimir Ulyanov – for that was his proper name – came top of his class, winning the gold medal at the Simbirsk Classical Gymnasium, but then immersed himself in revolutionary books. In truth, simply by association with his brother, he became a marked man, denied entrance to the country's top universities and closely monitored by the authorities. The events of May 1887, says Sebestyen, 'seemed to drain away all the cheerfulness, lightness of manner, and good humour that had characterised his early life. He was beginning to become the highly disciplined, tightly contained man people would know as Lenin.' His younger brother Dmitry said, 'Vladimir became grimly restrained, strict, closed up in himself, highly focused.'[16]

Vladimir became transformed, intent on revenge and revolution, full of hatred for the tsarist regime and its bourgeois 'lickspittles'. On 25 October 1917, he seized supreme power in Russia.

Margaret Thatcher: Transformed for unreasonable success

Margaret Thatcher managed the difficult feat of becoming prime minister without having had a transforming experience. In the third year of office she was the epitome of *reasonable* success, having always wanted a career in politics; and as someone who started as a Conservative admirer of Churchill at the time of his greatness, she was strongly opposed to socialism. She always worked hard and had a clear idea of her objectives, and although her ascent to power was sudden, unexpected and rather lucky, her plodding determination and simple focus on unchanging beliefs paid off.

Unlike Lenin and unlike Mandela – whom, incidentally, she later helped to free from prison – there was, up to 1982, no important discontinuity in her character or career. True, the translation from Kesteven and Grantham Girls' School in Lincolnshire to Oxford marked a dramatic change of environment. Oxford gave her confidence and self-belief, but it did not transform the young Margaret Roberts as one might have expected. One of her best and most even-handed biographers, John Campbell, says that university 'opened doors to her and set her on the way to a political career. Yet Oxford was not for her, as it was for so many others, a golden period of youthful experiment and self-discovery. In the four years she spent there she made no lasting friendships, underwent no intellectual awakening ... The most remarkable thing about her Oxford career, in fact, was how little the experience seemed to change her.'[17]

How important was it that Margaret Roberts met and eventually married Denis Thatcher, a prosperous manager and owner of a family paint and chemicals business? Denis had been a distinguished soldier during the Second World War, and although considerably older than his wife-to-be, he had a certain 'style and dash' and drove a Jaguar.[18] Marrying Denis was a shrewd and important step for Margaret – she left behind the austerity and cultural vacuum of her lower-middle-class provincial roots for a wealthier life in the Home Counties, and was free to pursue both her political ambitions and her training as a barrister without needing to worry about money. But did being Mrs Thatcher rather than Miss Roberts transform the inner Margaret? It seems doubtful. Thatcher herself said it was 'certainly not' love at first sight.[19] John Campbell says, 'Both were dedicated to their own careers, which neither ever curtailed for the other.'[20]

The last two pivotal events in Thatcher's life before 1982 – which nevertheless fell well short of personal transformation – were her election as Conservative Party Leader in 1975, and her victory in the first general election thereafter, in 1979. Both were fortuitous. The former event owed everything to three factors – the extreme unpopularity with Conservative MPs of Ted Heath, the leader she ousted, who had lost three out of four general elections, and who was gratuitously rude to everyone; the failure of nerve amongst other possible challengers to Heath; and her own courage and ambition, a constant part of her nature.

Her win as Conservative leader was a conundrum, with

strong overtones of *faute de mieux*. 'We've gone mad,' said Sir Ian Gilmour, a prominent minister, 'She won't last ... she can't last.'[21] The Labour Party were delighted at her election, rejoicing that she was 'bloody unelectable'.[22] Within her own party, 'Her position remained insecure for the whole period 1975–79 ... A powerful section of the party, including most of Heath's senior colleagues whom she was obliged to retain in her Shadow Cabinet, remained conspicuously uncommitted to her.'[23]

'Thatcher was in a weak position,' says Professor David Cannadine. 'Tory grandees such as Lord Carrington, Sir Ian Gilmour, Christopher Soames, and William Whitelaw looked down on her, on account of her gender and her lowly social origins, condescensions vividly articulated in Whitelaw's description of her as "governessy". It was the same in the Conservative Research Department, where Thatcher was described as "Hilda" or "milk-snatcher" ... Thatcher did not seem a plausible prime minister in waiting.'[24]

Yet Thatcher was again assisted by external events – the Labour Party's tiny majority eaten away by by-election losses, leaving the government dependent on other political parties; the appalling economic record and extremism of many leading Labour figures while in office from 1974–79; the failure of Jim Callaghan, the Labour prime minister, to call an election in the autumn of 1978, when he would probably have won it; and luckiest of all for Thatcher, the 1978–79 'winter of discontent', when thanks to striking workers demanding huge pay increases, rubbish piled to high heaven, ambulance drivers refused to take the sick to hospital, the dead were not buried, and petrol ran out. The Labour government lost all control – any Conservative leader would have won under these circumstances.

So when she became prime minister in 1979, expectations of Thatcher were muted. She had to depend on a Cabinet of Tory ministers, most of whom were contemptuous or unsympathetic. Though dealt a difficult hand, Margaret Thatcher proceeded to make an extraordinary mess of her first two years as PM.

Professor Cannadine sums up: 'She was genuinely unsure of herself now that she had obtained the supreme office . . . By the end of 1979 inflation was [rising] . . . even higher, and business confidence had collapsed. By the summer of 1980 prices had risen 22 per cent in a year, gross domestic product was down 5.5 per cent in two years, and unemployment stood at 2.7 million, an increase of one million in the previous twelve months . . . interest rates were raised from 14 to 17 per cent, the highest level ever. By the spring of 1981 it did not seem as though anything the Thatcher government was doing was working. Stagflation was intensifying, prices and wages were still rising out of control, but so too was unemployment . . . her chances of surviving until the next election, let alone of winning it, seemed minimal.'[25]

Only she and three other cabinet ministers, out of a total of twenty-three, backed her hard-line economic strategy. The prime minister suffered from 'physical and mental exhaustion, harsh public image and alienation from her friends'. When Thatcher finally sacked three of her most vocal critics within the Cabinet, one of them, Ian Gilmour, told journalists, 'It does no harm to throw the occasional man overboard, but it does not do much good if you are steering full speed ahead for the rocks.'[26]

There were riots protesting against unemployment in London, Liverpool and elsewhere. Lord Hailsham, the veteran lord chancellor, told Thatcher that Herbert Hoover had succeeded in destroying the Republican Party by his policy of austerity and sound money in the Great Depression of the 1930s – she could destroy the Conservatives the same way.[27]

Thatcher insisted on sticking to her economic plan, which she claimed would eventually work; but most ministers and other observers reckoned there would be no long term if the short-term pain had not dissipated before a general election.

That seemed unlikely. New political developments threatened Thatcher yet further. In March 1982, four prominent Labour figures, dismayed by the Labour Party's further lurch to the left, started the Social Democratic Party (SDP) and formed an alliance with the Liberal Party. The electoral results were stunning, with the Alliance taking the lead in the opinion polls – at one time polling 50 per cent, with Labour and the Tories pushed down to 23 per cent each. Thatcher's approval rating plummeted to 25 per cent, making her the most unpopular prime minister since polling began. Three devastating by-election losses in rock-solid Tory seats came in quick succession; in the last of them, in March 1982, Roy Jenkins, the SDP leader, won a famous victory at Glasgow, Hillhead, and seemed likely to become the next prime minister.

Into this bear pit dropped a seismic event of terrible proportions for Britain's standing in the world. Encouraged by British defence cuts, and a sense Britain would not defend its few remaining colonies, rumours began circulating towards the end of March 1982 that the Argentine dictator, General Galtieri, was about to invade Britain's Falkland Islands, an outpost in the Southern Atlantic where eighteen hundred fiercely loyal British subjects lived.

The Argentine invasion happened on 2 April 1982, unopposed. When she heard about it, Thatcher said it was 'the worst moment of my life'.[28] The defence minister, John Nott, told Thatcher that recapturing the islands – just three hundred miles from Argentina, but eight *thousand* miles from Britain – was practically impossible.

THATCHER: 'You'll have to take them [the Falkland Islands] back.'

NOTT: 'We can't.'
THATCHER: 'You'll have to.'[29]

Into this deadlock stepped Admiral Henry Leach, the head of the British navy, who asked for her permission to assemble a task force to retake the islands.

THATCHER: 'Can we do it?'
ADMIRAL LEACH: 'We can, Prime Minister, and though it
    is not my place to say this, we must.'
THATCHER: 'Why do you say that?'
LEACH: 'Because if we don't do it, if we pussyfoot – we
    will be living in a totally different country whose word
    will count for nothing.'

With a rueful half-smile, the prime minister gave permission to assemble the task force.[30]

Thatcher had very little diplomatic leverage, and it seemed likely that her career would be over in a few days. In the House of Commons Enoch Powell spelt out the challenge to Mrs Thatcher. The Soviets had half-mockingly called her the Iron Lady, and Powell taunted: 'In the next week or two, this House, this nation, and the right honourable Lady herself will learn of what metal she is made.' Alan Clark noted in his dairy 'how low she held her head, how *knotted* with pain and apprehension' she seemed as Powell spoke.[31]

On April 5 and 6 the task force sailed from Portsmouth with military music and wives weeping. Despite Admiral Leach's optimism, many military experts considered the chances of retaking the islands were minimal; the US navy said it was 'a futile and impossible effort which could not succeed ... a military impossibility'.[32]

For the six weeks that it took the task force to reach the south

Atlantic, the focus shifted to non–stop diplomatic activity. To her immense irritation and frustration, Thatcher found that America wanted to avoid taking sides between Britain and Argentina.

The American position was complex and contradictory. President Reagan and his secretary of state, Alexander Haig, appeared to want any available peaceful outcome, though Haig privately urged the president to side with Argentina; Jeanne Kirkpatrick, the US permanent representative to the United Nations, openly supported Argentina against 'colonial' Britain; while Secretary of Defense Caspar Weinberger backed Britain. He secretly provided the use of America's Ascension Island in the mid–Atlantic for refuelling, along with Sidewinder missiles and full access to US intelligence – without which winning the war would indeed have been impossible.

Thatcher played a blinder with Haig and Reagan. It was a delicate balance; she could not accept a ceasefire or a solution that would reward Argentina's aggression, such as joint British–Argentine sovereignty. But at the same time, she could not afford to alienate the USA by appearing intransigent.[33]

Reagan constantly begged her to agree a ceasefire. Thatcher resisted all the peace-mongering American and British bureaucrats, adamant that a military victory was the only acceptable solution.[34] With a natural affinity for the armed forces, she saw that they got everything they wanted. Her very ignorance of military matters helped, making her for once a very good listener. Philip Goodhart, a former soldier and defence minister, said, 'She wouldn't have done it [invaded] if she'd been a man and in the armed forces during the war. Then she'd have been aware how dreadfully wrong everything was likely to go.'[35]

Instead of attempting to land near Port Stanley, as the Argentines expected, and helped by bad weather, the task force reached San Carlos Bay undetected. On 21 May nearly five thousand men were safely put ashore.

Argentine troops outnumbered the British by over two to one, but the former were conscripts and not used to the Falklands' bitter weather. On 14 June British troops recaptured Port Stanley and on 15 June eleven thousand Argentine men surrendered. The war was over; Thatcher was triumphantly vindicated.

'Although Thatcher gave full credit to the service chiefs,' says Cannadine, 'she was the supreme architect and beneficiary of their victory. She had taken huge military and political risks, but her resolution and determination had never wavered.'[36]

How the Falklands experience transformed Thatcher

- **It gave her new, transcendent self-confidence.** The Falklands crisis was the time of her life, said Robert Armstrong, when 'she lived most intensely'.[37] She was sure that only she could have done it. It was the defining moment, the greatest triumph of her whole career.
- **She thought it proved that Britain could regain its greatness.** After her Falklands triumph, she went back to Downing Street, mingling with the people, young and old, singing *Rule Britannia*. 'It was their triumph,' she said. 'We have ceased to be a nation in retreat.'[38]
- As Charles Moore said, her mindset was 'both conservative and revolutionary. She saw herself as restoring an inherent British greatness ... At the same time, she saw herself as bringing about enormous change.'[39]
- **She went from being on probation with her Tory colleagues to complete dominance over them.**[40]
- **The full Thatcherite agenda to save Britain from socialism was now able to emerge.**
- **Finally, the Falklands experience made Thatcher**

dangerously over-confident, intransigent and unwilling to listen to close colleagues. Her success in war made her increasingly intolerant, autocratic and unable to compromise.

Why a transforming experience is necessary for unreasonable success

Reasonable success can follow from a linear and ordered career plan – doing all the 'right' things. But following a conventional path won't lead to *un*reasonable success.

On the other hand, unreasonable success can spring from one or more intense experiences which call forth unsuspected talents or latent character. The seeds of extraordinary personal achievement are watered and germinate during a time of extreme weather – a personal crisis or other learning and testing period which marks a profound discontinuity in your self-belief, expectations, rare knowledge, direction, certainty, focus and potential.

- Without a transforming experience you are unlikely to attain unreasonable success.
- It is possible to engineer a transforming experience for yourself. So position yourself in the slipstream of events where the right kind of transforming experience is most likely.

The players in this book did not consciously engineer their own transforming experiences. You are more fortunate. By learning from their experiences, you can plot a transforming experience which may catapult you to unreasonable success.

Bill Bain – the transformations
of a history researcher

Bill Bain never intended to be a strategy consultant, or work in business. Born in 1937 in rural Tennessee, he studied history at Vanderbilt. Bain loved history and started a postgraduate degree, aiming to become a history teacher.

But two transformations quite fortuitously turned him into a rich man and a formidable weapon in consulting and private equity. Although he is now dead and largely forgotten, Bain perhaps had more influence on global business practice than any other individual in the twentieth century.

Tired of tedious research, he cast around for other options, and at the age of twenty-six landed a plum job as Vanderbilt's development director, charged with raising funds for the university from corporate chiefs. He got to know the bosses of many famous companies, including Chemical Bank, J. P. Morgan, Kodak and the Bank of New York.

It was Bain's first exposure to the giddy heights of corporate America; he discovered that he could interact smoothly with its chief executives. 'I was fascinated by how they got there,' he said. 'I liked every one of those guys a lot, and they liked me. I felt very comfortable with them,' sharing common interests such as 'sports, women, business, competition, goals'.[41]

The Vanderbilt post gave Bain confidence in dealing in a very different and exclusive social world; he must have been gratified at his skill in getting corporate chiefs to part with money for a good cause. Since Bill was highly commercial and very interested in money, he may well have wondered whether there was a way to monetise his empathy with top business folk and break into the corporate world which he found so exciting and intellectually stimulating.

It turned out there was. Bill's second transformation flowed seamlessly and fortuitously from his first. While fund-raising, Bill met Vanderbilt alumnus Bruce Henderson. Bruce was impressed with Bain's charm and ability to handle meetings. In 1967, he approached Bain about possibly joining BCG. He said that though Bill had no business experience, Bruce needed 'someone very smart, who understands and can work with and motivate senior executives and be respected by them'. Bain was invited to Boston to meet BCG's three top vice-presidents. At the end of the day, Bruce passed Bill copies of their evaluations – as Bain tells the story they saw him as 'a guy who hadn't gone to business school and was bright enough, but so too were a lot of, oh, priests, who you clearly weren't going to hire'.[42]

Henderson hired Bain anyway, trained him personally on trips – I like the story that Bruce taught Bill the principles of depreciation while on a flight – and put him on some of BCG's biggest clients, where he excelled. Henderson took Bain with him on his pitches for new business.

Bain even succeeded in getting Henderson – a rotten sales-man, excessively opinionated, lacking in empathy, prone to veer off on irrelevant intellectual tangents – to start by asking the top executives questions, rather than launching into Brucian blather. Bain and Henderson meshed well together, and Henderson even responded to pointed coaching from Bain.

Bain went from strength to strength. He was put in charge of work for Texas Instruments and Black & Decker, BCG's biggest clients. In 1969 Bain added a third mega-client by selling Union Carbide a comprehensive, six-month portfolio review. He told them, 'We're going to put all your businesses along one axis, all your competitors along another; we're going to put all that together and tell you the structure of the industry and what's going to happen.' As Bain often did when selling business at quite unprecedented fee levels, he implied this was standard BCG practice.

The fourth monthly meeting with the client representative, Warren Anderson, was delayed by several hours. While kicking their heels in Union Carbide offices, Bain and his project leader, Dick Lochridge, summarised all their client's business units on a single sheet of paper. That was the prototype for the famous 'growth-share matrix', the Boston Box that would eventually feature cash cows, dogs, question marks and stars. By plotting the position of each of Union Carbide's businesses on two dimensions – the future market growth, and how large they were relative to their largest competitor ('relative market share') – they encapsulated the relative attraction and issues for all business units.

When they walked into the meeting, Bain said, 'Warren, we have a lot to tell you, but here,' – he flourished the chart – 'is your portfolio.' Anderson was enchanted.[43]

That chart was the key to BCG's success for the next ten years, and to Bain & Company's good fortune for even longer.

The whole experience of working at BCG between 1967 and 1973 was the vital second transformation of Bill Bain; but the transformation would not have been complete if not for one fateful, bizarre, yet entirely characteristic action Bruce Henderson took in 1970. He was a fanatical believer in the value of competition, so he divided BCG into three profit centres – effectively three mini-companies, each known by a colour: red, green, and blue. Bain was made leader of team blue, leaving him free to experiment. Soon his team accounted for more revenue and profit than the other teams combined.

By 1973, Bain was sure he could make far more money and have more fun by setting up his own shop. Henderson felt devastated and betrayed, but he took no legal action to stop Bain. Today, the three global consulting behemoths are McKinsey, BCG and Bain.

Helena Rubinstein's transforming experience

In May 1896, a diminutive, vivacious, pretty young woman with exquisite skin, speaking Polish, Yiddish and some German, boarded the *Prinz Regent Leopold* in Genoa, a ship bound for Australia via Naples, Alexandria, Aden, Port Said and Bombay. She travelled saloon class, roughly equivalent to business class on planes today. Though she was twenty-four, she put her age on the manifest as twenty – the first instance of a lifetime's practice of revising and romanticising her history. She charmed well-connected passengers and attracted admirers, as though born to a life of leisure.

The truth was otherwise. Helena Rubinstein had been born on 25 December 1872 in the Jewish city of Kazimierz, next to the larger and more prosperous Polish city of Kraków. Her father was a bookish and introverted merchant who ran a general store; her mother was devout and domineering. Money was tight, and her mother planned to marry off her eight daughters, starting with Helena, to gentlemen who could pay a substantial dowry.

Helena Rubinstein had other ideas. She left home, moving to Vienna to stay with an uncle and aunt. He and his three brothers were flourishing furriers, and Rubinstein worked in their store for two years, skilfully selling customers the most expensive furs. She liked working in the luxury retail trade, but even cosmopolitan Vienna seemed too small for her. Her cousin Eva in Australia had just divorced her husband and needed help with her three small children. Rubinstein decided to emigrate, taking with her, so the story goes, a dozen little pots of home-made face cream from her mother.

After three frustrating years in Australia as a domestic serv-ant, she became a waitress at two smart cafés in Melbourne. Outgoing and flirtatious, she soon met four friends who changed her life.

They were the painter Cyril Dillon; Abel Isaacson, a successful, smartly dressed wine merchant; Herbert Farrow, a rich printer; and most important of all, John Thompson, who was a big tea importer. As the four got to know Rubinstein, she revealed her plan to sell pots of face cream based on her secret Polish formula, and to open a beauty salon to save Australian women from the ravages of sun and age.

Her four admirers liked the idea, and gave her practical advice and help – Dillon the artist gave her the logo for her packaging, based on an Egyptian motif, and designed her brochures, which Farrow printed for her. Thompson taught her how to display, market and advertise her goods. For a time, she became his mistress. Most likely, Thompson and Isaacson bankrolled her.

The salon opened near the Winter Gardens around 1903, when she was thirty-one.[44] It was an instant hit, due to the quality, presentation and packaging of the face cream; the romantic, mid-European heritage which she fabricated around it; her effective fear-based press copy; pseudo-scientific inventions; cultivation of wealthy clients; assiduous wooing of journalists and her peasant-princess commercial acumen. 'There are no ugly women,' she would declare, 'only lazy ones.' If you could afford her deliberately expensive potions, for once she told the truth.

The transforming experiences of Walt Disney and Bruce Henderson

Disney and Henderson had this in common – their vital transforming experience came *after* they set up the ventures for which they became famous.

We saw how Disney escaped from Chicago to set up a small animation studio in Hollywood. The studio's breakthrough came five years later, with the invention of Mickey Mouse. The Mouse transformed Walt Disney.

What made the experience so intense, however, was not exhilaration, but sheer *desperation* to save the Disney studio. Disney was working speculatively, without a backer. He ran all over Hollywood trying to flog *Plane Crazy*, the first Mickey Mouse movie. He and his brother Roy had to refinance their mortgages to raise more money, yet time ticked relentlessly on.

The closer they came to disaster, the more deeply impressed on them the Mickey Mouse experience became, and the sweeter was the eventual triumph. Disney felt vindicated, and acquired a self-fulfilling faith in his genius and destiny.

Bruce Henderson's consulting venture was slow to take off. After a year or so in business he 'had six employees and virtually no reputation'.[45] They had nothing much to say. Yet Bruce knew more than he realised.

He had worked for the Leland Electric Company of Dayton, Ohio. Leland dominated its tightly defined business segment – making explosion-proof motors to go into gasoline pumps. Because of this background, when Henderson was hired by Westinghouse, he was assigned to its small-motors business, which made a wide array of products, some of which competed with Leland. Bruce could approximately recall Leland's costs, prices and profits on the overlapping products, and he compared these to those of Westinghouse. He was amazed to discover that Leland made a good profit on its small motors, while Westinghouse lost money.

How could this be? Both firms had the same prices; but Leland's costs were *much* lower than those of Westinghouse. The two firms had similar raw material and labour costs. Bruce suspected the disparity came from Leland's much higher market share in that segment. Somehow Leland found ways to make its small motors more efficiently than its rivals, because of higher volumes.[46]

In 1964, Henderson sold his first large project to the Norton Company of Worcester, Massachusetts. Norton made grinding wheels, some sold in huge volumes to car-makers and other large firms, and others sold in small numbers to more specialised manufacturers. Norton's prices were going down and its costs were going up. The consultants quickly cracked the case: Norton was under attack from smaller rivals who were picking off the high-volume products for the likes of the car-makers and gaining market share by cutting price. Meanwhile Norton was increasingly being left with the specialised products for smaller customers, on which the unit costs were higher and they lost money.[47]

The Boston team came up with some hypotheses that were to change business strategy forever:

- Costs for any firm are not generally similar across all their products, even if these appear to be similar (e.g. 'small motors' or 'grinding wheels').
- Prices across different products and to different customers may, however, be the same. If this is true, the high-volume products and customers will be more profitable.
- Market share in carefully defined business segments (e.g., not 'grinding wheels', but 'grinding wheels for car-makers') is very valuable, because higher volume *of the same product* means lower unit costs.
- A company probably has very different costs and profit margins across different products, depending on their volume in the correctly defined product/customer segment. It may make a lot of money on a few products and lose a bundle on most.
- Typically, companies' product lines are too broad. They

should focus only on the ones where they are the market leaders or have the lowest unit costs – these two are usually the same.

- A small company facing a bigger rival *must* segment the market and focus on one area or a few where it can become the largest in that segment, having the highest volumes of the relevant products and customers, and therefore the lowest costs.

- Price is a potent competitive weapon. If lower prices enable a firm to gain market share and become the largest in a segment, and therefore have lower costs than any rival at that point, it is worth selling at a loss in the short term to build volume and competitive advantage.

- Companies should strive to become and remain the lowest-cost competitor. Gain market share, then constantly reduce costs and prices to force rivals out of your heartland markets because they can't make money there.

Bruce Henderson's transforming experience was not the founding of his company, nor its delayed success. Rather, it was the evolution of the two grand tools of business strategy – the Experience Curve (1966) and Boston Box (1969) – and the beautifully elegant logic underlying and connecting them. Henderson's transformation can therefore be dated precisely to 1966–69, when he was over fifty.

All the dots, all the random insights that had been bubbling away in the recesses of his mind for decades, miraculously joined up. Henderson and BCG spoke with new authority – high market share meant low costs and high profits. He was a man possessed, still cranky, yet suddenly fulfilled.

Three patterns of transforming experiences in business

Transformations that occur in an unusual firm, before you start a new venture

There was Jeff Bezos, working out the plan for Amazon while still working in that most remarkable of firms, D. E. Shaw & Co, one of the very few that knew how much the internet was going to change the world. Before Amazon was even born, Bezos was transformed, equipped, almost Messianic.

There was Bill Bain, still within BCG, already transformed, already happily piloting the approach he would perfect in his own domain.

This first model is the best – you can acquire ideas and authority, and start to experiment, while still employed by someone else. You become transformed on their dime. The firm you found is not really a start-up, more a continuation and personalisation – *your* personalisation – of a validated prototype. The new venture can be relatively low-risk, yet still high-return, both financially and, more important, psychically.

Work for a strange, singular, surprising – and surprisingly successful – company. Look for one that is growing fast; that does things differently from its larger rivals; that focuses on a special subset of customers and that knows something the rivals do not know. Attain rare knowledge and confidence from what the firm knows.

Next, work out how to use that special knowledge in a different way, just as Bezos did.

Then reach for the stars.

Be transformed by starting your own show

Helena Rubinstein knew what she wanted to do – the formula for her face cream, how to source local ingredients, the salon she wanted to create, the right customers. Her friends taught her how to package, merchandise and promote the products. She knew that rich women would only trust an expensive product. She knew how to chat up customers and journalists.

Once she pressed the button – instant transformation!

Fantastic. But rare.

Typically, new outfits wobble around like drunks at a party, intoxicated by their patter, yet failing to connect. They feel good. Then the hangover.

Transformation after near-failure

This is the most painful, prolonged and elusive kind of trans-formation. It can happen in the nick of time, just before the cash runs out, but more often it does not happen at all. Bruce Henderson waffles about long-term planning, a total dead end, while his colleagues invent the Boston Box. Walt Disney can't sell Mickey Mouse, and teeters towards his final bankruptcy. Until he makes the rodent speak.

Desperation can fuel invention. Reasonable solutions are dead. You give up, or fabricate unreasonable ones. Oblivion beckons, unless you invent the concepts of strategy, or that talking mouse. You insert your last coin in that damn fruit machine; you gasp at three gold bars. Of course, you were a genius all along.

If at first you don't succeed, give up. Unless you have a guardian angel, writing the last act of silly Hollywood feel-good movies.

My advice? Go for the first means of transformation. And if

your first 'fantastic' firm doesn't transform you, move on to the second ... until you really are transformed by new knowledge and authority.

How were other players transformed?

- A bit like Bezos or Bain, **Leonardo** was lucky enough to work in an amazing company. Leonardo's father knew Andrea del Verrocchio, a painter, sculptor and engineer, whose studio-shop was famous in Florence. At fourteen, Leonardo was apprenticed to Verrocchio.

  As well as mass-producing art, furniture, books, maps and globes, Verrocchio also undertook commissions. He created a tomb for the Medici; a bronze statue of Christ and Saint Thomas; another of David, one arm and hand resting on his hip, a sword dangling from the other arm, smirking, perhaps, over the severed head of Goliath.

  Verrocchio taught Leonardo how to draw and paint, capture light and shade, depict the human body. Verrocchio let him paint a dog and an angel in two of his own works.[48]
- **Bob Dylan**'s transforming experience was to reach New York as a raw but incredibly self-assured teenager, perform folk songs in clubs and pubs, and somehow land a contract with Colombia Records – setting out on the path to becoming an icon.
- **Joanne Rowling**'s transforming experience can be viewed either as the most rapid in this book, or as the most protracted. Her transformation began in June 1990, when she was twenty-four, and lasted a mere four hours. She was on a train from Manchester to London, and it broke down. Staring out of the window, she had an inspired vision of a little boy on another train, heading for a special boarding school for wizards. 'All of a sudden,' she said, 'the idea for

Harry [Potter] just appeared in my mind's eye. I can't tell you why or what triggered it. But I saw the idea of Harry and the wizard school very plainly. I suddenly had this basic idea of a boy who didn't know who he was, who didn't know he was a wizard until he got his invitation to wizard school. I have never been so excited by an idea.'[49]

Despite her excitement, Rowling's transformation was not completed on her stalled train. Her first book, *Harry Potter and the Philosopher's Stone*, was not published until seven years after her first dream of the boy. Rowling's transformation is best viewed as a drama in three acts:

Act One was her vision on the train.

Act Two was the writing of the book, started the very evening of the train ride, but not completed until 1995, five years later.

Act Three was getting published, which did not happen until 30 June 1997. Only then was J. K. Rowling's transformation complete and secure.

As we will see in Chapter 10, between Act One and Act Three, she had many setbacks, which would have overwhelmed a less determined person, or one who had a less intense belief in the future of Harry Potter and Joanne Rowling.

• **Albert Einstein** was transformed by the four papers he wrote in 1905 tearing down the old certainties of physics which had endured since Isaac Newton, culminating in his paper on Special Relativity, titled *On the Electrodynamics of Moving Bodies*. One sunny day in Bern, after nearly giving up writing the paper, Einstein said he 'suddenly understood the key to the problem' which was that *there was no such thing as absolute time.*[50]

Having sent the article off, he and his partner Mileva Maric celebrated until they were, as Einstein said, 'dead drunk under the table'. There was not a moment of doubt in Einstein's mind that he had changed physics forever, or that experimental data would eventually prove him right (they did). But unlike Dylan, Einstein did not receive the academic equivalent of a recording contract, and although he would very much have preferred a professorship, the lack of one did not diminish his certainty one iota.

It was enough that Max Planck, 'Europe's revered monarch of theoretical physics',[51] wrote warmly to Einstein and started to lecture on relativity. Einstein was transformed, and although competing demands on his time included playing enthusiastically with his three-year-old son, performing every week in a string quartet − and, oh yes, continuing to work eight hours a day, six days a week, in the Patent Office − he threw himself into a new orgy of deep thinking and learned papers.

Like Bruce Henderson when he had discovered the Experience Curve, like Jeff Bezos when he and David Shaw worked out the blueprint for Amazon (and before Bezos left Shaw to start the new venture), like Bill Bain before he deserted Bruce Henderson to found Bain & Company, Einstein had been transformed. Like them all, he *knew* that he was privy to insights nobody else had, and that he would change the world. Similar transforming certainty affected three other people we have already met in these pages − **Steve Jobs, Paul of Tarsus**, and **Viktor Frankl**.

- **Steve Jobs'** transformation falls into my third category of business transformations, those that happen *after* founding their company. Apple was founded in 1976, but it wasn't until the summer of 1979 that Jobs got religion, that he saw the future of personal computing. And it wasn't at Apple; it was at Xerox PARC, the Silicon Valley lab designing Xerox's entrance to the personal computer market. The

Xerox boffins had invented the graphical user interface which for the first time allowed a computer desktop, on which icons representing documents could be displayed. The user could access everything on the screen by moving a mouse, drop files into folders and print a document from the screen.

Driving fast from Xerox PARC to Apple's campus in Cupertino, Jobs kept shouting to his colleagues, 'THIS IS IT!', stressing each word. 'We've got to do it!' And they did – far better and cheaper than Xerox – with the Lisa and the Macintosh.

- **Paul**'s vivid and disturbing encounter with Jesus, alive in the third heaven and as real to Paul as if he was next to him, was the vision which made him the most effective evangelist the world has ever seen.

- Before he was sent to the camps, **Viktor Frankl** believed he had cracked the insights which had eluded his precursors, Freud and Adler. Freud's psychoanalysis required introspection and sought the 'will to pleasure'; Adler's psychology spotlighted the 'will to power'. But Frankl saw humans' main motivating force as the will to meaning, the search for meaning in life. The key to meaning was free will. Even in terrible circumstances, individuals still retained the freedom to interpret their circumstances and create meaning from them.

On arrival at Auschwitz, and separated from his wife, father, mother and brother – who all perished in the camps – Frankl lost all his possessions and the precious manuscript of the book he was about to publish. He might well have given way to despair and effective suicide. But he took the freedom to see the camps as a test – his mission was to remember the themes of his book, to note them down on scraps of paper, to think of life beyond the Nazis, when he could expound his ideas in lecture theatres – and above all, to *survive and live the truth*, so that all of this might be possible. We are not on Earth, he reasoned, to judge what is happening to us, but to ask what life expects and requires of us, to fulfil our potential.

Frankl found light in the darkness. 'Man is that being who invented the gas chambers,' he wrote. 'However, he is also that being who entered those gas chambers upright, with the Lord's Prayer or the Shema Yisrael on his lips.' He fixated on thoughts of his dear wife; when a bird hopped in front of him, he saw it as her living incarnation. What transformed Frankl was finding meaning in hell.

We close with a completely different transforming experience.

The ultimate postmodern myth: Madonna's perpetual transformation

In 1844 Karl Marx said of Napoleon that he perfected the French revolution 'by substituting permanent war for permanent revolution'. In the twentieth century Leon Trotsky adopted the catchphrase 'permanent revolution' to excuse the twists and turns of Soviet terror. But with Madonna, we have reached the ultimate in personal transformation – perpetual transformation. It is not enough to have one, two or three personal transformations if you want to become and remain for decades perhaps the most famous woman in the world. For that, nothing less than permanent transformation will do – perpetual reinvention with a new identity or reason to talk about you all the time.

Enjoy the verdict of British journalist Ruth Picardie:

Our biggest hero was, of course, Madonna, after she emerged from the Charlene Atlas school of personal reconstruction, transformed from tubby pop star into a goddess. Suddenly, contradiction was in vogue. Madonna dressed like the star of a soft-porn fantasy, but her biggest fans – and friends – were women. The world's most potent sex object, she was also the mistress of her image and identity, whose principal creative pleasure came from reinventing herself as other icons, from Marilyn Monroe to Mae West. Swearing, sex-crazed, offensive and Catholic, we liked her so much we were prepared to tolerate her poor taste in men.[52]

Madonna embraced many different spheres of activity; and within any given domain, she changed tack time and time again, embracing different and sometimes completely opposite images, causing endless controversy and if possible offence, making the modern quest for the 'real' Madonna a lot harder than the medieval quest for the Holy Grail. Curiously, this made Madonna seem not inauthentic but more mysterious and deeper, endowed with ironic detachment.

Academics claim that Madonna is 'postmodern'.[53] What they mean is that she can be taken either at face value, or as a deliberate poseur, ricocheting from persona to persona and role to role without even the tiniest bit of consistency. By mocking her pretensions, yet simultaneously promoting them, she claims immunity from falsehood. Even when trouncing the truth, she does not lie; she simply encapsulates paradox, and, like Pontius Pilate, asks 'What *is* truth?'

Madonna transcends entertainment categories and stereotypes such as virgin or vamp, saint or prostitute, dominatrix or little girl, and now even the elegant lady of a certain age. She somehow manages to appeal simultaneously to the mass pop market *and* to particular niches, such as teenage girls, gay people, the wild side of sadomasochism, and very importantly what we might term, at our own risk, intelligent feminists. Madonna will not settle for certain segments of the market; she wants it all. 'Even when I was a little girl,' she says, 'I wanted the whole world to know who I was, to love me, and be affected by me.'[54]

Madonna Louise Ciccone was born on 16 August 1958, near Detroit. Her father was an engineer; her mother, a French-Canadian Catholic, died when Madonna was five years old. As a teenager she was mad about dancing, studying the subject briefly at the University of Michigan before dropping out to head for Manhattan. She mixed with musicians, DJs, artists and gay men, and had a brief but important interlude in Paris, where she was feted by the two producers of Patrick Hernandez, who had a global disco hit with *Born to Be Alive*. Back in New York in 1982, Madonna had a small dance-floor hit with her first single, and a top twenty hit the next year. Her first album, *Madonna*, reached number eight, and by the end of 1984, at the age of 26, she had sold a million records.

Not bad, but not enough for someone transcendently ambitious. Then the personal transformations began.

- Madonna's first transformation was into the persona of 'Boy Toy'. What on Earth is a boy toy? The clues come in the 1985 movie *Desperately Seeking Susan*. The role Madonna played is outwardly that of a fearless underground New York type. She dresses in black leather, black lace, with silver metal belts inscribed Boy Toy, and an entire junk shop of beads, bangles, bracelets, necklaces, lurid makeup and crucifixes. Her appearance was cheap and easy to copy; millions of young girls did.
- The zenith of Madonna's acting career was *Evita* (1996), where she milked the parallels between her cult and that of Eva Perón. 'You will see,' Madonna crowed, 'that I am Evita.'
- Like Madonna, Perón was a hero from zero, desperately

hungry for fame and power, constantly transforming herself. Perón was promiscuous, sexy, corrupt, yet, she said, 'the Madonna of the poor'. Madonna made herself look and move spookily like Perón. To win the role, Madonna saw off many more accomplished actresses, including Michelle Pfeiffer, Barbra Streisand and Meryl Streep. Madonna's *Don't Cry for Me, Argentina* was number one in dozens of countries.

- Each album was a peg for the latest Madonna reincarnation. Her second album, *Like a Virgin* (1984), featured the curiously but carefully named song *Material Girl*, where she dresses like Marilyn Monroe and performs a pastiche of parodies from the old movie *Gentlemen Prefer Blondes*, notably the classic scene where Marilyn sings *Diamonds Are a Girl's Best Friend*.

- Legendary video-maker Herb Ritts produced *Cherish* (1989), where Madonna frolics in the sea with beautiful male mermaids. She falls in love with one; he leaves the ocean to live with her. There are artful echoes of the movies *From Here to Eternity* (1953) and *Splash* (1984), and of David Bowie's exquisite *China Girl* video (1983).

- *Open Your Heart* (1990) had feminists up in arms, and many television channels banned it. It features a peepshow and a variety of booths displayed voyeuristically. In one, two ravishing twin sailors entwine, while Madonna struts knowingly. To close, Madonna kisses a twelve-year-old boy on the lips, taking him into the sunset.

- And then there is fashion. With a built-in audience, both rich and poor, she sets trends and fashions, all increasing her exposure and her bank balance. She shifts vast quantities of T-shirts and other high-margin, cheap apparel for chains such as H&M, yet also is a professional model at the top end. She has promoted and been promoted by

Jean-Paul Gaultier, Gianni Versace, Dolce & Gabbana, Oliver Thieskens and Christian Dior.

- Madonna the author – *Sex, the Book* came out on 21 October 1992. The print run was an astonishing one million, and all copies were quickly sold. Since then, Madonna has written or sponsored nine other books, including a series of illustrated children's books.

- As she has grown older, Madonna's publicity machine has not flagged. Apart from carefully controlled appearances on selected chat shows, she steals the show at many other events. In the 2003 MTV Video Awards she kissed Britney Spears suggestively, proclaiming, 'I am the mommy pop star and she is the baby pop star; I'm kissing her to pass my energy to her.'

- In the past two decades, attention has focused increasingly on Madonna's volatile love and family life, intertwined with philanthropy and promoted with full media glare. At the 2005 Live Aid concert for Africa, she performed for 200,000 people in London's Hyde Park. Then she sponsored Raising Malawi, an organisation to help destitute orphans in that country. She fought a public battle to adopt David, a one-year-old orphan. After prevailing over resistance from the Malawian government, she gave David a £5000 rocking horse from Harrods. In 2017 she adopted Malawian four-year-old twin sisters and moved her family to Lisbon.

- She breaks record after record for her albums, videos, and tours, making money from plain and simple pop music.

- Finally, Madonna is also a businesswoman and producer. She produces nearly all her own work, as well as that of many other singers, including British bands The Prodigy and Erasure.[55] In the music world, she is renowned for her canny business head.

Madonna is to performance talent what Amazon is to consumer goods – she is different because she covers the waterfront, somehow managing to provide excellent value for the attention she takes.

She is the ultimate in personal brand creation. Over four decades, she has hogged the limelight. Age and ennui must eventually take their toll. But not yet. In her sixties, she is not merely standing, but still frolicking.

If you have no capital and little skill or interest in acquiring it, and no wish to start a business, yet still crave unreasonable fame and fortune, study Madonna carefully. She is your role model. She shows how to multiply ordinary talent on an exponential scale, producing extraordinary results.

Summary and conclusion

All our players had a personal transformation – an event which changed them profoundly, connecting them with their destiny. They acquired rare new knowledge, rare determination, rare self-confidence and certain other indefinable but omnipotent psychic gifts which made them George Bernard Shaw's 'unreasonable man' or woman, in contention for unreasonable success.[56]

The personal transformations explored in this chapter were all unique. Some were strange indeed – getting a 'download' while stuck on a broken-down train, the hanging of an elder brother, the invasion of a country you governed, being sent to a concentration camp, and even a life-changing vision of the Risen Christ.

In business, personal transformation is more typically associated with working for or creating a most unusual company.

With very few exceptions, our players did not know they were heading for transformation, nor consciously choose their transforming experiences. But you can, and if you aspire to unreasonable success, you should.

The next chapter is perhaps the most important of all. It describes not the ways you achieve your world-changing object-ive, but rather what that breakthrough achievement is going to be. It is about the *what*, not the *how*; and it is the most vital decision you will ever make.

Transforming experience

- Deliberately engineer possible transforming experiences
- Search for defining moments – major events fuelling a sense of purpose and destiny
- Become a different person because of transforming experiences

Landmark 4: One Breakthrough Achievement

Churchill led Britain into total war without much thought for the morrow: he said he had 'only one single purpose – the destruction of Hitler – and that his life was much simplified thereby'.

—ROBERT TOMBS

What is a breakthrough achievement?

It's one that changes the world, for good or ill. It is the difference the players made in their life – what important things they made happen which wouldn't have happened without them.

There are four cardinal characteristics of a breakthrough achievement:

- No one has done it before.
- It encapsulates *why* each player left a permanent mark on the world.

- Most of the players' breakthrough achievements were forms of invention.
- The achievements were highly personal and part and parcel of the individual's character and idiosyncrasies. Perhaps their greatest achievement was to express themselves in a way which could not be ignored.

A breakthrough achievement can never be totally unwound. It becomes part of history, part of the environment, part of the flow of life far into the future.

The inventors

It came as something of a revelation to me that the breakthrough achievements of seventeen of twenty players were a form of creation, or more precisely, invention.

Jeff Bezos illustrates this. His breakthrough obsession and achievement was his peculiar vision for Amazon – the internet's 'everything store' marked by unbeatable prices and customer service.

Bezos made his vision a reality in a special, very unusual way. Do you realise how different Amazon is from almost all other companies? Can you imagine the fights there must have been in the boardroom when investors and managers wanted to raise prices so that the share price could be underpinned by real profits?

Bezos alone clung to the creed that if you provide extraordinarily low prices and high customer service, your ultimate reward will be massive. Part of Bezos' achievement comes from being pig-headed and dictatorial – he preaches; he insists that business should be done his way. There is a cult of Jeff at Amazon, just as there was – some would say, there still is – a cult of Steve at Apple. We can understand the Bezos cult from this – in March 2000 Amazon was worth $30 billion. Not bad. But today it hovers around $800 billion – twenty-seven times as much.

Writing in 2013 – when Amazon was worth a fraction of today's value – Brad Stone, biographer of Amazon and Bezos, was prescient: 'The future of the company becomes easy to predict. The answer to almost every conceivable question is yes ... Jeff Bezos will do what he has always done. He will attempt to move faster, work his employees harder, make bolder bets, and pursue both big inventions and small ones, all to achieve his grand vision for Amazon – that it be not just an everything store, but ultimately an everything company.'[1]

As with Bezos, **Steve Jobs**' breakthrough achievement was to create Apple as he envisioned it, to mould its DNA, charting its mission as a revolutionary digital simplifier. Under Jobs, Apple made devices never previously conceived, devices that are intuitive, superbly useful, beautiful, a joy to use. Walter Isaacson says that Jobs 'built the world's most creative company ... to infuse into its DNA the design sensibilities, perfectionism, and imagination that make it likely to be, even decades from now, the company that thrives best at the intersection of artistry and technology.'[2]

What about **Bruce Henderson**? He invented business strategy as we know it today, guiding BCG towards its two epoch-making displays, the Experience Curve and the Boston Box. He begat a unique and important company.

Henderson innovated in the *product* of strategy. **Bill Bain** innovated in the *process* of consulting – he made it work better for consulting and client firms alike, by making assignments long and open-ended, vastly boosting the profits of the client firm. Bain's value to the world flowed from inventing a fresh formula, crafting two new institutions – Bain & Company and Bain Capital. Bain showed how to transform stodgy blue-chip companies *and* young ventures so that they became prodigiously more valuable to their owners and customers.

What was cosmetics queen **Helena Rubinstein**'s break-through achievement?

Like Bezos, Jobs, Bain and Henderson, Rubinstein was above all an *inventor*. She created the modern notion of female beauty with a jar of face cream. Despite, or perhaps because of, all her fabrications, what she created was rock-solid reality – a regimen for women to protect and enhance their skin and looks. She also started the company which first promoted this idea, and made it reverberate around the world, creating a premium brand which has lasted more than a century.

Walt Disney demonstrated the same pattern of extraordinary creation: invention of his studio; the invention and reinvention of Mickey Mouse, the three little pigs, Bambi, Snow White and the seven dwarfs, and Brer Rabbit, among countless others; the invention of talking cartoon characters where the speech and action were seamlessly integrated; and later, the invention of Disneyland and its progeny, a monument to America's pure and unsullied fictional past and to its technology-fuelled future. Disneyland remains a supremely American work of art to rival or surpass the beautifully camp castles erected by King Ludwig the Second of Bavaria, who anticipated Hollywood by nearly a century.

Disney was a harnesser and creator of visual and kinetic imagination, giving generations of children and adults part of their cultural heritage, and a spur to further originality and invention by many other 'imagineers', including many authors, film-makers and artists most beloved by children and adults today. His inventions are Disney's legacy to the world, why he will always be remembered, and why, like every successful creator of unique characters, he still augments our imagination.

Invention, then, is probably the most common template for

unreasonable success in business. Yet is it so very different out-side business?

When **Leonardo** was thirty, he wrote a letter to the duke of Milan, asking for a job. He listed his expertise in engineer-ing, covering a wide gamut of skills – the design of armoured vehicles, bridges, cannons, public buildings and waterways. Only at the end of the letter, almost as a post-script, did he add, 'Likewise in painting, I can do everything possible.'[3]

Leonardo was not only an artist, but a polymath to boot. He was the quintessential Renaissance figure: part scientist; part thinker; part draughtsman, researcher and instructor in anat-omy; designer of a prototype tank and flying machine; military engineer; student of the flight of birds; architect of monuments; hydraulic engineer; but above all sculptor and painter. New knowledge informed his work.

Like our business players, Leonardo was a unique *inventor*. His destiny was to be Leonardo.

J. K. Rowling's breakthrough was to invent the world of Harry Potter, which has captivated millions of children throughout the world.

Madonna's primary achievement was also to invent – and constantly reinvent – herself; to create and embody the Madonna Myth. There is a recognisable Madonna brand, just as there is a Leonardo brand, a Bob Dylan brand, a Walt Disney brand, a Salvador Dalí brand, a Picasso brand, a Leonard Cohen brand and a Bowie brand. They all share this paradox – they are simultaneously varied in their work and it evolved markedly over time, yet each one's whole range of output *could not be the work of anyone else.* They are their work and their work is them.

The idea of 'one breakthrough achievement' is a great deal more complex and open-ended than the simple idea of 'focus'. Companies such as Amazon, Apple or Disney do not 'focus' on a few consumer products with a long lifespan, in the way that, for instance, Coca-Cola, Heinz or Mars do. Rather, the new creative companies continually invent and reinvent new products and services. The same can be said of players such as Leonardo, Madonna, Jobs, Bezos, Dylan, Disney, Picasso, Dalí or Paul of Tarsus. They all struggle for and achieve new heights of creativity and insight that demonstrate uniqueness and integrity – they stand for something and occupy a singular competitive niche. In business terms, they have one hundred per cent share of their segment.

There are millions of companies in the world, but only one Amazon, one Disney, one Apple, one BCG, one Bain & Company. There are seven billion individuals on the planet, but only one Madonna, one Bezos, one Dylan.

Bob Dylan is a singer-poet with intense attitude – perhaps the most pre-eminent of the genre. He had something to say, he said it memorably, and at least two of his anthems will endure.

Albert Einstein's distinctive approach, which marked him out from other great physicists of the twentieth century, was his reliance on concepts and thought experiments rather than conducting experiments or working through voluminous data to gather insight. Like nobody since Newton, Einstein proceeded by deep thinking from first principles – he proceeded from irrefutable axioms and observations proven beyond doubt, building on each one to move towards a new hypothesis about the nature of the universe. Einstein's breakthrough was his theory of relativity, altering forever the face of the Earth. In his own way, in his own sphere, Bruce Henderson did precisely the same thing, building a new theory of competition from first principles. It is a powerful method based purely on intensely hard thinking, fuelled by curiosity and imagination, not by new analysis and data; and, if you aspire to breakthrough invention, I commend it to you. Breakthrough achievements do not require genius; they can be the offspring of hard thinking by the likes of Henderson; and, I make bold to assert, by you and me.

Lenin created Russian communism, the first time Marx's theory was tried in practice. Lenin made his followers believe that they could supplant the tsars and rule Russia through a ruthless dictatorship of a few thousand disciplined and committed revolutionaries, backed up by the police and army. After his coup d'état on 25 November 1917, Lenin would not give up power. In Russia's first free elections, Lenin's Bolsheviks did badly, winning only 24 per cent of the vote, to the 39 per cent won by the moderate and democratic Socialist Revolutionaries.

On 5 January 1918 Lenin declared martial law, filling Petrograd with troops and Red Guards; they shot unarmed protestors demonstrating in favour of the elected Assembly. When the Bolsheviks lost the first vote in the Assembly, they walked out and returned with the Red Guards, who drove the delegates out. Lenin dissolved the Assembly and started a reign of terror. Before long there was a one-party communist state, which lasted until 1989. Arguably, directly, and through his influence on Hitler, Mao and other revolutionaries, Lenin had more influence on the twentieth century than anyone else.

Viktor Frankl's claim to fame was that he invented logotherapy, better called the psychology of meaning, and paved the way for today's 'positive psychology', associated with Martin Seligman and others. We all come into life with a unique set of potential meanings which we might fulfil, whatever our circumstances. We always have free will, and there is no true freedom without responsibility.

Should we care about success and happiness? No, he says; the more you make them a target, the more you are going to miss them. 'Happiness must happen – and the same holds for

success – you have to let it happen by not caring about it ...
listen to what your conscience commands ... and carry it out
to the best of your knowledge. Then you will live to see that in
the long run – in the long run, I say! – success will follow you
precisely because you had forgotten to think about it.'[4]

On the first day of 1936, **John Maynard Keynes** wrote to
George Bernard Shaw, saying that the book he would publish
later that year would 'largely revolutionize – not, I suppose, at
once, but in the course of the next ten years – the way the world
thinks about economic problems'.[5] It was no idle boast.

Until 1936, it was generally accepted that in recessions, high
unemployment was unavoidable. Keynes said it wasn't – that
government or central banks could step in to invest and create
demand, and so multiply the benefit from that investment. Once
the economy had picked up, government could withdraw to
the sidelines, raising taxes in good times for investment in the
next recession.

Removing unemployment, therefore, did not have to come
at the expense of freedom or efficiency. Keynes pioneered a
new theory of economics, at once kinder and more effective.
He devised a way to avoid mass unemployment without being
enslaved by communism or fascism.

St Paul's breakthrough was to give irrevocable impetus to
the movement we now know as Christianity, which would not
otherwise have become a world religion.

Paul identified a new and much larger target market for what,
until he changed it, was a tiny Jewish sect going nowhere. He
was the first religious leader in the world to offer a message of
supreme, universal optimism; and he provided the first and best
written account of the new faith.

Instead of the Jews, Paul's target market was the whole
Roman Empire, the hub of the known world. Paul's optimism
rested on the promise of God's love, and eternal life for anyone

who believed in Christ. Paul's letters, which were intended to solve immediate problems rather than define a faith, have nevertheless been the central inspiration for thinking Christians for more than nineteen centuries.

Did Paul intend to start a new religion?

No. He expected the end of the world very soon.

Did Paul – whatever his intentions – create a new religion?

Yes. Perhaps he would have been appalled, perhaps delighted, perhaps just bemused.

Now for the last of our inventors in this chapter . . .

Otto von Bismarck: The gospel of strategic opportunism

Bismarck was the greatest European statesman of the nineteenth century. He united Germany, redrawing the map of Europe as he saw fit. Though largely forgotten today, Bismarck's approach to getting his way – what I call 'strategic opportunism' – can be copied by you or me with great results.

He was born on 1 April 1815 on a rural, aristocratic estate in Prussia, then the largest of many separate German states. After university in Göttingen and Berlin, he dabbled in politics. At the age of thirty-six, quite unexpectedly, he was made the Prussian delegate to the federal Diet (parliament) in Frankfurt, where the German states talked to each other and to their Big Brother, Austria. He scored a coup by refusing to allow Austria to join the *Zollverein*, the free trade area created by the German states, which was to prove the foundation of German industrial success. Excluded from this common market, Austria remained relatively backward.

After eight years in Frankfurt, Bismarck's career suffered an apparently terminal blow in 1859, after the new regent, Prince William, took over the Prussian government. He thought Bismarck was a wild reactionary, and packed him off as Prussian ambassador first to Russia and then to France. Then, suddenly, Bismarck got his big break.

When William became king in 1861, he fell into conflict with the Prussian Diet. Neither monarch nor parliament had dominance. The king appointed ministers, but the Diet could reject their proposals. In 1862 parliament overwhelmingly rejected the budget proposed by the king's ministers, causing deadlock. The prime minister, Albrecht von Roon, hoped that Bismarck could provide a solution, and worked hard to get William and Bismarck in the same room. On 18 September he wired Bismarck to come at once to meet William.

The king did not know this, and had no wish to see Bismarck. On 20 September Roon tried to persuade William to see Bismarck. The king said tartly that Bismarck might be better able than Roon to unplug the deadlock, but that is was moot because 'of course Bismarck is not here'. 'He *is* here,' Roon replied, 'and ready to serve your Majesty.'

William had to see Bismarck, who pounced at precisely the right moment. The issue, he told the king, was simple – 'Royal government or the supremacy of parliament.'

Exasperated by the Diet, and seeing no other route forward, William reluctantly agreed to give Bismarck a try, making him prime minister. This utterly transformed Bismarck – and before long, the balance of power in Europe.

'The transformation,' says historian A. J. P. Taylor, 'began as soon as he entered office. He came into power with the urgent conviction that a great national upheaval was at hand.'

'Bismarck was 47 when he became prime minister. No man has ever taken supreme office with a more slender background of experience.' Never a minister, he was unsuitable for high office on many grounds, and seemed to be a stop-gap caretaker.[6] Yet Bismarck stayed at the helm for twenty-seven years, getting his way on every major issue.

How did he do it?

His strategic opportunism – which I have emulated, and commend to you as a route to unreasonable success – combined two elements usually seen as contradictory:

- Extreme determination on strategy, yoked together with
- Extreme flexibility on the means and timing of action, reacting to random events and grasping any opportunity they presented to advance his strategic objectives.

Bismarck did not plan events. Despite being impulsive and nervous, he forced himself to wait patiently for the right moment to seize the initiative.

'Events,' he said, 'are stronger than the plans of men.' 'Man cannot create the current of events. He can only float with it and steer.'[7]

Bismarck's aim was to unite the whole of Germany – then divided into a multiplicity of independent states – into one empire run by Prussia – and himself. Bismarck, says A. J. P. Taylor, 'held that Europe would not be at peace until her peoples had been sorted out into nationalities, or, as he preferred to put it, into "tribes". Bismarck did not regard nationalism as high or moral; he merely accepted it as inevitable and wished to be on the winning side.'[8]

Nationalism had another attraction for Bismarck – it was popular with the political class throughout Germany. Riding the wave of nationalism was the route to greater power for Prussia and himself. The liberal members of parliament, who were always influential and often the majority, were staunch nationalists.

In his first nine years as prime minister, Bismarck went from triumph to triumph, winning three short wars against Denmark (1864), Austria (1866) and France (1870–71). In 1867, Bismarck corralled the twenty-one German states north of the river Main into the North German Confederation, with the Prussian king as president and Bismarck as chancellor.

Events continued to smile on Bismarck. Napoleon III, the French emperor, had followed an adventurous and unsuccessful foreign policy; his regime was on the slide and needed a foreign success to shore it up. Out of the blue, something odd happened in Madrid. The Spanish throne was offered to Prince Leopold of Hohenzollern, a son of King William of Prussia, who reluctantly accepted. On 2 July 1870, word reached Paris that Leopold was about to become King of Spain. The new French foreign minister, Gramont, saw this as his opportunity to humiliate Prussia and restore France's prestige in Europe. On 6 July he threatened Prussia with war unless Leopold agreed not to take the throne of Spain. This was an impertinent and unreasonable demand. War looked likely, and Bismarck hoped it would provide the opportunity he needed.

But the plot of history – like our own lives – is not a straight line; it zig-zags. The crisis disappeared as soon as it had flared up. Neither Leopold nor William wanted the former to get involved in Spanish affairs. They decided that Leopold should withdraw.

France 1, Prussia 0. Bismarck was miserable.

Then France scored an own goal. On 13 July, Napoleon III and Gramont rekindled the dying embers of the fire by giving King William a new ultimatum – he must apologise for Leopold's candidature, and promise that it would never be revived; or else France would declare war on Prussia.

William, who was at his palace in Ems, sensibly rejected these demands, yet reiterated that Leopold's candidature was dead.

Only now did Bismarck act. Unlike William, he realised that France *wanted* a war, however thin the pretext. And Bismarck reckoned that Prussia could win the war, if supported by the other German states, and then unite Germany – something France would otherwise have resisted.

With the draft of William's response from Ems in front of him, Bismarck edited out William's conciliatory phrases and stressed the real issue: France had made outrageous demands on threat of war, and William had rejected them. He then despatched the famous 'Ems telegram' to Napoleon and Gramont, who declared war on Prussia.

All Germany – even Bismarck's left-wing opponents – backed the war enthusiastically. With troops from the other German states, Prussia defeated France very quickly. William was proclaimed German Emperor on 18 January 1871 at Versailles, with German troops still on French soil.

Bismarck had achieved his life's ambition. From then on, all he wanted was to preserve the peace of Europe and stay in power, which he did happily for the next two decades.

The three outliers

The three outliers are Churchill, Thatcher and Mandela, because they were not primarily inventors. I say 'not primarily' because a case can be made that all three *were* pioneers of a new approach. Churchill arguably invented – and certainly carried to eventual success – anti-Nazism. Mandela reinvented the ANC as a party of government rather than protest and armed struggle. As for Thatcher, she invented and solidified Thatcherism as a new way of combating socialism and running a free-market economy.

The problem with saying these three players were inventors is not so much what it asserts, as what it leaves out; namely, quite exceptional practical accomplishments and leadership in unique circumstances.

Churchill's destiny

Churchill was always a charismatic and exciting politician whose eloquence was second to none. Yet he didn't come into his own until he became prime minister in Britain's direst emergency. That event, and the years 1940–45, marked the transformation of Churchill from political failure to saviour of the world; the time when, as he later wrote, he 'walked with destiny'.[9]

What exactly was his breakthrough achievement? It started in 1932, and was not fully developed until victory in 1945. It was stopping Hitler by all the means at his disposal – fact-gathering, insight, oratory, intrigue, obstinacy, willpower, obsession, all of which were deployed, but without apparent effect for many years.

Even before Hitler came to power, Churchill told the House of Commons the danger posed by Germany. 'Do not delude yourselves,' he told them on 23 November 1932, about Germany's wish to rearm, 'that all that Germany is asking for is equal status ... All these bands of sturdy Teutonic youths, marching through the streets and roads of Germany, with the light of desire in their eyes to suffer for their Fatherland, are not looking for status. They are looking for weapons and, when they have the weapons, believe me they will then ask for the return of lost territories and lost colonies, and when that demand is made, it cannot fail to shake and possibly shatter to their foundations every one of the countries I have mentioned' – France, Belgium, Romania, Czechoslovakia and Yugoslavia – 'and some other countries I have not mentioned.'

'I say quite frankly, though I may shock the House,' Churchill continued, 'that I would rather see another ten or twenty years of one-sided peace, than see a war between equally well-matched powers.'[10]

On 16 March 1933, after Hitler had become chancellor,

Churchill said that the news from Germany was increasingly ominous. 'When we watch with surprise and distress the tumultuous insurgence of ferocity and war spirit, the pitiless treatment of minorities, the denial of the normal protections of civilised society to large numbers of individuals solely on the grounds of race,' he said, we should not expect those fierce passions to be confined only within Germany.[11]

In another speech, on 13 April 1933, Churchill told parliament it was 'extremely dangerous to talk lightly about German rearmament and say that, if the Germans choose to do it, no one can stop them ... The rise of Germany to anything like military equality with France, Poland or the small States, means a renewal of a general European war.' He went on to draw attention to the removal of all Jews from public office, Hitler's campaign of anti-Jewish propaganda, and the opening of a concentration camp at Dachau for Jews and other 'enemies' of the Nazis. If these 'odious conditions now ruling in Germany' were extended to Poland, the result would be 'another persecution and pogrom of Jews begun in this new area'.[12]

It was not until Hitler had broken every promise and invaded country after country – as predicted by Churchill – and seemed poised to invade Britain, that the British political establishment suddenly woke up. In May 1940, after years of collective deafness, they most reluctantly made Churchill prime minister, simply because he had been proved right about the existential threat from Hitler, and was the only man who knew how to counter it. Churchill then added other qualities: the ability to inspire almost the entire British people, and success – yes, in the nick of time and with some help from his enemy the Japanese – in wooing and winning over President Roosevelt, without whose help he knew he could not succeed. Finally, Churchill proved to be a formidable warlord.

These attributes, all vital, were blended and marshalled by Churchill in the service of one all-consuming mission, to save Britain and the world from Nazi subjugation.

Churchill did not need to be an inventor; his mission was more than that. He did not need to invent a philosophy, a political party, a system, or anything else – he just had to *be Churchill*, the one person, probably the only person, who could rally the world to defeat Hitler.

Churchill shows that a breakthrough achievement can be derived from, and can become identical to, a unique self-defined mission into which we pour our heart and soul.

You may want to ask yourself:

- **What could I invent** that would transform our lives and those of many other people?
- **What personal mission** would energise me and transform my impact?

Did Churchill sit down by a pond at his lovely home in Chartwell, and as a change from painting, decide he needed a personal mission which would take over his life and make him a towering figure on the world stage? Of course not! He happened to go to Germany for completely personal reasons and saw what was happening: the gangs of angry German young men terrorising any Jews or communists they could find, the raw energy waiting for Hitler to take command of it for his perverted purposes. He was outraged that this could happen in the land of Goethe and Beethoven, a place with a thousand years of learning and culture, and he was afraid for the future of Europe and the independence of the British Empire: all could fall under the Nazi jackboot.

He realised something the rest of the ruling class didn't – that Hitler could be stopped, and had to be stopped before it was too late. All Churchill's eloquence, contacts and force of personality were not enough to make his case until Hitler made it for him.

Thatcher's mission

Thatcher's achievement was to slay the dragon of socialism, reverse Britain's decline, and make Britons proud of their country again. She reveals herself in her memoirs:

> Chatham [British prime minister from 1766 to 1768] famously remarked, 'I know that I can save this country and that no one else can.' It would have been presumptuous to have compared myself to Chatham. But if I am honest, I must admit that my exhilaration came from a similar inner conviction.[13]

Through a combination of extraordinary courage and supreme luck, Thatcher achieved her mission. She was almost certainly right – nobody else could have done that, certainly not in the way she did, and probably not at all. Almost no one else in the political class of the 1970s and 1980s would even have tried.

Mandela's achievement

And what of our final outlier, Nelson Mandela?

You will recall we left him after his first transformation: his escape to Johannesburg and exposure to the leading lights of the African National Congress (ANC), resulting in his new self-image as a freedom fighter. Mandela had to undergo one very painful but essential further transformation before he could fulfil his mission: his imprisonment for twenty-seven years after being convicted of conspiracy to overthrow the state. The first eighteen years of his confinement, from 1964 to 1982, were spent at the harsh camp on Robben Island, a short boat trip from Cape Town but a world away. When I made the obligatory pilgrimage to the ugly island in the 1990s, I couldn't believe how tiny his cell was, nor how anyone could maintain their dignity under such circumstances.

On Robben Island he became, in the eyes of the ANC, the South African apartheid regime, the world, and – most import- ant, though he never said this – in his own eyes, the undisputed *de facto* leader of the ANC; and it became apparent to the more intelligent leaders of the governing Nationalist Party – a pretty thin but crucial crust on the unsavoury pie of South African politics – that here was a man with whom they could perhaps do business.[14]

From 1971 onwards, a small but steadily growing stream of visitors made their way to Mandela's cell on Robben Island, mostly 'authorities' seeking to test out his attitude towards a possible deal between the regime and the ANC.[15] Mandela handled these meetings adroitly, with a mixture of personal pragmatism and firm insistence that any deal must involve one person, one vote for all South Africans. Only Mandela could have done this – his personal charm, modesty and humanity took the edge off his uncompromising political stance, and eventually convinced his visitors that brutal civil war could be averted by conceding what Mandela required. Both sides rightly feared horrible violence from the other.[16]

On 2 February 1990 President Frederik Willem de Klerk announced the dismantling of apartheid and lifted the bans on the ANC, the Communist Party and other illegal organ- isations, paving the way for democracy. I have talked to 'F. W.' about those events – he is convinced that only he and Mandela could have bridged the chasm between the two sides. That was Mandela's sublime achievement.

Summary and conclusion

The breakthrough achievement of each player obviously depended on their unique circumstances and aspirations. But there are three important general findings:

- By far the most common type of breakthrough achievement is invention. For most of the players, all their other achievements and efforts pale into insignificance when set alongside their single decisive invention. What might you invent?
- Besides invention, strategic achievements seem most likely to arise from an overwhelming sense of destiny, mission, or desire to bridge seemingly irreconcilable gulfs of ideology, attitude or vested interests. Do you have any of these strong feelings? If so, nurture them. Singular achievement comes from singular convictions.
- Strategic opportunism is one attractive route to a break-through achievement. You must know precisely what you want to achieve, but wait for the footsteps of opportunity to be audible before you strike.
- The killer combination is extreme determination coupled with extreme flexibility regarding means and timing. If you are single-minded, yet patient, you will know the perfect time to act. Until then, keep your powder dry.

Your breakthrough achievement awaits. But how do you find it?

Before this chapter, we looked at three landmarks which helped our players on the road to unreasonable success. This chapter has been different. In it, we have described the specific unique impact of each player on the world – what they did to change it. We have also seen the features of the breakthrough achievement which were common to all players; they invented something – a radical or revolutionary idea or objective – and knew how to carry it to fruition. They personified the idea, too, so that it was, and still is, associated with them.

This may be a blinding glimpse of the obvious. Yet it may have some profound and counter-intuitive implications for anyone aspiring to great consequences:

- Your skills – and improving them – are not the point. Far more important is **what you try to do** – the originality and reach of your mission, goal, destiny, whatever you call it, and your tenacity, nay, fanaticism, and luck in seeing it through to completion.
- Your objective must be **new**, **revolutionary**, **imaginative** and almost laughably **ambitious**.
- It must also be incarnated within your personality – it must **come from the soul**.
- Ultimately, the '**what**' – in Lenin's stirring phrase, 'What is to be done?' – is more vital than the '**how**'. This landmark is the what. The other eight landmarks are the how.

Yet the how is also vital. The first three chapters described three 'hows', and the next five will outline the other 'hows'. With the end of this chapter we have reached the heart and high ground of the book, and we can represent the structure of unreasonable success in this chart.

One breakthrough achievement

What will it be?
1. A new 'invention'?
2. A personal mission?
Desire deeply. Wait. Pounce.

Self Belief.

OLYMPIAN
EXPECTA...

ONE
BREAKTHROUGH
ACHIEVEMENT

MAKE YOUR OWN TRAIL

FIND & DRIVE
YOUR OWN

PERSONAL
VEHICLE

THRIV...
ON
SETBACK...

TRANSFORMING EXPERIENCES

distort reality

ACQUIRE

Unique

intuition

8

Landmark 5: Make Your Own Trail

You don't want to be the best at what you do; you want
to be the only one.

—JERRY GARCIA

Nobody can become unreasonably successful by doing what
everyone – or anyone – else is doing. At some stage in their
career, all our players left behind established paths and ploughed
their own furrow.

Before they did that in the real world, they did it in their
own minds. They came up with the theory before putting it
into practice. They developed their own unique philosophy
and started to behave according to its dictates. They began to
act differently.

Unreasonably successful people construct their own proprietary mental map to guide their steps. They create their
own segment, which reflects their personality, their objective

and their way of working, all at the same time. Nobody else can enter their skin; nobody else can enter their segment; it is impenetrable, because they fill it, and nobody else can.

The business philosopher-monarchs

We can see this easily in the case of **Jeff Bezos**. It's hard to describe Bezos except in terms of his own philosophy and vision for Amazon – the internet's everything store with unbeatable prices and customer service. A business philosophy is not unusual – but what is rare is dedication to a philosophy, even when it appears to conflict with commercial common sense.

Companies – especially new ones, where capital is vital and costly, and the imperative is reaching cash break-even as soon as possible – almost never put their customers' interests above those of their shareholders and employees. There is a struggle for survival which prevents that. There is always a tension between the long term and the short term, and the pragmatic corporate leader must strike a balance. In the short term it may be necessary to secure a company's profitability and standing with its funders, even if this means compromising on customer service and value, because otherwise there may be no long-term future.

But the problem with pragmatism is that it rapidly becomes a habit, and short-term gratification – expressed in profits, cash and the praise which goes with them – becomes a drug that drives out long-term customer-related aspirations. It takes a rare visionary – people such as Henry Ford, Ray Kroc of McDonald's, Ingvar Kamprad of IKEA, and Southwest Airlines' Herb Kelleher – to insist on rock-bottom prices; or, as with Steve Jobs, fantastic products and a simple, intuitive customer experience. It takes an exceptional person to take on the risk of this approach – the risk of going bust.

Bezos belongs in both camps. He is a price-simplifier and a

proposition-simplifier. He wants customers to get a price never seen before, even if it means that break-even is deferred, and he also wants rapid expansion, to lower costs and prices, which might put the company in peril. At the same time he wants consumers to experience the joy of excellent products and service, at whatever cost to the company. Few businesspeople really believe in the creed of either the price-simplifier or the proposition-simplifier; yet Bezos believes in both.

In 1996, his favourite 'Jeffism' was Get Big Fast. The company that got the lead in online book retailing would probably keep it, would have the lowest unit costs and prices, the most customers, and could offer them even better service, and then move into other categories. But 'when you are small,' he warned, 'someone bigger can always come along and take away what you have'.[1] So he told Howard Schultz, founder of Starbucks, 'We are going to take this thing to the moon.'[2]

But getting big required more warehouse space, and Amazon's book distributors ran out of it and didn't want to invest in more. For Bezos, this was not a problem. Amazon would build its own warehouses. He hired Walmart's head of distribution, Jimmy Wright, who showed Bezos the plans for a huge new warehouse in Nevada. Bezos pronounced it 'beautiful', so Wright asked whose approval he needed and what return on investment would be required.

Bezos: 'Don't worry about that.'

Wright: 'Don't I have to get approval to do this?'

Bezos: 'You just did.'[3]

That year alone, Wright spent over $300m – a huge sum then – on warehouses.

By early 1998, Bezos wanted to go beyond books and enter new product categories. Music and DVDs proved successful, but electronics less so, and toys were a disaster. Meanwhile, Bezos resisted every attempt by the board and his financial people to say when his seven expensive distribution centres would pay for themselves or when the company would break even – 'If you're planning more than twenty minutes ahead in this game, you're wasting your time.'[4]

In 2000, Amazon was set to lose a billion dollars, and the company worked hard to raise a convertible loan of $672 million. The terms were tough on Amazon, but Warren Jenson, the new chief financial officer, insisted that the company take the money. A month later dot-com stocks cratered. Without the loan, Amazon would have disappeared.

Bezos hacked his own trail in dangerous territory, and was nearly eaten by bears. He and Amazon shareholders were spookily lucky. Still, without his bold and near-foolhardy philosophy, and his limpet-like attachment to it, Bezos and all who sailed with him would not have reached the New World, nor would their everything store have made them so unreasonably rich.

Bruce Henderson did not take the same financial risks as Bezos, nor reap a comparable bonanza. Yet it is doubtful that Bezos would have evolved his own ideology without Henderson's pioneering work on the importance of having far higher market share than any rival, and consequently the lowest costs and prices. Because of his indirect impact on many, many entrepreneurs such as Bezos, Henderson probably had an even greater impact on the world. His beautifully elegant and simple model of competition is commonplace today, but before him, it had eluded every single economist, business professor and consultant in the world.

And what about **Bill Bain**? Surely his philosophy must be too similar to Henderson's for us to say that he truly made his own trail? Not at all. It's true that Bain began to incubate his revolutionary approach to consulting within BCG, yet his vision was totally original and clashed with the DNA Bruce Henderson had begat. Bain's iconoclasm had six interlocking planks:

- An extremely close relationship with the client organisation, and particularly its head.
- Equality of status between the client organisation and the consulting firm (Bain & Company), and between the client's CEO and the lead partner from Bain handling the client.
- A long-term and continuous relationship, completely at odds with the consulting industry norm of specific and intermittent projects.
- Exclusivity between the client organisation and Bain & Company both ways – as Bain told prospective clients, 'We won't work with your competitors, and you won't work with ours.'
- Focus on increasing the value of the company organisation – strategy was the means to the end, not the end in itself; conversely, to Bain, 'strategy' meant 'anything that we can help with which will increase the value of the client firm'.
- Bill Bain believed in a top-down, quasi-military chain of command, both within his own firm, and in the client. What the lead Bain partner and the client CEO agreed should be done, would be done, by fiat, through the client organisation and in parallel with the Bain & Company organisation.

No other consulting firm on Earth worked this way.

The Bain philosophy was audacious in the extreme. You can instantly see the benefits for Bain & Company – long assignments and ever-increasing consulting fees within the client company meant huge inbuilt growth and profitability.

Yet it wouldn't have worked if it didn't reflect the reality that consultants could be vastly more useful within such a relationship. They could understand the company better than it understood itself, and ensure that the chief executive could implement whatever was necessary for radical profit improvement, without brooking opposition from powerful internal executives. These were 'barons' – heads of functions such as manufacturing or marketing, or of country operations – excoriated by Bain because they often acted to protect themselves and their people from profit-maximising change.

When I defected from BCG to Bain & Company, I was amazed at how utterly dissimilar the two outfits were. They used the same intellectual capital, but in totally contrasting ways. Bain & Company worked within clients in a much more intensive, expensive and remorseless way, leaving very little to chance – so achieving extraordinary results. This path was one Bill Bain created in his head and then concreted over, turning the trail into a vast international motorway system where super-ambitious – and often paranoid – corporate chiefs could break all speed limits on the way to their destination. The business world has never been the same since.

Steve Jobs provides further evidence that unreasonable success comes from the pursuit of an original dream.

If Jobs had never been reinstated as the leader of Apple, he would have been remembered as the Moses who led his people to the promised land of laptops. But after his return in 1997, Jobs also graced Planet Apple and Planet Earth with a dazzling array of beautiful miniature and mobile devices which did things previously unimagined. He bequeathed to the universe the most creative Starship Enterprise it had ever seen.

Eerie parallels can be drawn between Steve Jobs and **Walt Disney**. Jobs was thrown out of his own company because he marched too much to his own tune, while Disney disliked the corporate ethos which shackled his studio and creativity in the late 1930s and 1940s.

After 1945, Disney wanted to get back to making films,

and to recover his reputation as an innovating folk artist. 'The thing I resent most,' he said, 'is people who want to keep me in well-worn grooves.' He became interested in the surreal work of Salvador Dalí and started a partnership with him – he told a journalist 'we have to keep breaking new trails', which involved plumbing the inner soul, the psychological reality which under-lay all action.[5]

In 1946, Disney and Dalí spent countless happy hours together collaborating on *Destino*, a proposed surreal movie. One of their ideas involved the god Jupiter morphing into a sun-dial which becomes a hand covered in ants. The ants turn into bike riders; next, a bell turns into a girl and then into dandelion puffs. Finally, a baseball game transforms itself into a ballet. But Disney's accountants and board directors turned *Destino* down, and Disney himself grew increasingly frustrated.

He longed for the simplicity and direct contact with his people he'd enjoyed earlier. His dissatisfaction led to the next great leap forward, which was something that only Disney could have conceived and executed: the idea of 'creating an entire miniature turn-of-the-century village – a means to convey comforting, enduring American values when everyone was spooked by the bomb.'[6]

He assembled a team of designers, architects and engineers – his 'imagineers' – to create Disneyland. The park would be beautiful, with trees, flowers and benches, cut off from the flawed world outside, which would be invisible from the park. Hollywood met an idealised Mid-Western nirvana. Disneyland would have neither employees nor customers, but a 'cast' of clean-cut players hosting and guiding his 'guests' through the park. The whole experience was conceived as a kind of movie – 'this is scene one, this is scene two, this is scene three'.[7]

His brother Roy and the other directors thought that they should stick to their knitting, and that Disney had lost his marbles. So he financed Disneyland himself, through a company he set up called WED – his initials – before eventually striking a deal to roll Disneyland back into the Disney company. It turned out to be their salvation.

If anyone did it all his way, it was Walter Elias Disney.

A list of **Helena Rubinstein**'s innovations gives some sense of her originality: the first beauty salon; the first commercial face cream; the first beauty entrepreneur to use 'modern' advertising and marketing techniques; the first global beauty empire; the first to evolve a full line of beauty products including lipstick, moisturisers and the world's first waterproof mascara; and the first beauty salon to offer personal treatments.

Above all, she originated personality marketing, where she used her own legend, force of personality and reputation to publicise her business around the world. She was indefatigable and omnipresent even in her nineties. The list of people she made famous includes Christian Dior, Christóbel Balenciaga, Paul Poiret, Coco Chanel, Elsa Schiaparelli, Guy Laroche and Yves Saint Laurent.

Dior, for instance, had run an art gallery which Rubinstein patronised, but when he went bust after the Wall Street crash, she encouraged him to take up couture, sitting in the front row of the Paris catwalk show which launched him in 1947. Many years later, in 1962, Rubinstein helped to launch YSL at *his* first fashion show.

She also promoted Jean Cocteau, Truman Capote, Christian Bérard and Man Ray. She was close to Gary Cooper, the Gabor sisters, Gore Vidal, Salvador Dalí and goodness knows how many other celebrities. She was invited to the White House by President Roosevelt, and was guest of honour for Israel's prime minister David Ben-Gurion.

Rubinstein was photographed by Cecil Beaton; sketched by Picasso, whom she had known since the end of the First World

War and often visited at his studio; photographed by Dora Maar, Picasso's mistress and muse; and painted by Dalí, Helleu, Laurencin and Vertès. Graham Sutherland, already famous for his brilliant portraits of Winston Churchill and Somerset Maugham, begged her to pose for him – it would be his first painting of a woman. His portrait captured her as a formidable and imperious empress. She disliked it intensely, but was mollified on hearing that the Queen and Queen Mother had visited the Tate to see the work.

When in Paris, the whole *belle monde* spent summer evenings eating and drinking in her rooftop garden. She sponsored a modern art competition in 1938, and was photographed with the judges – who included Matisse, Braque and Léger – as well as with the winner, Cubist sculptor Henri Laurens. She served caviar on gold crockery to André Malraux and Baron Elie de Rothschild.

Living in New York in her eighties, she became a television star, fronting a popular show featuring Imogene Coca and Sid Caesar. She would say in her trademark Eastern European accent, 'I'm Helena Rubinstein. Give me ten minutes of your time and I'll make you look ten years younger.' She was imitated by cabaret artists, caricatured by cartoons, greeted affectionately by cabbies, and widely known as 'the Jewish Queen Victoria'.

Marie Curie: Trailblazer extraordinaire

Let's catch up here with the last of our players, Marie Curie. She overcame enormous barriers – poverty, and discrimination both as a woman and as a Pole living under Russian oppression – to create a uniquely valuable niche in the world as a pioneer-discoverer in both physics and chemistry. She was one of the most important scientists of the late nineteenth and the twentieth century, and one of the most high-minded and selfless.

She was born Marya Sklodovski in Warsaw, Poland, on 7 November 1867. Her father came from a family of distinguished but impoverished country squires, and held the position of under-inspector and professor of mathematics and physics at a school controlled by the Russian state. Her musically talented mother had been headmistress of a prestigious private girls' school, but retired when Marya was a baby to look after her five children. Despite a close-knit and happy family life, the family was soon hit by three hammer-blows.

Shortly after Marya was born, her mother exhibited the first symptoms of tuberculosis. To protect Marya, her mother never held her close or kissed her.[8] Then, in 1873, when the family returned from a summer holiday and Marya was five, her father found an official envelope on his desk, informing him that the Russian authorities had demoted him, cut his pay and taken away his right to live in the family home that had come with the job. The professor responded by leaving the school and renting accommodation large enough to house the family and up to ten boy boarders, whom he taught at home.

This too led to tragedy. One of the boarders contracted typhus, which then infected two of Marya's sisters, Zosia and Bronya. As Eva Curie, Marya's younger daughter, later wrote, 'What horrible weeks! In one room the mother tried to control her spasms of coughing [from tuberculosis]; in another two little girls shook and moaned with fever.'[9] Bronya recovered, but Zosia died. On top of this, when Marya was ten, her mother died from her dreadful disease.

As a child, Marya was precocious. When she was four, her elder sister Bronya was halting through an exercise reading to their parents, when Marya snatched the book from Bronya and read the sentence perfectly. Seeing her parents' stupefied faces, and Bronya's sulky look, Marya suddenly realised she had committed a blunder. Through a flood of tears, the four-year-old blurted out, 'Beg pardon. Pardon! I didn't do it on purpose. It's not my fault – it's not Bronya's fault! It's only because it was so easy!'[10] Marya rapidly became fluent in Russian as well as Polish, and demonstrated a near-perfect memory. She graduated from secondary school at fifteen, first in her class and with a gold medal. As a woman, however, university in Poland was barred to her.

After a year of rejuvenation and fun amongst her many relatives in the Polish countryside, Marya returned to Warsaw, took up tutoring, and along with Bronya took courses in the underground university – translated variously as 'flying' or 'floating' university – which provided low-cost, part-time instruction from qualified instructors, held secretly in private homes to dodge harassment by the police. Between the ages of eighteen and twenty-one, she worked as a governess, to save money, with the dream of eventually going to university in Paris.

On 5 November 1891, two days before her twenty-fourth birthday, Marie (as she came to be known, adopting the French version of her name) registered as a student at the Sorbonne, part of the University of Paris. This was Marie's first transforming experience. Eva Curie imagines her mother's reaction: 'She had her place in the experimental laboratories, where, guided and advised, she could handle apparatus without fumbling and succeed in some simple experiments. Manya [Marya, Marie] was now – oh, delight – a student in the Faculty of Science.'[11]

Indeed, it was a golden time for a female foreign student hungry for knowledge to absorb it like a sponge. The Sorbonne's eminent professors respected intellect and the thirst for discovery above all, regardless of nationality or gender. Amongst the faculty who taught Marie personally were Gabriel Lippman, the Nobel prize-winner in physics, and the brilliant mathematician, physicist and polymath Henri Poincaré.[12] Although she initially lodged free of charge with Bronya, she found her sister's new husband too irritating and time-consuming – 'my little brother-in-law had the habit of disturbing me endlessly'.[13] Marie relocated to a sixth-floor garret close to the university, with no heat, no lighting, no cooking facilities and no water.[14] She lived on air, often neglecting to eat; close to starvation at times, but happy to feast on her studies. In June 1893, she gained a degree in physics from the Sorbonne, first in her class; and in July 1984 another degree in mathematics, in second place.[15]

Then came Marie's second transforming experience – meeting Pierre Curie. They met at the beginning of 1894, and married on 26 July 1895.[16] When they met, Marie was twenty-six and Pierre was thirty-four, and a professor at the School of Industrial Physics and Chemistry in Paris.[17] Their intense love affair transformed Marie's effectiveness in three crucial ways:

- Pierre, although not quite an equal scientific partner, was a knowledgeable, intelligent, imaginative and productive collaborator for Marie.
- Their marriage gave Marie French citizenship, which smoothed the path to academic positions and attention in the French world of science, and anchored her in Paris, a vibrant centre of research and discovery in physics and chemistry – rather than, as she had originally intended, reverting to the backwater of her homeland.
- Most important of all, Marie gained scientific credibility as part of a husband-and-wife team, which was an accepted and familiar model amongst French, German and Anglo-Saxon scientists in the late nineteenth century.[18] A single woman, however brilliant, even in Paris, and especially if not French, would face barriers to research facilities and credibility that were much lower for a woman married to a man already within the magic circle of French science.

The next key towards Marie Curie's breakthrough achievement was the idiosyncratic theoretical and experimental field she chose to develop, hacking a trail never pursued before. Advances in science, as in any other field, including business, seem to me to involve a common pattern of intuitive and experimental exploration.

- The first stage is to take a new field – or market – which is exciting and pregnant with possibilities, because knowledge is being discovered quickly, particularly knowledge or ideas which seem to contradict established theory or procedures. Part of the apparent genius of scientific or other discoveries is the choice of broad field from which to branch out into new speculation and discovery.
- The next steps are progressively to narrow the field of enquiry, by building on the discoveries of the most unconventional and creative enquirers, and applying their insights, alone or in a new permutation, to a new avenue of speculation and experimentation, that could lead to a dramatically different picture of how the world works.

  For example, Albert Einstein's first step towards genius was to realise that quantum mechanics was *the* hot scientific topic that could and would subvert the classical theory of physics that had held sway for two centuries since Isaac Newton. Einstein's next step towards greatness was to recognise that Philipp Lenard, writing in 1901, had made experiments that undermined the accepted wave theory of light. Einstein's third great insight was to consider Lenard's experiments together with Max Planck's work describing the curve of radiation wavelengths at different temperatures. Einstein thus found a simple way to describe the relation between the size of microscopic quanta of matter and the wavelength of radiation. Light, he finally realised, could be described not just as waves, but also as point-like particles, which he called 'light quanta'.[19] It was a short final hop for Einstein to outline the special theory of relativity, which finally demolished the theoretical picture of the universe Newton had so powerfully constructed.

- The third step is to take the new theoretical model and prove it experimentally and/or with new data relevant to the new model.

These three steps were precisely how Curie blazed a totally new and proprietary scientific trail.

- Her first step was to focus on the hot new area of x-rays and radiation. X-rays were discovered by Wilhelm Röntgen in 1895, and he demonstrated that they could penetrate human flesh but not bones. He was awarded the first Nobel prize in physics in 1901 for his research on x-rays. In 1896 Henri Becquerel experimented with uranium salts and demonstrated that they could produce radiation, rays that could penetrate like x-rays.[20]
- It was Becquerel's new type of ray that Curie followed up as a subject for her Ph.D. thesis. She adopted this subject specifically because, although it utterly intrigued her, to her surprise it had not made any ripples with scientists or the general public. She decided to explore Becquerel's breakthrough further, not just theoretically, but also experimentally. She asked: what caused the radiation? She had an intuition, a hypothesis, 'that the emission of the rays is an atomic property of the uranium, whatever the physical or chemical conditions of the salt were. Any substance containing uranium is much more active in emitting rays, as it contains more of this element.'[21]

She proved through experiments that the stock

explanation of radiation – that it must be generated, like all chemical reactions where light or heat is generated, by an interaction between molecules – was plain wrong. She established that radiation must simply be a property of the atom itself. The more uranium, the more radiation. To make this clear, she invented the term 'radioactivity'.[22]

Now the pieces began to fall into place. Perhaps uranium was not the point, not the end of the trail. As Eva Curie recounts in her biography of her mother, 'She questioned: Even though the phenomenon [of radioactivity] had only been observed with uranium, nothing proved that uranium was the only chemical element capable of emitting such radiation. Why should not other bodies possess the same power?'[23]

The search was on: Curie resolved to examine all known chemical bodies. She examined two minerals which contained uranium: chalcolite and pitchblende, which is a uranium ore. Lo and behold, each of them was more radioactive than uranium itself, twice and four times more respectively. So, it couldn't be that uranium itself was the explanation of radioactivity. Now Curie made another leap of intuition: that the answer wasn't chalcolite or pitchblende either, but rather that 'there must be some unknown substance, very active, in these minerals. My husband agreed with me and I urged that we search at once for this hypothetical substance, thinking that in beginning this work we were to enter the path of a new science which we should follow for all our future.'[24]

Through hypothesis followed by experimentation, Curie had carved a new superhighway through the impenetrable mystery of chemistry. Her path led herself and Pierre before long to discover two new elements, two new substances, both previously unsuspected, which were the king and queen of radioactivity. They produced a substance that was 330 times more radioactive than uranium. They still didn't have the pure form of the product, but they were sure that they had discovered a new chemical element, and in July 1898 announced the birth of polonium, named in honour of Marie's native land.[25]

In December 1898, they went public with a second new element, radium, which was 900 times more radioactive than uranium.[26] In 1902, Curie separated one-tenth of a gram of radium from a ton of pitchblende.[27] She finally succeeded in isolating pure radium in 1910.[28]

In 1903, Pierre Curie proved that radium could cure growths, tumours and certain types of cancer, by destroying diseased cells faster than healthy cells.[29] Marie and Pierre paved the way for the emergence of a radium industry. Radium became a very valuable mineral, where demand for medical purposes outstripped supply, and the price rose astronomically; but the Curies never patented any of their discoveries, nor tried to profit from them.

Two other trailblazers: Churchill and Mandela

Winston Churchill took a long time to find his destined path. He thought for decades that his speaking prowess would propel him to power. Yet his eloquence did not produce the desired results. 'The very nature' of Churchill's oratory, says historian David Cannadine, 'made it harder, not easier, for him to get to the very top in public life'.[30]

Churchill went over the top for too many different – even conflicting – causes, so he seemed 'a man of unstable temperament and defective judgment, completely lacking in any real sense of proportion'.[31] His 'ornate phraseology', as Jan Smuts put it, 'soared above the sober and often intransigent facts of reality'.[32]

In one of Churchill's overworked phrases, 'the abyss' was always nigh; his colours were always vivid, nay lurid; the survival of Britain and the civilised world was always under threat, sometimes from quite imaginary foes, such as the trade unions, Gandhi, even the prosaic and mild Clement Atlee. 'To speak with the tongues of men and angels,' Asquith said of Churchill, 'is no good if a man does not inspire trust.'

It was not his speaking prowess that won the day for Churchill, but Hitler – and Churchill's abhorrence of him, together with his prescient accuracy about the threat. By 1940, Churchill's solitary trail had become the escape route for the whole free world.

> Hitler knows that he will have to break us in this island or lose the war. If we can stand up to him, all Europe may be free, and the life of the world may move forward into broad, sunlit uplands. But if we fail, then the whole world, including the United States, will sink into the abyss of a new Dark Age ... Let us therefore brace ourselves to our duties, and so bear ourselves that, if the British Empire and Commonwealth last for a thousand years, men will still say, 'This was their finest hour.'[33]

After being wrong for so long, Churchill was pitch-perfect here.

We close this chapter with another great tyranny-buster. **Nelson Mandela**'s long years in prison gave him time to find his destiny. While marooned on the repulsive Robben Island, Mandela realised that the only constructive course forward for all South Africans – the *only* feasible path of peace and reconciliation – was to do a deal with his gaolers.

Mandela was the first ANC leader to see that compromise would be necessary. Peace required them to repudiate communism, to accept the current wealth distribution in South Africa, and to convince the other side that black government could be peaceful. In 1986 Mandela was able to meet a delegation of 'eminent persons' from the British Commonwealth. He told them, 'I am a South African nationalist, not a communist; nationalists come in every hue and colour, and I am firmly committed to a non-racial society. I believe in the Freedom Charter, which embodies principles of democracy and human rights, and is not a blueprint for socialism. The white minority should feel a sense of security in any new South Africa.'[34]

Mandela had a unique blend of charm and iron resolve. Journalist Richard Stengel, who shadowed Mandela for three years, noted this extraordinary quality. 'He is a power charmer,' Stengel attests, 'confident that he will charm you, by whatever means possible. He is attentive, courtly, winning, and . . . seductive . . . He will learn as much as possible about you before meeting you.'[35]

The charm alone would not have worked. 'He will always stand up for what he believes is right,' says Stengel, 'with a stubbornness that is virtually unbending. I often heard him say, "This isn't right" . . . I heard him say it directly to South African President F. W. de Klerk about the constitutional negotiations. He used the phrase for years on Robben Island when talking to a guard or the head of the prison. *This isn't right.* In a very basic way, this intolerance of injustice was what goaded him.'[36]

His moral rectitude, his appeal to human decency, his maturity and absence of resentment at his appalling treatment, his capacity to see the good in everyone, and to compromise on everything except one person, one vote and equality before the law, his unstated but deep Christian convictions – all of these made it possible for him to achieve a settlement which would have eluded anyone else on his side. He was everyone's friend; but he was nobody's fool.

Mandela and the regime both knew that he alone must be the ANC negotiator. By 1985, Mandela and four comrades had been moved to share decent quarters at Pollsmoor prison, near Cape Town. But after a spell in hospital, Nelson was moved away from his friends to a new wing. 'I was not happy to be separated from my colleagues and I missed my garden and sunny terrace,' he wrote. 'But ... I resolved to do something I had been pondering for a long time: begin discussions with the government ... If we did not start a dialogue soon, both sides would be plunged into a dark night of oppression, violence and war.'[37]

This was brave. It went against ANC policy, and what he had said for decades. It could divide the ANC and undermine its bargaining power. Mandela kept the rest of the ANC in the dark: 'I chose to tell no one what I was about to do. Not my colleagues upstairs nor those in Lusaka.'[38] 'Oliver Tambo and the ANC,' he continued, 'had called for the people of South Africa to render the country ungovernable, and the people were responding.'[39]

In closing his book as he takes over as South African president, Mandela strikes a high moral tone that would seem false from almost anybody else: 'Man's goodness is a flame that can be hidden but never extinguished ... Freedom is indivisible ... For to be free is not merely to cast off one's chains, but to live in a way that respects and enhances the freedom of others.'[40] Because the men who ran South Africa were afraid of retribution, and yet trusted Mandela to shield them from it, fifty million South Africans of all colours tasted freedom. Mandela's words were not empty rhetoric; they were the plain truth, and I saw it at the time with my own eyes.

Summary and conclusion

Mandela and the other players testify to our themes so far – self-belief, incredibly high expectations, transforming experiences, a single transforming achievement, and a solitary, imaginative and uncompromising trail. Success, when it comes, appears completely unreasonable – or at least surprising.

Yet there may, after all, be some hidden subterranean rhyme or reason in the universe. Depth of willpower, depth of belief, depth of reach, depth of experience, depth of transforming skill and depth of character – good or bad – are needed to create change. Unreasonable success requires a singular path, and a singular personality.

Our players were or are larger than life. All were profoundly original. Most were highly eccentric. To be ultra-successful requires the verve to be utterly different.

To be unreasonably successful you need your own philosophy and deeply grounded beliefs. You need unique and authentic convictions before the world will take serious notice of you.

Not only do you need to make your own trail. We are about to discover that you also need your own personal vehicle to drive towards your destination.

Make your own trail

- High ambition often defined early or at start of career
- Devise and follow own trail
- Increasing focus over time
- Develop unique philosophy

9

Landmark 6: Find and Drive Your Personal Vehicle

At last I had authority to give directions over the whole scene. I felt as if I had been walking with destiny, and that all of my past life had been but a preparation for this hour and this trial.

—WINSTON CHURCHILL

This chapter presents a simple but vital finding that is often neglected – for unreasonable success, we need our personal vehicle. All our players had a vehicle which multiplied their impact hundreds or thousands of times.

There are two types of vehicle which can give unreasonable success. The first type is useful; the second is indispensable.

Type 1: Pool vehicles

The first type of vehicle is something which already exists in your environment, something external or extraneous to you, which you can leap on and from which you can derive great benefit. I call these 'pool vehicles' because I worked in an oil refinery and we had pick-up trucks to drive around its sprawling estate. Pool vehicles could be used by any manager.

In your career, a pool vehicle is something in the environment that can help you. It won't guarantee success, but it is a good start. What is there around you – knowledge, world-view, technology or other trends – which you can use as a launch pad?

Here are examples of pool vehicles the players used.

For **Bill Bain**, it was the theories of business strategy that had been originated by the Boston Consulting Group. BCG put its ideas such as the Boston Box out into the public domain to build reputation and sell business. When Bill Bain started Bain & Company, he was able to use all BCG's concepts. They were high-octane stuff, fuelling a whole new industry.

Jeff Bezos also used the BCG ideas to develop his philosophy for Amazon, especially dominant market share, and lowest costs and prices. Bezos also benefitted from two other pool vehicles – internet retailing and 'Californian Venture Capital Syndrome', which values growth above short-term profits, supporting Amazon's losses for long years, allowing a focus on customer experience and low prices.

Otto von Bismarck rode the rise of nationalism in the nineteenth century. This was his pool vehicle to turn Germany from a fragmented cluster of dozens of independent states into a unified superpower dominating central Europe. The popularity he gained by his unification of Germany pleased the liberal politicians and William, the Prussian King, and kept Bismarck in power for a generation.

Winston Churchill's pool vehicle was the rise of German National Socialism, Hitler's murderous anti-Semitism, and his own opposition to them. An environmental factor does not have to be appeased or promoted; it can also be a pool vehicle when it is opposed first or most vigorously.

Marie Curie's pool vehicle was the new field of x-rays and radiation.

The two pool vehicles which **Walt Disney** exploited so well were the rise of animated cartoons and, later, the rise of amusement parks. Disneyland was in many ways the opposite of traditional amusement parks, which Walt disdained as 'nasty, dirty places run by hard-faced men'. Without their existence he would probably not have had the idea for a pristine and uplifting park idealising the best of American small-town values.

Leonardo da Vinci would not have been Leonardo if he had not been born where and when he was. Renaissance Florence was his pool vehicle.

Bob Dylan's pool vehicle was the early 1960s folk movement in New York City, with its liberal-protest values, and self-importance, epitomised by his relationship with Joan Baez. He rode them until he became famous, then dumped them sharpish.

Albert Einstein benefited from the amazing new ideas in quantum mechanics in central Europe at the start of the twentieth century.

We've seen how **Bruce Henderson**'s revolutionary ideas did not arise in a vacuum. His long years spent in Westinghouse's purchasing department, and his discovery that rival firms did not have roughly equal costs, were the pool ideas available to any other intelligent manager with curiosity and a taste for profitable abstraction. As with Einstein, the raw material for radical new departures was floating around in the ether, accessible to anyone who could think hard about it.

Viktor Frankl benefitted from the theories of Freud and Adler, and the fashionable new growth market of psychoanalysis. Like Carl Jung, Frankl developed his own theories and practice – both arguably much better than those of their predecessors – but the ideas about the unconscious mind were already current.

For **Steve Jobs**, the pool vehicle was the emergence of the first personal computers in the early 1970s, together with the dramatically lower cost and higher capacity of superconductors and the unprecedented power unleashed by new software.

John Maynard Keynes' pool vehicles were the Treaty of Versailles, which he famously opposed in *The Economic Consequences of the Peace*, the Great Depression, and the resulting rise of communism and fascism, which provoked him to discover civilised ways of curbing unemployment.

Lenin's pool ideas were the French Revolution's notions, updated by Karl Marx, which Lenin adapted to critique the ramshackle autocracy of Tsarist Russia.

Madonna draws on the pool ideas of the archetypical American femme fatale, and a lot else besides. Her stock-in-trade is to reinterpret, update and incarnate previous American sex idols.

The African National Congress (ANC) was founded on 8 January 1912, six and a half years before **Nelson Mandela** was born. It was his pool vehicle once he became a freedom fighter.

Paul of Tarsus merged centuries-old philosophical and religious ideas from Jewish and Greek traditions.

J. K. Rowling benefitted from the emergence of mystery and fantasy literature, such as the work of C. S. Lewis and J. R. R. Tolkien, and from children's literature of various types where children experienced great adventures. She was a great reader as a child, and has said that she was particularly influenced by Edith Nesbit's *The Railway Children* and *The Story of the Treasure Seekers*, and by Lewis' *Chronicles of Narnia*.[1] Another book which fired Rowling's imagination, and has parallels with the Harry Potter stories, is *The Little White Horse* by Elizabeth Goudge. In this book, as Rowling has acknowledged, 'the heroine was quite plain', as was Harry Potter. Goudge 'also included details of what her characters were eating'. Rowling was to give generous helpings of what was eaten at Hogwarts.[2]

Helena Rubinstein may or may not have taken pots of her mother's home-made face cream from Poland to Australia, and she was not the only woman to have been interested in using natural ingredients to preserve and enhance good skin – she was just the first to commercialise the idea.

Margaret Thatcher also had two sets of pool ideas: a conservative philosophy woven by the interlacing ideas of many philosophers and politicians, from Thomas Hobbes to Edmund Burke to Benjamin Disraeli and countless others; not a set of ideas unique to Thatcher alone, but a powerful heritage. More unusually, she also drew on classical liberal ideas which resurfaced within a wing of the Conservative Party in the 1970s, influenced by economist F. A. Hayek, propagated by the Institute of Economic Affairs, and preached by the eccentric, intellectual and other-worldly Keith Joseph, her political ally. Anyone could have appropriated these ideas and turned them into a modern political programme, but only Thatcher did so.

Type 2: Your personal vehicle

Pool vehicles are useful; but your own personal vehicle is essential. You must create something new which vastly increases your impact on the world.

The players used their vehicles for three reasons:

- **Leverage** – using the vehicles' power, wealth, manpower, reputation, intellectual property and influence.
- **Collaboration** – enabling the players to do what they couldn't do themselves or couldn't do well; supplying missing ingredients; building supporters.

- **Credibility and publicity** – helping the players to be taken seriously by backers, gatekeepers, enthusiasts, and finally the general public/customers/voters.

Personal vehicles for business leaders

For the business players, all three success factors were important.

Bill Bain built a very large consulting firm, consisting of hundreds and then thousands of high-powered consultants. He needed large of numbers of Bain consultants to talk to client executives throughout their organisation, to understand their perspective on the strategic issues as defined by Bain & Company; to gather data both inside the organisation and in the marketplace; to perform analyses; and then to present the findings to the client, while also nurturing the close relationship between Bain and the client company.

The collaboration he needed also came from his partners, the people who sold client assignments and masterminded them. In the early days of Bain & Company, Bill Bain withdrew from doing this himself – not because he couldn't, but because he didn't want to, and he spent his time (such of it as he allocated parsimoniously to his firm) dreaming of the future and managing his partners closely.

Without the likes of Ralph Willard, John Halpern and Mitt Romney, Bain & Company would not have been so spectacularly successful. I have never seen such a talented and effective team of people below the boss, or a team so loyal to Mr Big.

Incidentally, Bain did not buy them with money – he kept most of that for himself. He mentored and inspired them, simultaneously giving them free rein, yet retaining control.

Bain & Company's credibility came in a new way. Bain

created a cult of secrecy around his vehicle. For many years his firm had no brochure, no website, wrote no memos or reports, had no business cards, and shunned publicity like the plague. All his sales were made by direct pitches to chief executives, and by references from existing clients to their peers in other companies.

This was greatly facilitated by the interlocking nature of US boards, whose members mainly comprise CEOs and chairmen from other big companies, who act as non-executive directors. Bain would encourage his clients to talk about the high-quality work the company was doing when they met their fellow directors at board meetings – most of Bain's clients came this way. I participated in a board meeting of Dun & Bradstreet in New York, showing some of the work we had done in Europe. Following that presentation, two other companies whose CEOs were present became Bain clients.

Most basically, Bain & Company's authority flowed from its unique positioning and intimacy with clients.

Jeff Bezos needs the leverage of his Amazon army to an even greater extent than Bill Bain did. Bezos too places enormous importance on the quality and ambition of those he recruits. To get big fast required him to build an enormous organisation.

Collaboration was similarly vital. Because Bezos knew nothing about functions such as warehousing and logistics, when Amazon had to start investing very heavily in these Jeff hired the very best people he could find, backed them totally unless they failed, and fired them if they did.

Credibility was also vital. It came by becoming the largest online retailer by far – later the largest retailer period – of books, and then of other products. And as we saw earlier, Jeff's relentless focus on exceptional customer service and unbeatable prices underpinned Amazon's rapid expansion. Again, the business formula was also the vehicle.

Walt Disney started his studio with just one other cartoonist, the nerdy and introverted Ub Iwerks. Disney supplied the ideas, Iwerks the execution.

Mickey Mouse is the perfect example. Somehow, mice had entered Disney's unconscious mind. On a train from Chicago to Los Angeles he sketched a scenario for *Plane Crazy*, about a mouse who built a plane in order to woo a lady mouse. The storyline worked, but his drawing was hopeless. Iwerks redesigned the rodent, giving Mickey a curved posterior and a long nose, which made all the difference.

Like Bain & Company, **Bruce Henderson**'s BCG obtained leverage through its ever-expanding hierarchy of consultants. Henderson needed his top colleagues to sell and manage the work, and to provide continued innovation in ideas. BCG gained credibility through its concepts, its creativity and intellectual firepower, and its reputation for having 'invented strategy'. BCG overtook its rivals, driven by superior creativity and brainpower.

When **Steve Jobs** was fired from Apple, the vehicle he had co-founded and inculcated with his quest for elegant simplicity, he started two other companies, NeXT and Pixar, which became his vehicles for the next decade. At NeXT, says Walter Isaacson, Jobs 'was able to indulge all his instincts, both good and bad. He was unbound. The result was a series of spectacular products that were dazzling market flops. What prepared him for the great success he would have in Act III — (after he was restored as head of Apple in 1997) — was not his ouster from his Act I at Apple but his brilliant failures in Act II.'[3]

Neither NeXT nor Pixar proved to be good vehicles for Jobs. When he returned to Apple, he found a right mess; a whole series of projects and products, including the Newton handwriting recognition software, were loss-makers and cash-consumers. Apple had one product that was profitable and credible, the Macintosh. Jobs cut everything else, and then paused until his people created 'the next big thing', which proved to be the iPod and iTunes, and then all the delightful and simple new products they created. Apple had the DNA, and design capability, which Jobs greatly augmented, to go from strength to strength. Jobs took his rackety old vehicle, which was barely roadworthy in 1997, and endowed it with such a powerful new engine that it became for a time the most valuable vehicle in the world.

The lesson? Don't look for a new vehicle if the existing one has potential for success and can be radically reconditioned.

Helena Rubinstein built the first global cosmetics empire from the unlikely beachhead of Melbourne, Australia. After receiving early help from entrepreneur John Thompson and his friends, she was largely a one-woman band. She was the brand.

She did not pick a successor, and after she died, the empire without the empress sat lonely and soulless within Colgate–Palmolive. Only when L'Oréal bought Helena Rubinstein in 1988 did the vehicle find a sympathetic and luxury-focused owner. In 2007 Demi Moore – someone as 'strong, determined, smart and seductive' as Helena Rubinstein – became the public face of the brand, and sales took off again.

All the business leaders used their vehicles to vastly increase their reach, power and impact, without diminishing at all their idiosyncrasies, quirks or ability to mould each vehicle's DNA in their own likeness. Even if the player becomes a caricature of themselves, that's a kind of validation.

When a firm has co-founders – think of Gates and Allen; Jobs and Wozniak; Bill Bain and Patrick Graham – typically one of them becomes dominant through sheer force of personality. Even when the driver has big flaws – perhaps *especially* when this is true – the emergence of a single leader underpins success.

Personal vehicles for political leaders

For the players in politics, only leverage and credibility were vital.

Otto von Bismarck was appointed by the king: Bismarck alone could balance the different interests and power of king and parliament. Bismarck's vehicle was the Prussian and later German state and its military forces. He relied almost entirely on his own skills and judgement; he had subordinates but no collaborators. The three wars he won entrenched his prestige and power.

Winston Churchill's vehicle was the British state and Empire, their armies and his popular appeal as war leader.

Lenin, like his fellow Russian revolutionaries, enjoyed a comfortable bourgeois life in exile in England and Switzerland, spending happy hours drinking coffee and eating good food in cafés and restaurants; disputing the finer points of Marxist theory; walking in the countryside, hills and mountains; and, in Lenin's case, penning newspaper articles and books. Lenin was a heavyweight intellectual, for whom Marx's theories and his own were vital guides to the forthcoming revolution. The Marxist newspaper *Iskra* was Lenin's first way of burnishing his revolutionary credentials – when his rivals moved the paper to Geneva in a move to lessen his influence, Lenin promptly moved there too.[4]

Lenin's second vehicle was his 1902 book *What Is To Be Done?*[5] It put him in pole position as the leader-in-waiting of any future Russian revolution.[6]

At the Second Congress of the Russian Social Democratic Party, in 1903, Lenin started a dispute about what kind of party they should be. Lenin wanted 'a tightly organized, elite corps of dedicated professional revolutionaries under a highly central-ized leadership that imposed discipline on the members.'[7] His rival Martov wanted something a little looser. It was a battle of personalities, and Lenin was determined to become top dog. Martov told Lenin, 'That's a dictatorship you're proposing.' 'Yes,' Lenin said, 'there's no other way.'[8]

When it came to a vote of delegates, Lenin narrowly won support for his resolution. He immediately started calling his group the 'Bolsheviks' and Martov's the 'Mensheviks'. It was inspired because Bolshevik means 'majority' in Russian and Menshevik means 'minority'. The terms stuck, despite the Mensheviks generally being larger and more influential right up to the revolution of 1917. He didn't regret the great schism and huge bitterness he had created. Rather, he relished having his own vehicle and being its undisputed leader. Many tyrants in the twentieth century were to emulate him.

But these early vehicles were mere hors d'oeuvres for Lenin. He was truly inspirational, offering hope that the worst, the cruellest and the largest autocracy in the world could be overturned by a bunch of romantic and idealistic comrades. 'Some few thousand nobles have ruled Russia for centuries,' he said. 'Why not us?'[9] It seemed an impossible dream. Yet a series of extraordinary events – Russia's defeat in the First World War and a series of uprisings in 1917 – along with Lenin's unscrupulous genius and amazing luck, made it happen.

This is where **Nelson Mandela** stands apart from other terrorists. Mandela gained a reputation within the ANC as a hot-headed young man, urging increasingly daring acts of defiance. Oliver Tambo, his fellow ANC leader, described Mandela as 'passionate, emotional, sensitive, quickly stung to bitterness and retaliation'.[10]

The ANC was Mandela's key vehicle to prominence until an even more vital vehicle emerged: his time in prison. During these long years, Mandela gradually matured. In prison, says Richard Stengel, who collaborated with Mandela on his autobiography, 'he had to temper his responses to everything. There was little a prisoner could control. The one thing you could control – that you *had* to control – was yourself.'[11]

On Robben Island, Mandela established himself as the ANC prisoners' shop-steward, resisting the more blatant brutalities of the guards and establishing a viable *modus vivendi* between the two sides.[12]

Robben Island and Pollsmoor jails were Mandela's vehicle to the presidency of South Africa, the route along which reconciliation between oppressed and oppressor could progress. The regime and Mandela conducted this delicate dance with astonishing brio and skill, with results that almost nobody in the 1980s had believed possible – an orderly and largely peaceful transfer of power, and the emergence of genuine democracy.

Margaret Thatcher decided at an early age that the Conservative Party was going to be her vehicle for influence and power. In 1979, when she unexpectedly won the election and became prime minister, her vehicle became not just the party but the entire apparatus of the state.

But there was a problem. Most of the senior Tories in her Cabinet did not share her ideological fervour, so the vehicle was faulty, scarcely able to get out of second gear. That was why, as we have seen, the Falklands War came to her as a huge blessing in disguise. Unexpected triumph in the Falklands transformed both Thatcher and her prospects, and before long it transformed Britain too. The war was her turbo-charged vehicle, just as Bismarck's wars had been for him, and the Second World War had been for Churchill.

Note here the obvious point that whereas a successful war is a great political vehicle, it is also a very crude and chancy mechanism, and one probably best deployed in defence rather than attack. Napoleon III precipitated the Franco–Prussian War of 1870–71 to shore up his crumbling political capital, but he lost the war and the empire he had successfully ruled for more than two decades. Tony Blair's alliance with America in the Iraq War was militarily successful, but it only made the area more unstable and divided, and the war demolished his reputation. Although Bismarck pursued three wars, he hated war for its carnage and unpredictability, limited it as much as possible, and preserved peace in Europe throughout his last twenty years in power.

The difference between political and business vehicles

Collaboration is markedly less important for the statesmen than for the business leaders.

Those who run business empires, however autocratic their tendencies, typically need collaborators with different skills to balance or cover for their own weak spots. Business, not politics, is the real art of the possible. Business is more complex, multi-functional, dynamic and fast-changing, and more exposed to unpredictable competition.

Another difference: the business leaders *created* their personal vehicles, whereas this was less true for the political leaders. Churchill and Thatcher inherited their most important vehicles – the Conservative Party and the British state – adding only war leadership as a vital vehicle.

Bismarck was given the position of Prussian chancellor by the king, although he too used war as a vehicle and extended his power and reach with the North German Confederation.

Lenin caused a split in the Russian revolutionary party in exile, and effectively created the Bolsheviks as his own faction and the springboard for his dictatorship, though his writings were also key vehicles.

Mandela made his reputation within the ANC, but did not

choose his most important vehicle before assuming power – prison – though he too uniquely positioned himself as the one person who could reconcile the races and parties within South Africa. He refashioned the entire structure of South African politics; his presidency was totally different from everything which had gone before.

The most unreasonably successful political leaders were also the least typical or conventional. They crafted new sources of power in an almost entrepreneurial way.

Other players' personal vehicles

Marie Curie had several personal vehicles in her career, including the Radium Institute she set up in 1914, and her mobile x-ray units which she created to drive to the First World War battlefields. The units helped save the lives of an estimated million wounded soldiers, by identifying where bullets had lodged and surgery was needed. But her most important vehicle was radium, the magnificent, ultra-potent, but also dangerous new mineral which she identified and isolated.

Albert Einstein's vehicle, above all, was his early breakthrough on relativity, which transformed the picture of the universe bequeathed more than two centuries earlier by Isaac Newton. Like Newton, Einstein was a loner, a solitary genius. Neither of them required any collaboration to make their breakthroughs. The truth of Einstein's theories, later validated by astronomical calculations, was its own source of credibility. Thereafter, slowly at first, and with increasing momentum, universities in Europe and America vied to attract Einstein. But it was he who gave them credibility, not the other way around.

With **Viktor Frankl**, too, the vehicle was the message – 'man's main concern is not to gain pleasure or to avoid pain but rather to see a meaning in his life'.[13] 'Man considers only the stubble field of transitoriness, and overlooks the full granaries of the past, wherein he has salvaged once and for all his deeds, his joys, and also his sufferings. Nothing can be undone, and nothing can be done away with. I should say, *having been* is the surest kind of being.'[14]

And **John Maynard Keynes'** vehicles? Both King's College, Cambridge – the establishment – and the bohemian world of Bloomsbury were decorative and enjoyable vehicles for Keynes, but they were not representative of real life. Keynes' essential vehicle was his extraordinary brain, and the books it gave rise to, principally *The Economic Consequences of the Peace* in 1919 and his 1936 masterpiece *The General Theory of Employment, Interest and Money*. Keynes had no important collaborators, and no need of positions to buttress his sense of destiny.

Leonardo's studio – and above all his paintings and sculptures – were the only vehicles he needed.

J. K. Rowling's vehicle was Harry Potter and Hogwarts.

The personal vehicles of thinkers, writers and artists are different from those of both politicians and business leaders. The thinkers' vehicles are principally books or other publications, discoveries or inventions, or works of art. Other vehicles are largely ornamental or useful for publicity.

Our two musicians needed their vehicles for credibility and leverage.

Bob Dylan's first and most important vehicle was the folk movement. He became its most famous exponent, reinterpreting it for new and turbulent times. Other significant vehicles were Columbia Records and his albums and songs, which often achieved greater commercial success when recorded by other singers. Dylan's turbulent relationship with his fans served as a vehicle too. It gave him an air of mystery and controversy, and highlighted his battle for freedom and creativity, which required him time and time again to disappoint and puzzle his fans by moving on to new genres. Though the folk movement made Dylan, he refused to remain its faithful spokesman.

For reasons that are still a bit mysterious today, Columbia signed Dylan before he had any significant following, and that contract drew attention to him. Before long, however, it was the inherent authority of his music and lyrics which gave Dylan his success. In this he was like the thinkers. He was like Frankl, Leonardo, Einstein and Keynes – their personal vehicles were their dramatic insights, expressed in unforgettable images and words.

Madonna has a fleet of vehicles – record labels, videos, movies, her own business empire and, above all, her cultivation of the media. Madonna is always ready with a controversial pose or something newsworthy. She is needy – she needs leverage. She derives it through talented video producers, film directors, sound producers, and goodness knows who else. Her credibility flows from her permanent presence in the media.

Finally, **Paul of Tarsus**.

Without Jesus, Paul would have had nothing to preach. Equally, however, Paul so radically changed the Jewish sect who were followers and relatives of Jesus – giving it a mission to the whole world, and reinterpreting the significance of Jesus – that we should regard him as similar to the few entrepreneurs who started a world-dominant company, or to the few scientists, such as Newton or Einstein or Darwin, who gave us a completely different worldview.

Unlike the scientists, but like the entrepreneurs, Paul needed leverage. He couldn't start a new philosophy-religion and grow it exponentially without many followers, many new groups of believers, in many different towns around the Mediterranean. Not only did Paul need followers of Christ (and of himself); he also needed to indoctrinate them with his new message. He simplified the new way of life in his letters to the new groups of believers.

Paul was like our scientists and other thinkers – he had to change a worldview and create a new one. It is hard to sell the unfamiliar; it takes unique intellect and powers of persuasion.

Like the scientists, and unlike the entrepreneurs, Paul's message and credibility had to be personal. An entrepreneur's credibility and influence rest far more on his vehicle – his company and its products – than on his personality. You don't buy an Apple device because you admire Steve Jobs; you buy it because of what it does for you. You can believe that he was a total asshole, yet happily pay a premium price for his inventions. The credibility that matters for entrepreneurs is *not* personal; it is based around the brand and the product.

To become a Christian, you had to 'buy Paul' and his account of the significance of Christ and of his continuing living presence. All the great Christian leaders after Paul drew inspiration from Paul; his words resonated down the centuries, and still do.

But perhaps Paul's most important vehicle – which he never knew about, and without which he may have been forgotten or overshadowed – was the work of Marcion, the forgotten yet pivotal second-century evangelist. Marcion was a successful shipping magnate who went to Rome in AD 138 and who, after five years of reflection, published two books.

One was a reinterpretation of Paul's message, which contrasted the God of the Old Testament – a God of wrath – with the supreme and 'Unknown' God – a God of love. This God, Marcion said, first revealed himself by sending Jesus to Earth.

Marcion's other work was a canon – a compilation – of his 'approved' scriptures: the first 'New Testament'. It comprised just ten of Paul's letters and one gospel, a version of Luke.[15] Although other books were later admitted to the New Testament, Paul's predominance in its pages remained. Marcion ensured that Paul's message, and that of Jesus, which

Paul encapsulated and reinterpreted,* were the core of the new religion. Without Marcion, Christianity would have become a different religion, and most likely the Reformation and Protestantism would never have happened.[16]

The survival and propagation of important books – those containing the philosophy and insight of the likes of Aristotle, Plato and Socrates, as well as that of Jesus and Paul – was probably the most important single vehicle of Western civilisation as we know it today. As Churchill said, the only thing which survives for long centuries is books.

Personal vehicles of players

Player	Personal vehicles created
Bain	Bain & Company; the unique Bain consulting formula; recommendations from client CEOs to other CEOs; Bain Capital
Bezos	Amazon; the Bezos business formula for Amazon
Bismarck	The Prussian state and army; North German Confederation; German state and military; successful wars against Denmark, Austria and France
Churchill	His opposition to Hitler; British state and Empire; their armies and people
Curie	Radium

---

* It is not often realised, except by biblical scholars and historians, that the version of Jesus presented in the gospels was heavily influenced by what Paul wrote about Jesus and his significance. Paul's letters were almost certainly written before any of the four New Testament gospels.

Disney	Disney Studio; cartoons, movies and television; Mickey Mouse and later Disney characters; Disney's personal WED corporation; Disneyland
Dylan	The folk movement; Columbia Records; songs and albums; fans
Einstein	Theory of Relativity; Zurich, Prague, Berlin, Caltech, Berkeley and Princeton universities; media
Frankl	*Man's Search for Meaning*; lectures; awards; school of followers
Henderson	Boston Consulting Group (BCG); the Experience Curve and Boston Box concepts; Perspectives (short thought-pieces mailed to senior managers); BCG conferences
Jobs	Apple, NeXT and Pixar; Macintosh computers; Apple digital devices; Apple store; Apple apps
Keynes	*The Economic Consequences of the Peace*; King's College Cambridge; *The General Theory*
Lenin	*Iskra* (Russian revolutionary newspaper); *What Is To Be Done?*; Bolshevik party; Russian state; military and secret police
Leonardo	His studio in Florence; his paintings, sculptures
Madonna	Record labels; albums, videos, movies; media; personal business ventures
Mandela	ANC; Robben Island prison; South African state
Rowling	Harry Potter
Rubinstein	Eponymous cosmetics empire; advertising and media; personality marketing and personal networking

| Paul of Tarsus | City churches he founded; his letters (epistles) to them, *Acts of the Apostles*; Marcion and his pioneering New Testament canon |
| Thatcher | Conservative Party; British state and military; Falklands war; 'Thatcherism' programme in favour of free enterprise, against state business monopolies and abuses of trade union power |

Personal vehicles of players by category

Category	Typical personal vehicles
Business	Company founded; business formula
Politics	Political parties; the state; wars; clear focus on narrow goal
Thinkers	Discoveries or new concepts; books and journals; universities; artworks
Music	Record labels; songs; albums; gigs; videos; media and publicity
Religion	A hero/prophet; personal credo; simple concept; organisational skill; canon of approved writings (e.g. New Testament)

Now, you may be thinking, 'Isn't all this obvious? Naturally, an entrepreneur needs to start a company. Of course, a rock musician will need a record company and world-class songs to record, and so on. How does this help me turbo-charge my career?'

Well, it *is* obvious – but if you are a singer, do you already have a prestigious record label and access to great songs? If you are in business, have you started a company that is sufficiently different from any other, with a great business formula, like

Amazon or Apple or the Boston Consulting Group or Bain & Company or Helena Rubinstein or Walt Disney?

If you haven't, are you obsessed with the need to do so?

Summary and conclusion

A 'pool vehicle' which already exists is a useful start – something we can leap upon and use for our own purposes. If there is nothing in the environment which we want to use as a vehicle or anti-vehicle, we should change our environment to a more fertile one.

For unreasonable success, you must have your own personal vehicle. You cannot walk to unreasonable success. None of our players did so.

What is to be your vehicle?

Find and drive your personal vehicle

- Find your 'horse to ride'
- Nothing big can happen without one or more great vehicles
- The vehicle may be a movement, a network, an organisation, or a new positioning which strikes a chord
- Kick off by adopting or opposing a 'pool vehicle'
- Then find your personal vehicle and drive it to success

10

Landmark 7: Thrive on Setbacks

Success means going from failure to failure without loss
of enthusiasm.

—WINSTON CHURCHILL

Politicians rise by toils and struggles. They expect to
fall; they hope to rise again.

—WINSTON CHURCHILL

The excess energy released from overreaction to setbacks
is what innovates!

—NASSIM NICHOLAS TALEB

It is not enough to be resilient and get over setbacks; to be
unreasonably successful you must learn to positively thrive
on them. This is an art that all the players perfected. Consider
three standout cases.

The king of setbacks: Winston Churchill

Like his father Randolph Churchill, Winston seemed slated for glorious failure. His setbacks were so numerous that we must limit ourselves to the really serious ones.

The way that his manic, overflowing energy could overrule common sense, with grave results, is illustrated by Churchill's adventure in Antwerp from 3–7 October 1914, in the Great War of 1914–18. When the Germans advanced through Belgium, their objective was to take the great ports on the coast of France and Belgium. Their first port of call, as it were, was to advance on Antwerp. If Antwerp fell, it would mean the end of Belgium as a free country, and endanger the other ports – Ostend, Dunkirk, Calais and Boulogne, which the French were racing to fortify against the Germans.

Churchill proposed to the British Cabinet that he go to Antwerp to rally the Belgian troops and bring British re-inforcements. 'Once in Antwerp,' says biographer Roy Jenkins, Churchill 'threw himself, with a mixture of galvanic energy, total indifference to his own safety and considerable concern for his own comfort, into organising Belgium's resistance.'[1] He was enjoying himself so much that he suggested he should resign his Cabinet position and take over as military commander there.

It was a total fiasco. Antwerp held out against the German advance for just five days, long enough to help secure the other ports, but at large human cost. Churchill, said the *Morning Post* newspaper, a supporter of the Tory government, 'must have been mad to have thought that he could relieve Antwerp . . . by putting 8,000 half-trained troops into it'. Most of the Belgian army was lost, and around 2,500 British troops – many of them Churchill's untrained Naval Division – died, or were captured and interned.[2]

Much worse was to follow. Rightly critical of the impasse on the Western Front – 'sending our armies to chew barbed wire in Flanders', as he put it – Churchill proposed what he thought would be a casualty-light joint naval and military operation in the Dardanelles (part of the Ottoman Empire, in modern Turkey), aimed at threatening Constantinople (Istanbul), forcing Turkey to withdraw from the war and bringing Greece, Bulgaria and Romania into it on the side of Britain and France. The campaign, also known as Gallipoli, didn't work – in March 1915 troops were landed but soon after most were massacred, with over 114,000 British casualties.[3]

Churchill's reputation as a military strategist never fully recovered. Before long he was edged out of the government altogether. At forty years old Churchill told Lord Riddell, 'I am finished.' Churchill's doughty and ever-supportive wife Clementine ('Clemmie') confided to a friend, 'I thought he would die of grief.'[4]

Yet Churchill bounced back. He went into the British army in France as a major for six months, including a spell in the trenches – a new life to which he adapted well, fortified by extra supplies of sardines, chocolate, potted meats, corned beef, stilton cheese, cream, hams, dried fruits, steak pie, vintage brandy and peach brandy sent by Clemmie. He appreciated the comradeship and relative hardships, and his customary good humour returned. 'I have found happiness and content such as I have not known for many months,' he wrote to Clemmie. 'I have never been in better health and spirits.'[5]

Churchill was to have many further setbacks. In 1925, as chancellor of the exchequer, he made the appalling blunder of returning the pound sterling to the gold standard at the very high pre-war level, which British industry – especially the coal industry, which was already losing exports – could not sustain. Keynes wrote an influential pamphlet blaming Churchill, calling it *The Economic Consequences of Mr Churchill.*

This was unfair, since the whole financial establishment, the Conservative leaders and the Labour opposition, had foisted the policy on Churchill, who had strong doubts about its wisdom. Nonetheless, Churchill was responsible for the decision and the mud stuck.

What made matters worse was the General Strike of 1926, led by the million miners who suffered high unemployment as a result of the return to gold. Churchill forced the strikers into submission.

He had always wanted to become prime minister. In 1928 this prize seemed to be within his grasp. But in 1929 his party lost office, and when they returned two years later as the dominant strand in the National Government, Churchill was too contentious a figure to be included in the coalition.

His initial response was to detach himself from his political obsession. Just as Churchill had cut himself loose from politics by joining the army following his blunders of 1914 and 1915, in 1929 he left active politics, immersing himself in a two-year frenzy of highly lucrative writing, then a punishing lecture tour of America.

But whereas in 1916 a short break from politics worked wonders for Churchill's psyche, between 1929 and 1931 nemesis pursued him relentlessly. He nearly went bust following the Wall Street Crash of 1929. Still he was resilient; he redoubled his writing efforts to stay ahead of his creditors. Then in December 1931 he was knocked down by a car when walking across Fifth Avenue, suffering a severe scalp wound and two cracked ribs. Still Churchill went on. Before long he resumed his onerous speaking tour, returning to London in 1932 battered and bruised.

Churchill made things worse by throwing himself headlong into a new political obsession: opposition to a mild measure of self-government for India. 'It was largely because of the hostility

Churchill aroused by this ferocious and futile campaign,' wrote historian David Cannadine, 'that his closely argued and powerfully documented speeches against the Nazi threat attracted so much less notice than they deserved.'[6] In truth, Churchill knew very little about India.

By 1936 Churchill was in a bad way, occasionally depressed and drinking far too much, even by his liberal standards. He had, says Roy Jenkins, 'a sense of political impotence, of his talents wasted, of time passing him by'.[7]

Yet it was also at this time that Churchill hit his stride with ever more apocalyptic warnings about Hitler. And, miracle of miracles, as Churchill went more and more over the top, Hitler lent increasing credibility and vindication to his most determined enemy. After Hitler had deceived the British prime minister, Neville Chamberlain, by promises of peace at Munich in October 1938, and then torn up his commitments by invading Czechoslovakia in March 1939, Churchill was increasingly on a roll, and when war with Germany came in September 1939, he became nigh-unstoppable. At that time, he said in his memoirs, 'a very strong sense of calm' and 'serenity of mind' grew in him, together with an 'uplifted detachment from human and personal affairs'.[8]

How do we explain this remarkable man's ability not only to survive a whole catalogue of personal and political disasters, but to thrive on them, and to emerge on top form at the time of his nation's greatest crisis?

On 18 May 1940, Churchill expected an imminent German invasion of Britain. That night, his friend John 'Jock' Colville was with Churchill in the Upper War Room at Admiralty House. 'Winston was in excellent humour,' Colville recorded, because he 'is full of fight and thrives on crisis and adversity.'[9]

Churchill, buoyed by his self-belief and gargantuan expectations, had throughout his career an intense sense of personal drama, not despite, but rather *because of*, his setbacks. His career mattered, and if it went up and down like a yoyo, it just fed his sense of self-importance. What Winston did, what Winston said, mattered. He was either 'out' or 'in', and if one was the prelude to the other, being down would be followed by being up – and being *really* down was perhaps the condition and preparation for being *really* up. Churchill knew from history that life does not go in a straight line and being part of great events made every day vital.

Setbacks give feedback, so that we either change course entirely – a change of strategy – or redouble the conviction that we are right but realise we must change tactics in order to triumph. We can see this learning experience with Churchill. After his hostility to organised labour in the General Strike created fierce enemies, Churchill stopped his strident pro-capitalist crusade. In the 1930s he courted Labour and Liberal support for opposing Hitler and demanding rearmament. He knew that he was right about the threat to the world, and focused all his energies, his entire being, on defeating Hitler.

Paradoxically, setbacks can validate unconventional views and contribute to a sense of greatness. If you follow the herd, you are unremarkable. If you are controversial, you are noticed. Setbacks happen more frequently to people who take large risks. Risk-takers defy the majority view – that is why it is a risk. Risks have high downsides, but high upsides. And if we can survive defeats – not just through inbuilt resilience, but also because defeats give us feedback *and* validation – and continue to take high risks, we preserve the possibility of remarkable future success.

Churchill was wrong about Antwerp, disastrously wrong about Gallipoli, wrong about the gold standard, injudicious in his handling of the General Strike, wrong about India, then absolutely right about the existential threat from Hitler.

Surviving one defeat makes surviving the next defeat more bearable, easier and more likely. And eventually, if you keep pulling the one-arm bandit, you may reach your treasure – so long as you do not run out of currency, the currency of self-confidence and conviction.

Nassim Nicholas Taleb has written a fine book – in my opinion his best – which he called *Anti-fragile*, a term he coined. He opens the book thus:

> Wind extinguishes a candle and energizes fire.
>
> Likewise with randomness, uncertainty, chaos: you want to use them, not hide from them. You want to be the fire and wish for the wind . . .
>
> The mission is how to domesticate, even dominate, even conquer, the unseen, the opaque, and the inexplicable.[10]

Being anti-fragile does not mean being resilient – rather, it means positively benefitting from shocks, setbacks, risks and uncertainty. To innovate, he says, first get into trouble. Setbacks are a discovery mechanism; they also release excess energy, motivation and willpower. Exposure to failure is essential for success; we need 'the light of experience gained by disaster'.[11] Through imagination, courage and action, it is possible to get, in his wonderful phrase, 'the better half of luck'.[12]

This eloquently describes the actions of our players to a tee. It is not clear, however, that this attitude to risk, setbacks and disaster is the natural property of humans. Rather, it seems that resilience is the most that the great majority of people expect of themselves – the ability to withstand failures, not the ability to seek them out and triumph from them.

Yet our players, exemplified by Churchill, *were* anti-fragile. It is not that they wanted, either consciously or unconsciously, to experience huge problems. Instead, they took risks which ordinary people tend not to take, and they were able to benefit from setbacks which would have knocked most people for six.

They had the anti-fragile spirit. They were and are buccaneers, pirates and explorers, with a highly developed sense of their own potential and with strong anti-conventional opinions – they exhibit not just a strong ego, but also an ability to confront and confound adversity, with a curiosity about themselves and the world and a degree of stoicism which sets them apart from people who are merely big-headed and oblivious to risk and randomness. Our players sought out risks, *knowing that they were risks*, aware that they were swimming against the tide, confident that they could win, but aware of the possibility of failure and able not just to cope with it, but to find a way around it. They had and have the courage to benefit from adversity.

So too, perhaps, for us. The ability to thrive on setbacks, to reframe them in the most favourable and courageous light, to turn a blind eye to one's vulnerabilities, is a necessary condition for unreasonable success. The slings and arrows of outrageous fortune always operate when we travel in the hills of elevated ambition – if we want to win, we should regard them as our friends, and take the opportunity to sharpen our character and make it impervious to future setbacks. Once we have survived and prospered after the equivalent of Churchill's Dardanelles or Thatcher's Falklands, we become confident that we can turn any nasty shock to our advantage.

Jobs thrives on failure

In 1985 Steve Jobs was brutally fired from the company he had founded. 'The best thing ever to happen to Steve,' said Arthur Rock, the venture capitalist on Apple's board, 'was when we fired him, told him to get lost.'[13]

Jobs didn't see it that way. He had courted John Sculley, the Pepsi executive, and brought him into the company, and now Sculley had forced Jobs out of his own beloved firm. Jobs had a cute photo of himself and Sculley happily chatting in his office, and he hurled it across the floor, shattering the glass. Jobs sold all his shares – 11 per cent of Apple – bar one solitary share. This was not the action of a man planning a comeback. He was out, it seemed, forever.

Can you imagine what that must have done to the man who thought he was a genius, one of the enlightened ones who stalk the Earth, the man who had created the Macintosh – possibly, despite its weaknesses, the greatest product leap forward Silicon Valley had ever made – and was now frozen out of Apple? To add insult to injury, Apple shares soared almost 7 per cent when his departure was announced.

Yet Arthur Rock was right; despite the trauma, Jobs was truly anti-fragile. The shock of dismissal energised him mightily. Like Churchill, he immersed himself in other activity. He founded one new venture, and took over another.

The first was NeXT. The product was a high-end workstation sold only to colleges and universities. NeXT was a caricature of Jobs' search for a spectacular product, along with all his worst indulgences and habits. He started by paying $100,000 for a logo, a perfect black cube. Because the logo was so beautiful, Jobs insisted that the computer should also be a perfect cube, which was expensive to manufacture. Jobs built a fancy futuristic factory, complete with white walls, $20,000 black leather chairs, and an impossibly grand staircase which seemed to float in space – the head office had one of these too.

The product went on the market in mid-1989, some two years late. It had some great features, such as the Oxford dictionary and complete works of Shakespeare – 'what we've done', Jobs said at the launch, 'is made the first real digital books', the first advance in 'the state of the art of printed book technology since Gutenberg.'[14]

There were some problems. The computer had an optical read/write disk, but no backup floppy disk. The optical disk had high capacity but was slow. Bill Gates was hardly objective, but sadly accurate: 'This machine is crap. The optical disk has too low latency, the fucking case is too expensive. This thing is ridiculous.'[15] Jobs had promised his academic market that it would cost between $2000 and $3000, but it came out at $6500 — if you wanted a printer, it was another $2000, and $2500 for an external hard disk.

NeXT expected to sell its factory capacity of ten thousand computers a month. Only four hundred a month were sold. NeXT was a magnificent flop — Jobs at his most expansive, and least commercial. Yet the venture served a function for Jobs — it distracted him from being fired from Apple, it kept him in the digital game, it preserved his self-respect as a player in the brave new world, it gave him valuable lessons in how not to create a viable business, and most of all it eventually paved the way for his return to Apple, when it was in even worse straits than NeXT.

While NeXT limped on, Jobs' obsession with digital images and computer animation pulled him ever deeper into another massive learning experience. After leaving Apple, he had become the majority investor in Pixar, whose main product was the Pixar Image Computer. It sold for $125,000, mainly to digital animators and graphic designers — think Silicon Valley serving Hollywood — Disney was Pixar's biggest customer. Alongside the hardware, Pixar had two other products: software for the computer and a small sideline making animated movies.

While running NeXT, Jobs provided Pixar with ideas and board supervision, but neither were fruitful. By 1991 Pixar was in the intensive care ward — it could neither sell enough of its very expensive kit, nor invent a new mass-market product. Jobs had sunk nearly $50 million into Pixar. All three divisions were bleeding cash, and neither Jobs nor anyone else wanted to shovel more money into the bottomless pit.

Then serendipity intervened.

In 1988 John Lasseter, the creative genius behind Pixar's animated films, had made *Tin Toy*, a very short movie about a toy called Tinny and the boy who plays with the toy, seen from the latter's perspective. A brilliant little piece of work, *Tin Toy* became the first computer-generated film to win an Oscar. Lasseter and Jobs had become friends and soulmates – Jobs loved computer animation, and had bankrolled *Tin Toy*.

In 1991, Michael Eisner, the larger-than-life workaholic boss of Disney, and Jeffrey Katzenberg, head of the Disney film division, who had been hugely impressed by *Tin Toy*, tried to lure Lasseter back to Disney. But Lasseter was loyal to Jobs and told Disney no. Then Katzenberg tried to get Pixar to make films for Disney, and to give Disney exclusive rights to the Pixar 3-D animation technology. Jobs said no. Jobs was playing brinkmanship, because he knew something Katzenberg didn't – that Pixar was about to go bust. After vigorous talks, in May 1991 a deal was agreed – Disney would fund and own the first new movie they collaborated on, together with the characters in it. In return Pixar would get 12.5 per cent of box office receipts.

They agreed the new movie would be *Toy Story*, picking up on the idea of *Tin Toy*. The movie nearly didn't get completed – Disney and Pixar tussled for control of the storyline, neither side liked the work-in-progress, and the cost overruns were horrendous, with each side blaming the other.

Yet by the time *Toy Story* premiered in November 1991, it was a work of art. Jobs gambled Pixar's future on the film's success, taking Pixar public one week after its release.

You may know that *Toy Story* was a massive success, loved

by critics, cinema-goers and Pixar's bankers. Jobs insisted on an extravagant price for Pixar's shares – yet they almost doubled on the first day of trading. Jobs' stake, virtually worthless at the start of 1991, became worth $1.2 billion.

Now Pixar had the cash to go 50/50 with Disney for the costs and rewards of future movies. In 2006 Disney paid $7.4 billion in stock to acquire Pixar. Jobs' shares became worth nearly $6 billion.

'The loser now will be later to win.' One could understand if Jobs, a fanatical admirer of Dylan, came to love that line of Dylan more than any other. After *Toy Story* and the Pixar float in 1995, the next year saw another Jobs coup – he persuaded Apple to buy his ailing company NeXT as the price for his reinvolvement with Apple. Then in 1997, as Apple stared at the abyss of bankruptcy, the board begged Jobs to take the reins.

Like Churchill, Jobs was a man transformed by his decade in the wilderness. He was still the visionary, still the showman, still reaching for the stars, but his failures and lucky triumphs in NeXT and Pixar had made him much more realistic and commercial.

He now understood that to fulfil his destiny, he needed Apple as much as it needed him: 'The whole notion of how you build a company,' he said, 'is fascinating. When I got the chance to come back to Apple, I realized that I would be useless without the company, and that's why I decided to stay and rebuild it.'[16]

Jobs had become anti-fragile, a gambler who had twice been to the brink, yet came back stronger, poised for greatness.

Leonardo's greatest disappointment leads to his triumph

It is significant and excellent that the ability to thrive on setbacks is emphatically *not* the result of a lucky, sunny temperament.

Churchill had his 'black dog' – moments of despair and even depression. Jobs had his self-doubt and prickliness. He was profoundly affected by what he saw as the treachery of John Sculley, leading to Jobs' banishment from Apple, his baby, for more than a decade. We can see the coexistence of a troubled side to personality with the strength to rise above adversity even more vividly in our third case, that of Leonardo da Vinci.

When he was twenty-four, Leonardo suffered a sharp shock. He was one of four prominent young men who were anonymously 'denounced' for alleged sodomy with Jacopo Salterelli, who was seventeen, apprenticed as a goldsmith, and said to consort with men 'who request wickedness of him'.[17] No accuser came forward, so the case was dismissed, provided there were no further accusations. But a month later another denunciation alleged that the four had extensive sexual entanglements with Salterelli. If convicted, the penalties included imprisonment, exile or death. Again, no witnesses came forward, but it seems likely that Leonardo spent at least a night, and possibly up to two months, in prison.[18] There is little doubt that the incident marked Leonardo inwardly. 'When I made a Christ-child you put me in prison,' he later wrote in his notebook, 'and if I show him grown up you will be worse to me ... I am without any friends. If there is no love, what then?'[19] He felt abandoned by friends and family, and 'became more withdrawn, more "mysterious", than ever'.[20] Nevertheless, throughout his life, Leonardo had several extended relationships with young men.[21]

In his late twenties, Leonardo experienced a serious blow to his career, which appears to have arisen from, and further contributed to, despair and depression. In 1481, when Leonardo was twenty-nine, Pope Sixtus IV wanted to decorate his newly built Sistine Chapel, with no expense spared to make it the most beautiful monument. The Pope naturally asked Lorenzo de' Medici – 'Lorenzo the Magnificent' – who were the cream of Florence's artists, so that he could bring the best of them to Rome. Lorenzo obliged, sending a contingent of supreme talent, including Botticelli and many others, but excluding Leonardo.[22]

It seems that Leonardo believed he had made little impression on the world – 'while I thought that I was learning how to live, I have been learning to die', he jotted in his notebook, also quoting a phrase, 'our glories and our triumphs pass away', and a fragment from Dante, including the lines: 'Fame, without which man's life wastes out of mind/Leaving on earth no more memorial/Than foam in water or smoke upon the wind.'[23]

Completely devastated, Leonardo resolved to leave Florence and go to Milan. It was the best decision of his life, giving him new impetus and a broader definition of his talent. As Robert Greene explains, Leonardo's huge setback drove him to devise a new strategy: 'He would be more than an artist. He would also pursue all the crafts and sciences that interested him – architecture, military engineering, hydraulics, anatomy, sculpture.'[24] Before long, Leonardo had become integral to the court of Ludovico Sforza, duke of Milan, initially as a producer of flamboyant pageants, plays, and other entertainments, then as resident artist and engineer. He had splendid quarters in the Corte Vecchia, Milan's ancient palace, supported by a pleasing array of students and assistants. It was here, in the last five years of the fifteenth century, that he painted his masterpiece *The Last Supper*.

Setbacks experienced by other players

Marie Curie was dealt a lifetime of suffering and personal blows. When she was five, her sister Zosia died from typhus. Her mother had tuberculosis; she dared not touch or kiss Marie, and died when Marie was ten. As a student in Paris, she lived a life of abject poverty and sometimes near-starvation. Her adored husband and research partner, Pierre, was run over and killed in a Paris road accident. Marie Curie's research was often conducted in cold, dilapidated and thoroughly inhospitable sheds rather than proper laboratories. Her health was further endangered by not appreciating the dangerous contamination that radium emitted, resulting in near-blindness from cataracts. Throughout her life she suffered from discrimination as a woman, and from being born outside France in a country and family oppressed by Tsarist Russia. Through all these disasters and several others, Curie carried on indefatigably and creatively, without complaining, without self-promotion or self-glorification, marching on to new discoveries and practical humanitarian achievements far beyond any reasonable expectation, until she eventually succumbed to premature death caused by her beloved radium. If you are looking for suffering saints in this book, who had a huge positive impact on humanity, three stand out – Nelson Mandela, Paul of Tarsus, and last but not least, Marie Curie.

Joanne Rowling had her vision of Harry Potter in mid-1990, but in her mid-to-late twenties she was in a grim place. Her mother Anne, whom she loved dearly, died unexpectedly early, at the age of forty-five, from multiple sclerosis, in December 1990. Rowling felt 'torn apart'[25]. She went to Portugal, met and married Jorge Arantes in 1992, but the relationship deteriorated rapidly, with rumours of abuse. She escaped to Edinburgh the following year, clasping her infant daughter Jessica close to her, and also taking with her, after three and a half years of writing, just three chapters of her book. Mired in poverty, feeling trapped by her daughter, who slept badly, she slipped into the black hole of depression. 'It is that absence of being able to envisage that you will ever be able to be cheerful again,' Rowling said later, 'that very deadened feeling which is so very different from feeling sad.'[26]

And yet – the only thing that Rowling really had left, besides Jessica, the only thing besides her much-loved daughter that she really cared about, was the story of Harry Potter. And that proved magnetic enough to pull her out of hell. She took to visiting a café, Nicolson's, where the staff knew her and would allow her to make a single coffee last for an hour or two, while Jessica slept, and Jo (as she called herself) wrote furiously and productively about Harry. She had to finish the book, for the sake of her sanity. And she did. By the end of 1995, *Harry Potter and the Philosopher's Stone* was ready to send out to agents and publishers.

We know the outcome – just as Rowling's life up to then had been unreasonably awful, it then became unreasonably successful. For the sake of others, she generously put a cheerful gloss on it: 'The knowledge that you have emerged wiser and stronger from setbacks means that you are, ever after, secure in your ability to survive.'[27] While this is true, we may also draw this conclusion from the prime of Miss Jo Rowling – belief in your destiny and your project can overcome even poverty, a sad personal life and serious depression, and there is no surer therapy for the dark side of life. As with Churchill, Jobs and Leonardo, horrible setbacks can be best trumped by a change of scene, and by creative activity focused on a single breakthrough achievement.

Walt Disney went bankrupt when he was twenty, and nearly repeated that event when trying to finance his first Mickey Mouse movie. We also saw how he became disillusioned with the board of Disney in the late 1940s and 1950s and needed to recover, as he saw it, his earlier creativity and pizzazz. His dissatisfaction bordered on depression, yet led to his greatest ever leap forward: Disneyland, which he achieved in the teeth of opposition from his brother Roy and the Disney board, and only by going into heavy personal debt and finding sources of finance from outside his original firm, Disney Productions. He started a new company to fund Disney with the then-enormous sum of $20 million. He cashed in all his insurance policies and sold his second home. Roy Disney threatened Walt with legal action if he used the Disney name for the new theme park. Since Roy and Walt had always been close and stood shoulder to shoulder in all previous crises, this must have been traumatic for both brothers. Walt Disney would have lost everything if Disneyland had not worked.[28]

Margaret Thatcher described the invasion of the Falklands as the worst moment of her life. Yet that event led to her greatest triumph and personal transformation, and, as she saw it, the reversal of Britain's national decline.

Bruce Henderson was fired by Westinghouse and Arthur D. Little, becoming unemployed and apparently unemployable as he approached the age of fifty. He founded a consulting firm, but it trod water until Bill Bain, a maverick hired by Henderson against the advice of his most senior partners, invented the 'Boston Box' and the Experience Curve. Then, when the Boston Consulting Group seemed set for glory, Bill Bain, who ran the largest and most lucrative part of BCG, suddenly took his most successful consultants and clients away from Henderson by founding his own firm. Henderson thought that Bain owed everything to him, and was stunned by his desertion. 'It was war,' Henderson said, 'the Japanese bombing of Pearl Harbor. I felt more betrayed and robbed and desecrated than ever before in my life.'[29] Yet rebuilding BCG afterwards turned out to be Henderson's greatest hour, and BCG eventually eclipsed even the extraordinary record of Bain & Company.

Recall also how a life imprisonment sentence for **Nelson Mandela** turned him into the most renowned leader of the ANC, and eventually the saviour of South Africa. **Viktor Frankl**'s wife and other family members perished in Hitler's concentration camps, yet Frankl himself went on to become one of the most influential therapists and philosophers of the twentieth century. **Paul of Tarsus** suffered at least three shipwrecks, and multiple arrests and beatings, before he disappeared from view around AD 62. We do not know how he died. One tradition is that he was beheaded on the orders of Emperor Nero. Another story is that he ended his days as a missionary in Spain. Yet Paul was arguably the most influential shaper of Western civilisation, writing the deeply subversive and prophetic line – 'There is neither Greek nor Jew, slave nor free, male nor female, for you are all one in Christ Jesus.'[30] It was also largely because of Paul that Jesus Christ, whose ministry apparently ended in failure and crucifixion, became the most famous and revered personage in history.

Conclusion

There is a template for turning repeated reverses, eventually, into supreme triumph:

- Take big risks.
- Do not be dismayed if they don't work out.
- After a disaster, keep going, but switch gears.
- Reframe the disaster – deny that the failure was inevitable or your fault – 'it was always high risk so it's not surprising it failed'.
- Unless you keep your original objective, immerse yourself in something different.
- Setbacks give feedback. You need reverses, and are going to get them anyway. Use them to make you stronger, more robust to future failure, and to gain new experiences. The disasters also make the eventual triumph sweeter.
- Never give up hope. You can't know the future, but you

must *trust* it. Remain fulfilled and coolly confident; jump when the big break beckons.

- Feed an intense sense of personal drama. What you will achieve *matters*, not just personally, but to the world.
- Expect catastrophes to be followed by great rejoicing, all the greater for what went before. A novel or movie that ends in failure, failure, failure, failure, failure . . . ultimate failure – is not a very good story. Reject the script – improve it, transcend it. It can be done. It *must* be done. The audience expects it.

Thrive on setbacks. It is a way of thinking, a philosophy of life, and a self-conceit essential for unreasonable success.

THRIVE ON SETBACKS

Thrive on setbacks

- Failure is the key to future success
- Reframe the disaster and use feedback
- After a disaster keep going but switch gears
- Immerse yourself in something different
- Feed your sense of personal drama
- Become anti-fragile

11

Landmark 8: Acquire Unique Intuition

A hunch can be trusted if it can be explained ... it is information you don't know you possess.

—MAX GUNTHER

A hunch is only as good as the sum of past experience that produces it.

—DR NATALIE SHAINESS

Business thinking starts with an intuitive choice of assumptions. Its progress as analysis is intertwined with intuition. The final choice is always intuitive. If that were not true, all problems would be solved by mathematicians.

—BRUCE HENDERSON

ntuition is the killer advantage – the biological edge that humans have over other lifeforms. We can be rational creatures; indeed, the whole of science, civilisation and the unprecedented wealth of modern times appears to spring from knowledge and rational calculation. But this is wrong.

We can send rockets into space and bring them back safely to Earth. We can destroy ravaging diseases which have caused immense suffering. We can create thrilling new digital products based on knowledge that did not exist a generation ago. We can farm food at a tiny fraction of its real cost in the past and solve the seemingly intractable problem of starvation and malnutrition. We can do all this because of knowledge: some ancient, mainly modern.

Where, for example, did cheap power or food come from? From science, for sure; from theories which proved to be correct in practice; from the modern science of agriculture; from quantum mechanics; from Einstein's theories of relativity; and from many other wonderfully rational discoveries and inventions. Two hundred years ago we had none of these, and now we have them. So, where did these massive leaps come from?

From new knowledge, you will say, and you are right. But that is not the most important truth.

Before there is knowledge, there is something else which generates knowledge. This 'something else' can be called many things: theories, hypotheses, imagination, intuition, curiosity, the noting of anomalies in previous theories which don't work as well in practice as they should in theory, a new paradigm of science – and many other names.

This 'something else' is the peculiarity and the glory of humankind. It is not knowledge, but it is related to knowledge, and it results in new and better knowledge. But there is no way that a computer, or – for all its vaunted hype – artificial intelligence, can generate this wonderful new knowledge. We can call this something else 'not-quite-knowledge', 'implicit knowledge', or perhaps best of all 'hidden knowledge'.

The magical way that hidden knowledge turns into incredibly valuable knowledge – the way in which dross turns into gold, the alchemy of knowledge – is through a prior process. And I am going to call this by its most simple and familiar name. It is intuition which turns hidden knowledge into incredibly valuable knowledge.

Unreasonable success flows from intuition. Intuition converts the hidden knowledge we've picked up throughout our life from our unique experiences, creating incredibly valuable knowledge.

Developing unique intuition – turning your hidden knowledge into incredibly valuable knowledge – is about the most fun thing you can do in your life.

But there is a catch.

Good hunches require deep knowledge

'A new idea,' said Albert Einstein, 'comes suddenly and in a rather intuitive way. But intuition is nothing but the outcome of earlier intellectual experience.'[1]

Intuition is not random. The more you are an expert in a narrow field, and have deep wells of knowledge and experience in it; the more you think about it, clearly, and with curiosity, the better your hunches will be. Intuition is not the opposite of knowledge – it's adjacent to it, underpinned by it, the extension of it.

Good intuition is the articulation of hidden knowledge. It is a leap of imagination which captures the truth that, in a sense, you already knew. We take in vast amounts of unprocessed or semi-processed information all the time – we can't file it all, but it doesn't disappear. If you really need it and want it to solve a gap in your explicit knowledge, you may miraculously dredge it up from the depths of your mind.

We can state some guidelines in respect of intuition:

- Trust your intuition only in areas you know backwards, or about people you've known very well for a long time.
- Author and investor Max Gunther says, 'Never confuse a hope with a hunch ... I'm much more inclined to trust an intuition pointing to some outcome I don't want ... Be especially wary of any intuitive flash that seems to promise some outcome you want badly'.[2]
- Hone your intuition in your areas of special focus. Your most valuable hunches will be where you have developed unique knowledge already, and are using intuition to extend it.

Here are three striking examples.

The unique intuition of Churchill

Winston Churchill was one of the greatest statesmen of modern history, and he was one of the most intuitive. Now, that is not as wonderful as it sounds, because his intuition was often – in fact, usually – wrong. But then again, one of the most marvellous things about intuition is that ten intuitions proved wrong in practice cannot, if you keep going, in any way cancel out or even diminish the eleventh intuition which proves gloriously correct.

Having been wrong about Antwerp, the Dardanelles, the gold standard, the General Strike of 1926, the strength of Wall Street at the end of the 1920s, self-government for India, and much else besides, when he approached sixty-five, Churchill was proven right about one great intuition. He was right about

Hitler. He was right that Hitler, despite fatally deceptive appearances, was not an ordinary man.

Hitler was underestimated and misunderstood, because he
was so easy to under-estimate and misunderstand. In 1938,
Prime Minister Neville Chamberlain undertook the first two
flights of his life to conclude the Munich agreement with Hitler.
What did he think of him? Chamberlain did not say he was
evil, not even aggressive, extremist or cunning. No – his verdict
was that Hitler was very ordinary, 'entirely undistinguished' as
he put it.[3] A man you would not invite to dinner, or into your
Cabinet, but one you could trust to keep a bargain.

We know, of course, with hindsight, what a monster and
pathological liar – as well as a skilled and terrible enemy – Hitler
was, set on world conquest, the extermination of the Jews, and
the reduction of the world to slavery. But how few people in
the 1930s shared this view!

Many of the British great and good went to see Hitler in 1936, to
find out what he 'really' wanted. As historian Robert Tombs says:

> Arnold Toynbee [the distinguished historical theorist] pro-
> nounced him 'sincere' and passed on his offer to send troops
> to help defend Singapore. Lloyd George [the British war
> leader and prime minister during the First World War] was
> much impressed by 'the greatest German of the age'. [The
> Labour leader George] Lansbury was delighted to find Hitler
> 'a total abstainer, non-smoker and vegetarian who likes
> peace' – 'Germany needs peace ... Nobody understands
> this better than Herr Hitler' ... Anthony Eden, the Foreign
> Secretary, thought Hitler 'sincere' in wanting disarmament.
> Labour favoured a 'constructive policy of appeasement'. Few
> in Britain could take Nazi ideology seriously, assuming that
> *Mein Kampf* was largely bombast ... a mixture of [British]
> decency, prejudice, fear and self-deception stopped most ears.[4]

Two powerful deaf men were Neville Chamberlain and the pious and gentlemanly Lord Halifax, who became foreign secretary in February 1938. 'Chamberlain ... was convinced that he must and could do business with Hitler and Mussolini.'[5]

Having seen Chamberlain and Halifax at Munich in 1938, Hitler drew the obvious conclusion: 'Our enemies are small worms.' He knew he could do what he wanted.[6]

Churchill was the great exception. He had warned against Hitler and the Nazis from 1932. When Hitler marched his troops into the Rhineland on 7 March 1936, he said, 'The struggle for German equal rights can be regarded as closed ... We have no territorial claims to make in Europe.'[7] Churchill alone gave the right response: 'Let us free the world from the approach of a catastrophe, carrying with it calamity and tribulation, beyond the tongue of man to tell.'[8] Churchill said Hitler was lying – 'This Rhineland business is but a step, but a stage, is but an incident in this process' of preparing for further aggression.[9]

On 24 March 1938, Churchill warned that Hitler would inevitably move into Czechoslovakia, and that the British response of disarmament and trying to placate Hitler would inevitably fail terribly: 'I have watched this famous Island descending, incontinently, fecklessly, the stairway which leads to a dark gulf. It is a fine broad stairway at the beginning, but after a bit the carpet ends. A little further on there are only flagstones. And a little further on still these break beneath your feet.'[10]

Contrast the reactions of Churchill versus almost everyone else to the Munich Agreement between Hitler and Chamberlain in 1938. 'Chamberlain returned to England,' says Robert Tombs, 'as perhaps the most popular man in the world, mobbed by cheering crowds, and receiving 40,000 mainly congratulatory letters and hundreds of presents. He was suggested for a Nobel Peace Prize.'[11]

What did Churchill say? 'This is only the first step, the first foretaste of a bitter cup.'[12] And so it proved. Churchill was made prime minister in 1940 because his apocalyptic warnings about Hitler had proved so horribly accurate.

How did Churchill get Hitler so right, when almost everyone else got him so wrong? One reason was his understanding of Germany, having seen with his own eyes the Nazi thugs with the light of fanatical devotion to Hitler and German expansion in their eyes, on his trip there in 1932.

Churchill saw how popular Hitler was, how extreme he was, how the dictator marked the end of Christian civilisation in Germany and Europe, and how nothing but force could stop him. Churchill understood the dangers of placating Hitler because he had studied history, the history of peace and war, most carefully over centuries – indeed he had written hundreds of thousands of words on the subject. 'The whole history of the world,' Churchill said, 'is summed up in the fact that when nations are strong they are not always just, and when they wish to be just they are often no longer strong.'[13]

Churchill had hidden knowledge and turned it into incredibly valuable knowledge. He understood both the nature of Nazi Germany and the nature of warfare – that peace depended on strength and deterrence rather than on good intentions.

The unique intuition of Nelson Mandela

How did Mandela arrive at his view that the impasse between the ANC and South Africa's Nationalist government – the one that had imposed apartheid and sentenced him to life imprisonment – could be broken, and that he was the person to make the breakthrough – from his prison cell?

It seemed improbable. Both sides were ratcheting up violence – there was terror, murder and mayhem from the ANC and the security forces, feeding a vicious circle of embitterment and hatred. There were no civil institutions through which the principals could meet or establish dialogue – the ANC leaders were all in hiding, in exile or locked up.

The demands of the two sides could not be squared. I spent a chunk of time over several years consulting in South Africa to large companies. I never met anyone who said that a peaceful political solution could be reached – the only question was whether bloody revolution would come in five years or fifty. Why did Mandela feel otherwise?

Mandela's breakthrough was emotional and intuitive. It sprang from human contact and warmth, from growing trust and mutual respect which gradually incubated and arose between five people – Mandela and four leaders of the apartheid regime. It could not have happened at all unless Mandela had been in prison, and therefore available for strange clandestine meetings.

President P. W. Botha – dubbed 'The Great Crocodile' and reputed to be a resolute hardliner – was more intelligent and flexible than he appeared. 'You know,' he said to his ruthless justice and security minister, Koebie Coetsee, in 1985, 'we have painted ourselves into a corner' – he meant, made negotiations with the ANC impossible. 'Can you get us out?'[14] From then on, Botha and Coetsee pursued a dual-track policy of fierce repression while secretly exploring whether a compromise might be possible.

Negotiating with Oliver Tambo or other ANC leaders was useless, they felt, but perhaps, just perhaps, this Mandela fellow might be more pragmatic. They were intrigued by reports that filtered out of Robben Island that Mandela, once an immature hothead, had over the years become measured and good-natured, co-operating with the prison authorities to make conditions there just about tolerable. On becoming justice minister, Coetsee had commissioned a secret report on Mandela:

> There exists no doubt that Mandela commands all the qualities to be the Number One Black leader in South Africa. His time in prison has caused his psycho-political posture to increase rather than decrease, and with this he has acquired the characteristic prison-charisma of the contemporary liberation leader.[15]

In April 1982, Botha and Coetsee decided to transfer Mandela from Robben Island to Pollsmoor prison near Cape Town. 'Compared to Robben Island,' Mandela said, 'we were in a five-star hotel.'[16] In November 1985, Mandela was taken to hospital for surgery on an enlarged prostate gland. Botha agreed to let Coetsee conduct a surprise secret meeting with Mandela – the start of possible negotiations. 'For Mandela,' writes the anti-apartheid activist and friend Peter Hain, 'it was the opportunity for the dialogue he had sought for decades. If it went wrong, both men had much to lose.'[17]

Coetsee and Mandela – sworn enemies – entered a competition to see which of them could be more pleasant. 'He was a natural,' Coetsee reported, 'and I realized that from the moment I set eyes on him. He was a born leader. And he was affable.' Although a prisoner, 'he was clearly in command of his surroundings'.[18] Mandela impressed his visitor by his knowledge of early Afrikaner history – the history, conveniently, of a liberation struggle.

Coetsee told Botha that it opened a door 'to talk rather than to fight'.[19] Mandela later wrote that his ANC colleagues would condemn his decision to start negotiations – 'they would kill *my initiative* even before it was born. There are times when a leader must move out ahead of the flock.' (My italics.)[20]

Coetsee took the much-feared head of the National Intelligence Service, Neil Barnard, to meet Mandela, and they got on well. Barnard surprised everyone by declaring that 'a political settlement is the only answer to the problems of this country'.[21]

Finally, President Botha nailed his colours to the mast by meeting Mandela in May 1988 – the two adversaries got on famously, each determined to out-charm the other. 'I was tense about meeting Mr Botha,' Mandela confessed. 'I had heard many accounts of his ferocious temper.' But it went according to a Hollywood script. 'From the opposite side of his grand office, P. W. Botha walked towards me ... He had his hand out and was smiling broadly ... he completely disarmed me. He was unfailingly courteous, deferential, and friendly ... Now, I felt, there could be no turning back.'[22]

In 1989, President Botha had a stroke and was replaced by F. W. de Klerk. Mandela and de Klerk were to form a formidable partnership, ending in Mandela becoming president and de Klerk his deputy president and mentor.

Let's exclude intuition, and just think along conventional, rational, lines for a moment. Consider the truculent President Botha; his equally hard-line minister in charge of justice and security, Coetsee; the greatly feared boss of the government's spy force, Barnard; and the new President de Klerk, reckoned to be in the image of his predecessors. These were the most unlikely people for Mandela to trust, and seemed the least likely to accede to Mandela's demand for genuine, black-majority democracy.

Yet Mandela came, first to like them, then to hope that they might be reasonable, then eventually to trust in their goodwill and desire for a settlement. And in turn these four horsemen of the Afrikaans apocalypse, their hands dripping in blood, their eyes covered to conceal from themselves the sight of their own brutality, their minds trained to run on the straight tramlines of tribal loyalty, these four most improbable peacemakers, they came to like and trust Mandela.

This required intuition on their part too. They had to hope that Mandela could see their predicament, to understand their fears that black rule would mean wholesale slaughter, to trust that this old-timer could win over his intransigent colleagues and bring South Africans together in peace. If they got it wrong, if they set the reform train in motion, if Mandela fell by the wayside, if they stoked up black expectations by their apparent weakness – well, they would have given up power for descent into hell.

Bill Bain's unique intuition

Now for an example of extraordinary business intuition, which was hidden from everyone else. During his time at the Boston Consulting Group, Bill Bain, the ex-history researcher with no engineering or business qualifications, came to three momentous conclusions, all intuitions based on hidden knowledge.

The new ideas about 'business strategy' which Bruce Henderson and Bain pioneered were immensely valuable to companies. Bain called it 'playing three-dimensional chess'. The vital three dimensions were the 'three Cs': a firm's costs; its customers and how they segmented; and its competitors. There were right and wrong strategies, and the right ones could hugely multiply the value of a company.

This much was common ground between BCG and Bain & Company. But Bill went much further, to make the potential value of the strategy ideas real, to make them practical, and to implement them.

Client companies could not be changed by the BCG model of 'seagull consulting' – swooping down from Boston, depositing a new strategy in a presentation or report, and flying back to Boston. Clients simply could not implement a strategy by exhortation, followed by desertion.

The best way to make a new strategy happen was to transform the company through a personal alliance between the client chief executive and Bain & Company. Bain would only work for the top person in a company, because only he or she had the power to make the new strategy stick. To do that required the Bain consultants to work on all important strategic issues in the company, and to infiltrate the organisation so that its managers really understood the strategy and wanted to implement it.

This was how to multiply the profits and value of the client company – and the billings of Bain & Company. If Bain produced huge value for the company in terms of increased profits and market value, Bain could charge millions or even tens of millions of dollars a year in fees, because these were just a small slice of the value added.

Let's summarise what we have learned so far.

Winston Churchill:

- Possessed deep hidden knowledge about Hitler and Nazi Germany, and from his study of history, the importance of balance of power and deterrence of aggression.
- Imagined very early on the unimaginable, that Hitler could be a mortal threat to the British Empire, America and Western civilisation.
- Went strongly against the flow of opinion in his Tory establishment circles.
- Had a simple view and objective.

Nelson Mandela:

- Had deep hidden knowledge about his captors and their willingness to meet him halfway.
- Imagined early on the unimaginable, that there could be a peaceful transition of power to majority black rule.
- Contradicted all ANC strategy.
- Used charm and empathy with the enemy to advance his vision.

Bill Bain:

- Developed a unique intuition about how to boost the fortunes of companies and give consultants skin in the game.
- Imagined the unimaginable, namely a very close personal relationship between the leaders of Bain & Company and the top person in each client, leading to great changes in results for the client, and huge, ever-growing fees for Bain & Company.
- Contradicted the unanimity of all other consultants on how to run assignments.
- Provided a simple model of how to win consistently.

Key intuitions of other players

- **Lenin**'s great intuition was that precisely *because* Russia was a backward country ruled by a tiny elite – the tsars and their hangers-on – power could pass to another tiny minority, his revolutionary group, if they were ruthless and disciplined.
- **Otto von Bismarck**'s hidden knowledge was that there was a missing third element to political power in Prussia.

Before Bismarck became chancellor, power was shared between the king and parliament. Afterwards, the unimaginable happened, and Bismarck became the dominant third wheel in the machine – he ruled the parliament with the power of the king and his prestige in uniting Germany, but he ruled the king with his indispensability and his personality. 'It is not easy to be Kaiser under such a Chancellor,' said King William, with rueful wit.[23]

Bismarck's other great intuition was to hold back until the perfect time to strike. Biographer Volker Ullrich says, 'The ability to wait for the decisive instant, taking advantage of a uniquely favourable moment with determination – this was a skill Bismarck brought to the point of perfection.'[24]

- **Walt Disney**'s supreme intuition was to imagine and construct the unimaginable – a theme park that would epitomise the past, present and future of the United States in a way to which all American patriots could relate.

- **Albert Einstein**'s theories of relativity are the perfect example of intuition, which, though based on deep and extremely powerful knowledge – the revolutionary new field of quantum mechanics from the first years of the twentieth century – nevertheless required a leap of imagination in opposition to prevailing theory.

A visual image he had at the age of sixteen of himself riding a photon travelling at the speed of light was the start of long years of his thinking about relativity. On a beautiful day in Berne in 1905, Einstein was grappling with the inadequacies of existing theories of time in the universe. Then, as he told his friend Michelle Besso the following day, 'I've completely solved the problem.' It came to him suddenly, in the form of an image of moving trains. His totally original view of the universe – that there is no such thing as absolute time – came in a picture he saw in his mind. It was the fruit of intuition, not linear thinking.[25] Even when he came to write up his revolutionary paper, *On the Electrodynamics of Moving Bodies*, its message was mainly in the form of words and thought experiments, rather than in equations.[26]

'High-level intuition,' says Robert Greene, 'involves a process that is qualitatively different from rationality, but is even more accurate and perceptive. It accesses deeper parts of reality.'[27]

Einstein's thought experiments also illustrate something which is common to many of our players' intuitive break-throughs: they featured themselves in the drama which they conjured up. Churchill imagined himself opposing Hitler, a compliment which Hitler returned, condemning Churchill in the late 1930s, even before he attained any political office. Lenin imagined that he would be the ruler of Russia, just like the tsars, if he could strike at the right moment. Bismarck, similarly, dreamed of putting Austria in its place and harnessing the new power of nationalism to the Prussian cause, long before he became chancellor. Walt Disney participated physically in the design and construction of Disneyland, living above the fire station on the incipient Main Street, and leaving little notes such as 'paint this bench' or 'plant flower-bed here'. Bill Bain imagined himself in deep conversation with the boss of a big company before he nabbed them as a new client with an enormous budget. In his prison cell, years before seri-ous negotiations with his jailers began, Nelson Mandela saw himself as a nattily dressed president, bringing South Africans together in peace and reconciliation.

For our players, intuition was laced with personal longing and ambition. It was a clump of emotion, the convergence of aspiration, personal drive, homespun philosophy, understanding of the environment, and wild jumps of insight and ingenuity.

- We saw earlier (Chapter 8: Make your own trail) that **Marie Curie**'s discovery of two new minerals, polonium and radium, came from unique intuitions which were totally her own. In his tribute to her after her death, Albert Einstein singled out her ingenuity and intuition as her greatest quality.[28] Great intuition, based on unrivalled knowledge in their different domains, was the killer advantage possessed by both scientists.

- **John Maynard Keynes**' great work on *The General Theory of Employment, Interest and Money* was expressed in dense logic and equations, but it boiled down to one simple intuition, which had eluded all reputable economists – in a depression, the government should not cut, but rather should *raise*, its spending, in order to provide employment and keep the economy from contracting. In good times, the government should step out of the way, cut expenditure and let market forces work their magic. This became common practice; yet was unimaginable for policymakers until someone as respected as Keynes dared to say it.

- **Bob Dylan**'s intuition was that the folk movement could provide the stage to parade his poetic and artistic genius. He brushed aside the movement's provincialism and fuddy-duddy trappings, dragging it into the forefront of popular music and social protest. That done, Dylan also realised that he contained multitudes and could not remain shackled to folk tunes and protest activism – he had to 'keep on keepin' on', reinventing himself and his art. In every new step, he felt, there is decay if it is the final step. Enigma and poetry were more important than popularity; and they lasted longer.

- The first time **Joanne Rowling** thought of Harry Potter, it felt more like a revelation than an invention of her conscious mind. When she sat on her stalled train for hours, it was as if she were receiving a download from an external source, a glimpse of a reality that already existed. She felt she was learning about the boy – not named until later but visible in her mind, as if she were being given a picture and piecing together scraps of information about him. 'I simply sat and thought for four hours, while all the details bubbled in my brain, and this scrawny, black-haired, bespectacled boy ... became more and more real to me.' An air of mystery surrounded him – she knew he was an orphan, but not how or why. She pictured the school and many of its characters, later named as Ron Weasley, Hagrid the gamekeeper, and the school ghosts, Nearly Headless Nick and Peeves. The images came as inspiration from her unconscious mind.[29]

  This is a common experience of many highly creative people, in many different fields including poetry, writing plays or novels, mathematics, philosophy, the physical sciences and music. As we have seen, Albert Einstein gained insight into relativity from visual images which suddenly appeared to him.

  There are many other cases which have parallels to J. K. Rowling's 'download' of Harry Potter. The early nineteenth century Romantic poet, Samuel Taylor Coleridge, wrote what many consider his finest poem *Kubla Khan* after seeing a vision of a palace in Xanadu in a dream. Over 200 lines of the poem came to him in the dream, and when he woke up, all he had to do was write them down at once. 'All the images,' he said, 'rose up before me as *things* ... without any sensation of conscious effort.'[30]

  Wolfgang Amadeus Mozart had similar experiences. A

new piece of music, he said, came to him suddenly, and he heard it the piece not in sequence, but 'all at once'. 'All this inventing, this producing takes place in a pleasing lively dream ... the committing to paper is quickly done, for everything is already finished.'[31] Peter Ilych Tchaikovsky, the mathematician and polymath Henri Poincaré, the chemist Friedrich Kekulé, and many others report similar sources of inspiration, all, as Tchaikovsky said, seeming to come from 'that supernatural inexplicable force we call inspiration'.[32]

- **Helena Rubinstein** founded an industry on the simple belief that women could be converted to an enhanced view of their beauty and status through the application of skin cream and other cosmetics, and her conviction that women would pay through the nose for a quality product. She could be considered the first feminist of the modern consumer age.

- **Margaret Thatcher**'s great presentiment was that Britain's decline could be arrested by rolling back socialism, encouraging a new generation of creative entrepreneurs and renewing all that was best in Britain's illustrious history. She stood for a blend of British nationalism and market forces which cut across the entire waterfront of British political opinion – and that of her own party – but which worked.

- Finally, **Paul of Tarsus** caused the greatest shift in values in the great Roman Empire of his day, and for centuries after the fall of Rome. Paul's vision was simple, burningly intense, and at first so grandiose and unrealistic as to mark him out as mad: the idea that the Living Christ whom he encountered could conquer the empire which had crucified him, and that it could be accomplished by the power of Christ within ordinary people.

Conclusion and summary

You need intuition with these qualities:

- **It must be important.** Could it make a dent in the universe?
- **It must be unproven and original.** Otherwise it is a fact, not an intuition.
- **It must be imaginative.**
- **It must be simple.**
- **It must contradict the experts.**
- **Yet it must be based on deep knowledge.**
- **You must star in the intuition.** Your ambition and emotion are part of the package, part of the appeal, and an integral part of the driving force.

Your singular intuition will eventually arrive unexpectedly and suddenly. Will it to come, and it will come. Do not rush it. It is the intuition of a lifetime, which will transform and immeasurably enrich your life, your world, and the whole world beyond you.

It is worth willing; worth waiting for; and worth committing yourself to utterly.

Your final landmark is just around the corner. It is a superbly potent compound of all the strategies and attitudes that you have already explored.

Acquire unique intuition

- Develop hugely important intuitions based on deep knowledge in a narrow field that is growing fast
- Must be unproven and original
- Imagine the unimaginable
- The intuition becomes part of your personality and you are a 'star' in applying the intuition

Landmark 9: Distort Reality

In his presence, reality is malleable.

—BUD TRIBBLE on Steve Jobs

The spirit now wills his own will, and he who has been
lost to the world now conquers the world.

—FRIEDRICH NIETZSCHE

Blast medicine anyway. We've learned to tie into every
human organ except one – the brain. The brain is what life
is all about. That man can think any thought that we can,
and love, and hope, dream as much as we can.

—DOCTOR MCCOY in *Star Trek*, 'The Menagerie'

Visiting our final landmark, we discover that the difference
between unreasonable success and its absence is simple –
it rests on the self-fulfilling belief that current reality can, or
cannot, be overturned.

Star Trek has a lot to answer for. Steve Jobs was a 'Trekkie',

and was influenced by two episodes of 'Menagerie', broadcast
in November 1966, in which the Talosians, humanoid aliens,
use sheer mental force to create illusions indistinguishable from
reality. I think very hard, and I bend reality to my will. *Star Trek*
originated the phrase 'reality distortion field', which became
a favourite of Jobs and his coterie, as in Bud Tribble's explanation of how Jobs could get his team to meet quite impossible
deadlines:

> Steve has a reality distortion field. In his presence, reality
> is malleable. He can convince anyone of practically any-
> thing . . . It was dangerous to get caught in Steve's distortion
> field, but it was what led him to be able to change reality.[1]

Jobs' terminology may have been unique, but all the players exhibited a reality distortion field. They changed reality
because they thought they could. Not many people think this,
and therefore not many people do it. Or to quote the Apple
'Think Different' commercial of 1997, 'The people who are
crazy enough to think they can change the world are the
ones who do.'

If we want unreasonable success, we must first believe we can
change the world. Really believe we have our own personal
reality distortion field.

It won't always work, but on important occasions it can
change reality, if you believe. After all, what is extraordinary
achievement but bending existing reality to your vision and
your will, by persuading yourself and your key allies that it is
possible? Yet the very phrase, 'reality distortion field', as in 'I
have a reality distortion field', or 'Steve has a reality distortion
field', when spoken and recognised as a real force, can have the
power of a magic incantation.

Let's see how it worked for Jobs.

The biggest event in Apple in the twentieth century was the launch of the Macintosh in 1984. On 3 October 1983 the cover of *Business Week* led with the headline – 'Personal Computers: And the Winner is . . . IBM'. 'The battle for market supremacy is already over,' said the story inside. Jobs was determined to prove this wrong. To do so he wanted, as his colleague Andy Hertzfeld said, 'to do the greatest thing possible, or even a little greater'.[2]

This was where Jobs' reality distortion field came in. He told Larry Kenyon, an engineer working on the Macintosh prototype, that it was taking too long to start. Kenyon tried to explain to Jobs why it couldn't boot quicker, but Steve was having none of it. 'If it could save a person's life,' he interrupted, 'would you find a way to shave ten seconds off the boot time?' Jobs then multiplied ten seconds by the five million users of the Mac to show that it would save 300 million hours, which equalled 100 lifetimes saved a year.

Kenyon was impressed, and came back a few weeks later, having found a way to save twenty-eight seconds. As a colleague said, 'Steve had a way of motivating by looking at the bigger picture.'[3] If something was defined as vital, it therefore became possible. Jobs didn't have to know how to do it, just tell his people what was needed and that they could do it. They believed him, and they did it.

The reality distortion field worked on deadlines too. The Mac was due out in January 1984 and it was imperative to Jobs that there was no slippage. The problem was that the coding geniuses were late – shipment was due on 16 January, and a week before that they concluded that this was impossible – they needed an extra two weeks to get the software right.

Jobs was in New York for the press previews, and on a Sunday conference call the engineers back at head office gathered around the phone to break the bad news to him. The shipping could go ahead, the manager explained, but with 'demo' software, to be replaced with the real code two weeks later.

A long pause. The software wizards expected an explosion from Jobs. But he was calm. He told them how great they were, so they could get this done on time: 'You guys have been working on this stuff for months now, another couple weeks isn't going to make that much of a difference. You may as well get it over with. I'm going to ship the code a week from Monday, with your names on it.'[4]

The engineers did what they thought was impossible. At 8.30 that Monday morning, according to Isaacson, Jobs arrived at Apple to find Andy Hertzfeld 'sprawled nearly comatose on the couch' after three all-nighters. Jobs gave the okay to the software, the product shipped as planned, and Hertzfeld drove his blue Volkswagen Rabbit, with its licence plate MACWIZ, home to sleep.[5] The reality distortion field had worked again.

'Every once in a while,' Jobs said in 2007, in perhaps his greatest product introduction, 'a revolutionary product comes along that changes everything.' The first Mac, he went on, 'changed the whole computer industry'. The iPod 'changed the entire music industry'. 'Today,' he continued, 'we're introducing three revolutionary products of this class. The first one is a widescreen iPod with touch controls. The second is a revolutionary mobile phone. And the third is a breakthrough Internet communications device.' He repeated the three-fold litany. 'Are you getting it?' he challenged the audience. 'These are not three separate devices, this is one device, and we are calling it iPhone.'[6]

Three years later, Apple had sold ninety million iPhones at prices of $500 upwards, generating revenue of more than $45 billion, and, because of the high pricing, astronomical profits too. Apple scooped more than half of all mobile phone profits in the industry – surely a record for a new entrant to a market, garnered in a very short time, for total profit dominance of a market. Since then, it is largely the iPhone which has driven the unfathomable increase in the value of Apple. In financial terms this must be the most successful new product of all time.

Yet I don't think that if Jobs were alive today, he would take most pride from the numbers. He was always in the game to make 'insanely great' products, so simple and amazing that they are works of art.

The iPhone would never have been possible without Jobs' reality distortion field. Let's look at one vignette, just one illustration of how reality distortion made the iPhone near-perfect.

One of the iPhone's great innovations was its beautiful glass screen. Glass looks much better than plastic, but Jobs couldn't find a strong enough glass which would be resistant to scratches or breaking. Jobs approached Wendell Weeks, the head of Corning Glass, and discovered that they had invented an incredibly strong 'gorilla glass' in the 1960s, but had never been able to sell it. When Weeks described gorilla glass's properties, Jobs said he wanted it for the iPhone, to be launched in six months. Weeks said he couldn't: 'None of our plants make the glass now.'

Weeks was taken aback when Jobs told him, 'Don't be afraid. You can do it. Get your mind around it. You can do it.'

This was Jobs' reality distortion field in operation – what he really wanted, he had to have, and if it was impossible, that didn't matter, he'd get it anyway by telling Weeks that he could do it.

Now, Weeks was smart and self-assured, and he pushed back. 'Engineering challenges can't be overcome,' Weeks retorted, 'by a false sense of confidence.'

But still, Jobs' reality distortion field won the day. He persuaded Weeks that he really could do it. Weeks recounted this story to Walter Isaacson, Jobs' biographer, with a continuing sense of bemusement and astonishment: 'We did it in under six months. We produced a glass that had never been made. We put

our best scientists and engineers on it, and we just made it work.'
Isaacson saw this framed message in pride of place on Weeks'
desk, sent by Jobs the day the iPhone shipped: 'We couldn't have
done it without you.'[7]

The story should instruct those who claim that Jobs' reality
distortion field was just science-fiction-speak for bullying. For
sure, Jobs was a kind of bully, but a rare one – he bullied the
strong, not the weak. His team were stars. He made them believe
they were as incredibly, unbelievably good as they became. This
is an extreme version of the Matthew principle – 'To everyone
who has, will more be given, and he will have abundance.'[8] Jobs
manifested a super-abundance of talent and achievement, nay,
quite unreasonable achievement for a mere mortal.

Of course, there were limits. Jobs was not Christ. The reality
distortion field didn't work at NeXT, or on his cancer. Perhaps
the NeXT team was not stellar enough; perhaps the objectives
were not right. But at Apple, Jobs moved mountains by distorting reality, and there were two vital steps which we can
emulate – if we believe:

- Step 1 – Project extreme optimism and determination to
  redirect reality to fit your philosophy and objectives. Do
  what others think is impossible, or which never occurs to
  them. Defeat the conventional view of what is realistic and
  unrealistic. Sharpen your willpower and convince yourself
  it could change reality.
- Step 2 – Brainwash brilliant followers or collaborators into
  believing they can attain the impossible – because you say
  so, and you have a track record of being right.

Reality distortion becomes progressively less impossible – I
would not say 'easier' – the more you practise it and demonstrate
your powers of will and prediction.

Lessons from the reality distortion fields of other players

Though some followed just Step 1, and others used both steps, each of the players had a reality distortion field to some extent – and tellingly, in some different ways too:

Bill Bain was able to persuade his key lieutenants – including Mitt Romney – that they could sell budgets to leading American companies which stretched into seven and eight figures, at a time when the venerable, blue-chip, undisputed leader of the consulting industry, McKinsey, had budgets one-tenth as big. Like Jobs, he made the impossible sound logical – Bain & Company could make these companies worth billions more, so what was a budget of, say, $20 million a year?

Bruce Henderson had a different Talosian force-field. His uncanny nose for raw talent and his breakthrough map of strategy were complementary. People now say, 'oh, the Boston Consulting Group – they transformed business strategy', but they don't realise that the change Henderson enacted was equally, and necessarily, demographic.

Without GPS, without even paper maps, he led his people to Mount Sinai; but having arrived there he made it possible for the first time for twenty-something wet-behind-the-ears consultants like me to shift the fortunes of venerable corporate behemoths. It is as though Moses came down from the mountain to be met by the elders of Israel, only to pass them by and seek out the brightest and the best of their children and grandchildren. Henderson marked not just a financial, but also an age earthquake in business.

Youth and brains conquered capital and experience, or at least gave them a good and synergistic run for their money. The Talosians would have approved this dramatic victory of mind over matter. Bruce told us we could do it, and we did.

The aftershocks resonated far beyond the world of consulting, into investment banking, venture capital, and eventually into the last fortress of age and experience, general management, creating a new landscape dominated by bright young things armed with quantitative skills and ineluctable economic principles.

Jeff Bezos has a similar distortion field. He's changed the face of retailing, through faith in his own ideas and by mesmerising and indoctrinating the smartest young people he could find.

Walt Disney's studio followers, too, found that his magic rubbed off on them. Time and again, in his cartoons, characters, movies, and with Disneyland, Disney proved the power of imagination to reinterpret and reshape the world. As he said, 'It is kind of fun to do the impossible.'

Five of our six business players used both reality distortion steps. The only one to use just Step 1 was **Helena Rubinstein**, who reimagined her own past and antecedents, and gave her clients a new face and confidence, but did not create a cadre of powerful disciples.

What about our players operating outside business? They all violated the rules of their world, bending or replacing them with their own rules. Yet most of them were more like Rubinstein than the five other business players, distorting reality through their own mental powers without needing to invoke those of a cast of thousands or millions.

- **Otto von Bismarck** upended the nineteenth-century pecking order of European nations, raising Prussia–Germany above Austria, France and Russia. His mental domination worked on King William, the German parliamentarians, and the rulers of the other great powers. Unlike Jobs, Bezos, Bain, Henderson and Disney, Bismarck didn't work through a team he inspired to greatness, but solely through his own mesmerising intellect and personality. He changed reality by changing and expressing himself.

- The same applies to **Leonardo, Curie, Einstein, Frankl, Dylan, Rowling, Keynes, Mandela, Thatcher,** and on a less exalted plane probably to **Madonna.** Their reality-defying-and-redefining forces came from their superlative and sometimes super-human creativity. They redefined art, physics, psychology, the role of music in society, economics, and the distribution of power within South Africa and Britain.

- **Lenin** certainly exercised similar mental power. His genius was to make his small cadre of revolutionaries believe that, though they were few, they could seize total power.

His followers, however, were disciplined troops rather than prime movers in the drama of history. They were to obey rather than create, and if they did not obey, they were eliminated. Lenin was largely a Step 1 man, with enough Step 2 follower-belief-creation to get him into supreme power.

Winston Churchill: Defying reality in 1940

'The late Spring and early summer of 1940,' says Roy Jenkins 'was one of the most extraordinary, in some ways unreal, phases in the history of the [British] nation.'[9] After France fell to the Nazis, Britain stared invasion in the face. The foreign secretary, Lord Halifax, favoured a negotiated peace with Hitler. Only one man prevented surrender to Hitler.

Six or seven years later, that man claimed that, the night he became prime minister, he felt enormously confident of his 'destiny' to save Britain. 'As I went to bed about 3 a.m.,' Churchill was to write in *The Second World War,* 'I was conscious of a profound sense of walking with destiny, and that all my past

life had been but a preparation for this hour and for this trial . . .
I was sure I should not fail.'[10]

This can only have been half true. By 1946 or 1947, when
Churchill wrote this, he knew the outcome of the war. In May
1940, he may assuredly have felt a sense of destiny, but he knew
that Hitler was planning to invade England and that the outcome was dicey. If we go back to Churchill's speeches in 1940,
this is starkly apparent. In one half of his mind, he was fully
aware of the dangers; with the other half, he refused to contem-
plate defeat or any compromise with the evils of Nazism, and he
held out the prospect of ultimate victory after a titanic struggle.
He pulled out all the stops, for himself and the British people,
to defy the likely Nazi invasion and avoid surrender to Hitler.

On becoming prime minister, Churchill told the House
of Commons:

> I have nothing to offer but blood, toil, tears and sweat. We
> have before us an ordeal of the most grievous kind . . . You
> ask, what is our policy? I will say: it is to wage war, by sea,
> land and air, with all our might and all the strength that God
> can give us: to wage war against a monstrous tyranny, never
> surpassed in the dark, lamentable catalogue of human crime.
> That is our policy. You ask, what is our aim? I can answer in
> one word: it is victory, victory at all costs, victory in spite of
> all terror, victory, however long and hard the road may be;
> for without victory, there is no survival. Let that be realized;
> no survival for the British Empire, no survival for all that
> the British Empire has stood for, no survival for the urge and
> impulse of the ages, that Mankind will move forward towards
> its goal. But I take up my task with buoyancy and hope. I feel
> sure that our cause will not be suffered to fail among men. At
> this time I feel entitled to claim the aid of all, and I say, 'Come
> then, let us go forward together with our united strength.'[11]

While the War Cabinet was contemplating Lord Halifax's requests to consider a peace deal with Hitler, Churchill went to address a meeting of twenty-five ministers who were outside the Cabinet. He told them:

> It is idle to think that if we tried to make peace now we should get better terms from Germany than if we went on and fought it out . . . We should become a slave state through a British Government which would be Hitler's puppet . . . On the other side, we have immense resources and advantages. Therefore we shall go on and we shall fight it out . . . and if at the last the long story is to end, it were better it should end, not through surrender, but only when we are rolling senseless on the ground.'[12]

Churchill knew that defeat by Hitler was possible, even likely, and that the consequences would be terrible beyond belief. He also knew his destiny was to help the British people and Empire resist to the last man or woman.

In this almost-impossible task, Churchill was successful, which is why he is commonly accounted the best British prime minister of all time. Roy Jenkins summed it up: the national mood in 1940, he says, 'was not so much defiant as impregnable. The prospects were awful, but people pushed the consequences of defeat out of their collective mind . . . they chose to believe that the worst would not happen.' What Churchill did 'was to produce a euphoria of irrational belief in ultimate victory'.[13]

Churchill was not the preferred prime minister of the king, the Cabinet, or the Conservative Party, which had a large majority in the House of Commons. He could easily have been removed from office shortly after he took over, and there is evidence that Lord Halifax intrigued to make that happen. But, as Roy Jenkins says, Churchill's authority 'most stemmed from popular acclaim'.[14] David Low, the premier cartoonist of the age, and one of liberal-left inclination, published a cartoon which reflected and helped to further consolidate public opinion. Low specialised in satirical and cutting images, but this one, with the caption 'All behind you, Winston', was wholly laudatory. It showed Churchill, sleeves rolled up, striding unshakeably forward followed by all the key political figures of the day and behind them, most important of all, a mass of ordinary people.

Churchill was immensely powerful in rolling out his reality distortion machine. His sincerity and utter determination could not be doubted, and words evoked deeds. He made England's worst hour its finest; and it would not have come without his conviction, courage and confidence. He gulled the whole population into a collective delusion, which, against all odds, created the reality that history recorded.

The greatest reality distortion of all time?

Perhaps the most remarkable reality distortion of all belongs to **Paul of Tarsus**. He provided a new way of seeing the world, and transmitted that corpus of belief to an ever-growing number of people within the Roman Empire.

Whether or not we believe that he had supernatural help in the process, Paul certainly believed that he did. The technology of 'Christ Inside' proved amazingly real. God suddenly acquired a new location – inside people, within the human self. 'I no longer live,' Paul dared to tell his church in Galicia, 'but Christ lives in me.'[15] By believing that they had divine assistance, that their whole character and actions were directed by Jesus, the early Christians were given the confidence to change the world.

I don't think it is blasphemous, disrespectful or unduly credulous to suggest that Paul used the same two steps of reality distortion as our other players, or to posit that all the players' inspiration and power, whatever their ends and means, may have come at least partly from the miracle of the human brain and its ability to connect through the unconscious mind to transcendent forces of which we have little understanding.

You can, however, tap into those forces, and may need to, if you are to become unreasonably successful. To distort reality, you need to believe wholeheartedly that you can.

Summary and conclusion

The players changed reality because they believed they could. They demonstrated conclusively that reality is more malleable than is commonly believed. Yet it is only possible to change your world if you sincerely believe you can.

The players all exhibited extreme optimism and willpower to re-channel reality to match their philosophy and aspirations.

Many of the players – probably the ones who had the most unreasonable success – also brainwashed their followers and collaborators into believing that they too could distort reality. It may be that businesspeople, preachers and politicians are particularly prone to mobilise reality-defying belief in their followers, whereas scientists and artists need only defy reality in their own person.

What is clear is that if you are to change the world, you need to master the technology of reality distortion. Faith can overpower facts. It is not the meek or the powerful who shall inherit the Earth, but the unreasonable believers.

Distort reality

- Exhibit extreme optimism and determination to redirect reality to fit your philosophy and objectives
- Inspire followers to believe they can do the impossible

PART THREE

Lessons Learned

*My Journey and How You Too Can
Reach Unreasonable Success*

13

Self-Belief

I didn't have this map before I started my journey, and I hope that telling you how I staggered to reach the landmarks will enable you to avoid some of the troubles and cul-de-sacs I experienced.

How did I develop self-belief? It started with a humiliating experience, which turned out to be a lucky accident.

When I was nine, my parents and I visited Auntie Louise in Seaford, on the south coast of England. It was a trip we made as infrequently as politely possible, because although we loved my auntie, all three of us were scared stiff of her live-in companion, Miss Gates, an overbearing lady who had been endowed with far too much intelligence and far too little kindness. One day she grilled me about what I wanted to be when I grew up.

'I want to be a millionaire,' I blurted out. In fact, I had no idea what I wanted to be, but it was the first thing I thought of.

'That's silly,' she tut-tutted. 'It's completely unrealistic. Your father has no money to speak of, and never will. Why don't you think of something that you could work towards?'

'I want to be a millionaire,' I persisted petulantly.

'The boy has no common sense,' she announced to nobody in particular, before swishing out of the drawing-room.

Her curt quashing of my idea made me determined to prove her wrong. Perhaps it wasn't the best goal for me to choose, but I stuck to it. It made me serious about my schooling and my life — it gave me a dream to chase. I believed I could do it, though I doubted myself at times. But my decision focused me on what I reckoned was the first step on the ladder — doing well in tests and exams, which I had never done before. As I did well in these, my self-belief blossomed, along with my bloody-mindedness.

I now realise that nobody can really have self-belief in the abstract, except as a vague belief in their star. So your first lesson is that it can only flourish if you are motivated to reach a goal or destination. The particular goal is less important than having one, and knowing the steps necessary to get closer to it.

My exam performance and increasing self-confidence carried me into a plum job with Shell International when I was twenty-one. But though Shell promised a great way to see the world — or at least its oil and gas plants — and to retire early, I soon realised it was not a way to become seriously rich.

I asked the most successful people I knew what I should do. 'Go to business school in America,' they said. I enjoyed my time at Wharton in Philadelphia, but I didn't learn much about how to make money. Nor did the job I landed with the Boston Consulting Group, at least directly. I didn't have too much of an idea how to reach my goal, but my self-belief had burgeoned and I was still searching.

Your second lesson – really quite obvious in retrospect – is that self-belief can grow with little experiences of success, and with experimentation, such as when I went to America. There may be many routes to reaching one's goal – take one of them.

In my late twenties, my self-belief came under pressure. I was failing in my job at BCG – the firm valued analysis above all, and I wasn't very good at it. I redoubled my efforts, started working eighty hours a week, became a little chubby from eating junk food late at night when working, imperilled my relationship . . . and still floundered. I went through a year or two of increasing self-doubt, became thoroughly miserable, and eventually was asked to leave.

But, you know, I need not have worried. I should have given up on BCG earlier, and, as I eventually did, joined Bain & Company, a spin-off from BCG, which valued results and skills of persuasion above analysis and raw intellect. My self-doubt was very useful, and I should have listened to it earlier. It changed the route to my destination, and if I had been less pig-headed it might usefully have changed the goal itself.

Your third lesson is to listen to self-doubt – when it is clearly right – and to change tack accordingly. Self-doubt is constructive and should not be repressed. It's the friend of self-belief, not its foe.

Changing firms within the same industry led me to think quite deeply about why the two firms – BCG and Bain & Company – were both successful, yet in many ways dissimilar.

Experiencing success within Bain revived my earlier dream when I joined BCG – that sooner or later I might be a founder of a new strategy consulting venture. It might be risky and hard to make work, but if it did, perhaps I could make my fortune.

Your fourth lesson is to keep hoping, scheming and dreaming, while learning everything you can about your niche.

Summary

- Define a goal to incubate self-belief.
- Experiment to generate experiences of success.
- Listen to self-doubt.
- Keep dreaming and learning.

14

Olympian Expectations

Y ou may recall that the nine-year-old Koch decided to
become a millionaire. It was probably a childish reaction to
the brutal dismissal of the idea by Miss Gates, my aunt's companion. But it was Big Thinking and it conditioned, to some
degree, my whole life – from then on, my aim was to become
rich, and I always at least half-believed it, and measured myself
against progress towards that aim.

> There doesn't have to be a good reason for thinking big, but the
> first lesson on expectations is that your should get into the habit of
> doing it anyway – see the big picture and believe that you belong
> there; visualise what it will be like when you hit the big time. It
> won't be quite like that, but imagining it will help you get there.

My most important feedback came with unexpected success
in exams at the ages of ten, seventeen and twenty. Having

been admitted to Oxford University and then having received a top degree, I persuaded myself that I was some kind of deep thinker, able to look below the surface – initially of my subject, history, and later of business and ideas – and see the few things which were significant, and the vast majority which were not. Increasingly, throughout my life, I have seen my gift as reducing things to their essence and simplifying them.

My other sustaining presumption is the ability to make money – spurred on by the faith of a few friends that I could make a fortune. Jim Lawrence, one of my co-founding partners in LEK, labelled me firmly as a 'money-maker'. I believed this much more after he said so.

It is strange how expectations determine performance. Because I expected to make money in the long run, I regarded my many setbacks as aberrations and valuable feedback, not as discouragements.

All of us receive some praise and positive feedback from parents, teachers and playmates from the earliest stages of our lives. Your second lesson is that you should take the encouragement seriously. Let it expand your expectations of yourself: store the praise and our emotional response to it carefully in your memory bank; revisit it and augment it, adding interest to it like money in a bank. Genuine praise opens your heart and mind, and can widen, deepen and 'warm up' the part of your unconscious mind that deals with expectations.

When LEK started, we asked ourselves how fast to try to expand our tiny venture. What were the precedents?

We chose to see ourselves as an offshoot of two very successful firms. BCG had grown at 25 per cent a year, and Bain

& Company at an incredible 40 per cent. I wanted us to aim at 100 per cent, doubling every year. My partners' eyebrows shot up, reckoning that as usual I had gone over the top. Even then, I realised the importance of expectations. 'If we aim for 100 per cent,' I argued, 'that defines the ceiling. But if we target 25 or 40 per cent, *that* would set the ceiling. So, let's go for one hundred.'

This simplistic argument might not have won the day, but for an apparent problem. I had the job of recruiting junior consultants who had just graduated from leading universities, and we identified thirty excellent candidates. We thought at best five to ten of them would take our offer – we were a new and therefore risky firm, and faced plenty of competition from the successful established strategy houses. So we made offers to all thirty.

Twenty-eight accepted our offer.

At the time I think our total headcount was five, and we had no assignments to feed the new intake. Should we stick with the offers, and risk bankruptcy? Or retract them, and ruin our reputation with recruits? After much sucking of teeth, we took them all.

In the first six years of LEK, when I was there, our annual growth in headcount, revenues and profits all averaged around 100 per cent.

Your third lesson is that whether you have a new venture or are setting personal targets, it's a good idea to reach as high as you can just-plausibly believe. There are no guarantees, but it is surprising how often lofty expectations come to pass. Because they are more inspiring, and require more original and radical action, grand expectations can be easier to reach than modest ones. In the words of the Eagles, 'take it to the limit one more time'.

The first time I met Bill Bain, I was desperate to get a job and so listened very intently to what he said. As the prelude to a question, I repeated one of the things he'd said twenty minutes earlier. I was surprised when he said, 'You are a very good listener. That is very unusual.' Nobody had ever said that to me (perhaps because I wasn't!). Thereafter I made a point of listening carefully.

Bill Bain's comment later led me to advise the consultants at LEK to concentrate on what they were already good at, and I gave suggestions for what that might be. To one person I'd say it was analysis, to another insight, to a third succinct encapsulation of an issue, and so forth. I encouraged them to hone a single skill – one which could produce results far greater than the effort required – raising their expectation of what they could become and achieve.

> The fourth lesson is that you should be specific in your expectations of other people, whether they are friends, partners, co-workers or people working for you. And you should be clear with yourself too – what is the utmost you can aspire to and deliver?

To succeed, you need a serious intent to do so. Wake up each day determined that you will do something – anything, big or small, but something specific that you target for that day – to get closer to your destiny.

Once you have this serious intent, your chance of unreasonable success will rocket.

But be advised: unless you make your high success the most vital thing in your life, the thing you think about most and most intensely, it will elude you. The players in this book either had supportive spouses, or spouses dedicated to their own success, or else difficult relationships or no significant other. The players put their own career above all else, and if you want unreasonable success, you must do the same.

I repeat: serious intent means a permanent obsession with what you can do for the world. You should think about it every day. If you do, your unconscious mind will never stop thinking about it, whatever you are doing and even when you sleep. Every player thought about their success continually.

So must you.

Summary

- Think big.
- Take praise seriously. Compound it in your mind.
- Set the highest possible growth targets.
- Be explicit with high expectations of other people.

Self-belief and Olympian expectations are mutually reinforcing. If you believe in yourself, it's easier to have very high expectations of what you will achieve. If your expectations are Olympian, and you see yourself in the big picture, it's easier to elevate your self-belief.

What makes it easier is that self-belief and Olympian expectations stem from the same four sources:

- Background
- Praise
- Self-manufactured belief
- Transforming experiences.

You can't do anything about your background. But you can do something about the other three sources of belief. (We will talk about transforming experiences next.)

Praise, and basking in praise, generates self-belief. That applies to Olympian expectations too. To an important extent, the
genuine positive feedback you gain is under your control – you
need to deserve it! That means putting your efforts and intelligence into the one area where you can most easily excel. It's not
easy, but it's a lot easier than trying to be a good all-rounder.

15

Transforming Experiences

Søren Kierkegaard said, 'Life can only be understood backwards; but it must be lived forwards.'[1] This is true of transforming experiences. You can't know in advance whether a particular experience will truly transform you; you will only know afterwards if it has.

Here are some of the experiences I had up to the age of forty, which *might* have been transforming:

- I went hitch-hiking alone for fourteen weeks around eleven European countries when I was seven-teen.
- University – eighteen to twenty.
- My first two 'proper' jobs in business – twenty-one to twenty-four.
- Business school at Wharton, first time living abroad – twenty-four to twenty-five.
- Consultant at Boston Consulting Group (BCG) – twenty-five to twenty-nine.

- Consultant and partner at Bain & Company – twenty-nine to thirty-two.
- Co-founder of LEK – thirty-three to thirty-nine.

All these experiences left some imprint on me. But there is a high bar for a 'transforming experience'.

What makes a transforming experience?

- It must make you a different person from who you were before the experience.
- It must give you new, rare and profound knowledge which is used in your future career
- It must give you an order of magnitude more authority, confidence, effectiveness and value to other people.

By this demanding definition, my first transforming experience was Bain & Company, and my second was LEK. I learned a great deal at BCG which was to prove useful at Bain and LEK, but I was not successful there. It was only at Bain and LEK that I sold and operated very large and effective projects for corporate chiefs. As a founder at LEK I was able to give free rein to my ideas and theories.

The first lesson is that a transforming experience is a rare event, and, well . . . totally transforming. Ask yourself whether this has happened to you or not. How were you changed as a result?

What kinds of experiences can be transforming?

Now that you have the concept of a transforming experience, the second benefit is that you can speculate about the kind of experience that could make you mightily more successful. Consider, for example, the following types of potentially transforming experiences:

- Educational – go to the best college(s) for what you want to learn and do.
- Self-defined unique expertise – become *the* expert in a narrow subject which you define.
- Live in a different country and culture.
- Work as an apprentice for an expert in your target field.
- Finagle a job in an exceptional, innovative company, which:

    - knows something unique – such as BCG for Bill Bain, BCG and Bain & Company for me, or DESCO for Bezos
    - operates in a different market from any other firm, defined by customers, products, price, or technology (or permutations of these differences)
    - is growing very fast – 30 per cent at least, ideally doubling or better each year
    - comprises 'A' people – curious, demanding, and innovating.

- Start a company, club or network like this.

Further transformations

Writing this book has made me ask whether I should seek a further transforming experience. It's an inspiring and provocative question, but I don't know the answer. To help me answer that question, however, I've asked myself:

- Do I want further unreasonable success?
- What kind of new experience could make me many times more useful to the world?
- What would the new entity do that I care greatly about, and could have a massive impact relative to the effort and cost of starting it? What could refuel my sense of purpose and destiny in life?

The last lesson is that most successful people are not content to rest on their laurels. When you reach your destination, it may be time to ask yourself these kinds of questions, which could lead on to yet another adventure.

Summary

- If you haven't had a transforming experience, position yourself to make one more likely.
- Decide what kind of experience is most likely to transform you.
- Once you've had a transforming experience and success, you may want to seek another such experience.

16

One Breakthrough Achievement

When I was in my twenties and early thirties, I resolved to be one of the founders of a new consulting firm, but I didn't know when or with whom. I trusted this would be revealed to me at the right time.

When I was thirty-two and a partner of Bain & Company, I heard a strange rumour that two of the other partners had suddenly flown to Boston to see the firm's founder, Bill Bain. When I asked a friend in the office if this was true, he wouldn't confirm or deny it, but implied it was bad news.

I suddenly guessed, based on absolutely no evidence, that they had gone to resign. And if that was true, maybe they intended to set up their own firm.

And if that was true, it wasn't bad news, at least for me – it might be great news. The partners involved were good friends and colleagues.

They hadn't asked me to join them. There could be any number of reasons for this, ranging from 'they didn't think I would be any good' – an interpretation I obviously rejected – to 'they wanted to maintain secrecy' or 'they didn't think I would be interested', which struck me as highly plausible!

Their phones were off. Bingo! Since a partner not even receiving calls was unheard of, this was suspicious. For two of them to be doing this at the same time was amazing.

I jumped on my bike to Kew, where Iain Evans lived.

Getting in was a problem. I rang the doorbell. No response. I thumped the door. Nada. I shouted through the letterbox. Seeing that I wasn't going away, Iain's wife Zoe eventually came along. 'You'd better come in,' she said.

Iain and Jim Lawrence were there, shell-shocked by their ordeal. Bill Bain said they couldn't resign, it would end their careers, he would sue them. Bill kept them talking, until a beefy Bostonian bailiff came in to slap an injunction on them.

Three months later, we started LEK.

Co-founding LEK was my one breakthrough achievement.

Deciding our breakthrough achievement is the hardest thing anyone in search of unreasonable success can do. Some of us are lucky and have found it, often by accident. For some of us it may come in the next year or two. For others it may only become apparent in the far future. We can't hurry love, and we can't hurry this decision.

But greatness requires that we are crystal clear – at the right time – about what our breakthrough will be.

The first lesson is that the best way to get closer to knowing your achievement is to think deeply about what you may invent or personify.

It's remarkable that at least seventeen out of twenty players were inventors. Could you invent a new concept or valuable theory; product or service; company; charity; social, political, philosophical or religious movement; art form or other invention?

What could you become uniquely qualified to invent, perhaps as a result of your transforming experiences?

What do your personality, experience, practical skills, intellect, rare knowledge, curiosity, contacts, opportunities, values, ambition, imagination, creativity, and all your other personal characteristics, make you fit to pioneer?

The second lesson is this: if your transforming achievement is not to be some form of invention, could it arise from a mission to stop something bad or promote something good that already exists?

Do you have a deep-seated, visceral passion to start something that would be great for our community or society, or to stop something?

What do you believe in which makes you unusual or different?

Could you evolve a unique mission out of what you love or dislike?

The third lesson is that opportunity often comes in a disguised way. Keep your fixed objective in mind and wait for events to give you the break you need.
Bismarck said, 'Man cannot create the current of events. He can only float with it and steer.'

> Desire deeply.
> Wait.
> Pounce.
> It may take you years or even decades.
> But you must be ready when the call comes.

I have since used the capital gained from LEK to start, or accelerate the growth of, some remarkable companies, and have written a string of books which have had some influence. I take pride in these achievements. But they wouldn't have happened without my personal growth and privilege in helping to start and shape LEK and its community.[1]

Summary

- Could your breakthrough achievement be to start a great company, movement, school of thought or something else remarkable?
- Or could it be to personify an advance in science, the arts or popular culture?
- What would you like to achieve? Are you prepared to wait and listen until the quiet footsteps of providence tell you when to jump?

17

Make Your Own Trail

The opportunity to make my own trail came when I was the 'K' in LEK. We didn't find our own trail immediately – indeed we didn't see the need for it.

We believed in the Bain way, and saw LEK as a gentler, more British–European variant of our old firm. But pale imitations never work.

I was the partner most concerned with developing our own strategy. Almost by accident, we began to forge our own DNA. We hired a boatload of junior consultants, gave them a computer, and trained them to gather data and do quantitative analysis.

We floundered in our early months, when we tried to copy a winning formula. We succeeded when we created our own trail by inventing our own concepts and ways of raising profits.

The first lesson is to find a cause which is original or unpopular.

Early in my career as a strategy consultant, I decided to trademark my presentations by making them flamboyant. Though I say so myself, I became an exciting speaker. This didn't work wholly to my advantage at BCG – they thought I was being *too* original and sometimes off-message – but it did at Bain and LEK.

The second lesson is: you must *be different.*

In LEK, and all my later business interests, I've noticed that we succeeded when the following conditions applied, and we failed when they didn't:

- When we were number one in our market or niche, and therefore had lower costs.
- When we glommed onto the most profitable customers.
- When we went for simplicity – when our products were easier to use, more useful, or a joy to use.

The third lesson is that in business it is not enough to be different: you must be *profitably* different.

Summary

- Be original.
- Be different.
- Be *profitably* different.

18

Find and Drive Your Personal Vehicle

When I was twenty-five, and fresh out of business school, I joined BCG. I knew within weeks that this was a great business – ideas-led, highly prestigious but run by young people and the occasional old fogey with silvery hair who was the token grown-up able to speak on equal terms to our clients.

BCG was not just a company – it was the vanguard of a new movement, a new way of thinking about the battle between opposing firms, a crusade that would eventually spawn a whole new industry – strategy consulting – and alter the whole world of business, investment and consumption.

The first lesson is to start by adapting or opposing a 'pool vehicle' (see Chapter 9). Put yourself into the slipstream of a movement, a crusade or a new way of pursuing your field, and become expert in it.

It took me little time to work out that BCG was a hugely profitable business, growing very fast, yet requiring no external capital. Sadly, though, I couldn't own BCG. So, the young Koch decided there and then to become an owner of a strategy consulting firm in the future – that would be my vehicle.

> The second lesson is to identify what your own personal vehicle should look like. If you really want the vehicle, if you know what it will look like, and if you keep your desire near the top of your unconscious mind, it will arrive.

When I was thirty-three, and my vehicle hove into view in the shape of LEK, I asked myself whether I was ready to become co-founder of a serious global firm – that was what we intended – to rival the giants of BCG, Bain and McKinsey.

I pondered the question, and eventually decided I *was* ready, because:

- I really understood the concepts of strategy consulting and how to sell it.
- I could see a gap in the market for our first phase of success – we could build a British-based firm able to package and sell 'American' concepts in user-friendly ways to British and European bosses.
- Not only was there a gap in the market, but there was also a market in the gap – a big target market which was underserved. We could see something that our top competitors couldn't: that the decision-makers in British and European companies were often put off by American 'power salesmanship' and jargon, by a lack of intellectual subtlety,

and a failure to understand local nuances. We aimed to capitalise on that.

- Although we were a new outfit, LEK had partners who had worked for two of our top rival firms at a senior level, and we reckoned we would be at least the peers of the consultants we would be selling against.
- We were really excited about being in business for ourselves, taking whatever risks we wanted to, choosing who would work in our venture and reaping the rewards for ourselves and our people.
- We were confident about the economics of our new business if we could sell large chunks of business. We knew that strategy consulting was highly profitable, that it required no capital investment, and that it could be cash–positive very quickly.

The third lesson is to ask yourselves similar questions to decide if you are ready:

- Do you understand the market niche backwards?
- Can you see a gap in the market, and what is it?
- Is there a large enough market in the gap?
- Have you worked for one or more major competitors at a senior level?
- Can you see something your rivals can't?
- Does it excite you?
- Can the new vehicle become cash-positive and profitable quickly, and do you have enough capital to reach break-even (bearing in mind this nearly always takes longer than expected)?
- You should only launch your new vehicle when you are sure you are ready.

There were three partners in LEK – our last names were Lawrence, Evans and Koch. We were fortunate to have prior history in that we had worked well together in another firm and were friends.

Why, then, did we often have disagreements, sometimes even conflicts laden with strong emotion?

I now realise that we were not unusual. Every group of founders I've known has similar issues and rows. They happen because founders feel passionately about their business, and after years of working for other people, they want to have it their own way. That is often not possible if the founders don't see eye to eye.

One thing I know now is that just as two or three people can't drive a car, they can't drive a business vehicle either.

The fourth lesson is that it is better to have one driver of the vehicle, the dominant person chosen by the founders to lead it.

Eventually I left LEK because I wanted to turn it into an 'M&A' – mergers and acquisitions – consulting firm, and my partners didn't. Having failed to carry my view, I resigned after six years, took a bunch of money with me, and cheerfully pursued a new career.

To be honest, however, in hindsight I made a mistake in leaving LEK when I did. Vehicles are precious. I had lost mine. The partners who remained continued to make a great success out of LEK. I am obviously biased, but I believe that my vision for LEK would have made it an even more successful firm.

The fifth lesson is that if you are super-confident that your proposition is best for the vehicle, you should fight tenaciously for it, and grasp the nettle of leadership that I was too diffident to seize. If the vehicle is roadworthy and has great future potential, do not sell or surrender it too readily.

I think this applies beyond business, to other organisations, crusades or social movements. It is why they are always fragmenting, often in a positive way. Divergence is the organising principle of evolution and life generally.

At the time I didn't realise how important it was for me to have a personal vehicle that could multiply my own powers. It took me a long time to find a new personal vehicle because I didn't realise how necessary it was.

The sixth lesson is that disagreements among founders are endemic and should not come as a surprise, an affront, or a cause to be stressed and break friendships. Founders are powerful and independent personalities. If disagreements are profound, they should happily and amicably go their own ways.

The seventh lesson is that if you give up your personal vehicle, immediately start searching for the next one – you owe that to yourself and the world.

After I left LEK, armed with some useful capital, I eventually decided to use the concepts of strategy not to consult, but to do – to invest in new or young companies and use strategy to make them more valuable.

I bought stakes, often controlling stakes, in several small ventures that I believed could benefit from the concepts of strategy. Some of these ventures folded, some gave modest returns, but some multiplied my capital prodigiously. Each new venture was a new adventure for my collaborators and me.

> The final lesson is that a good way to define your next vehicle is to extend your experience and knowledge into a new yet adjacent field, where you can be a pioneer.

Summary

- Ride a pool vehicle – some trend in your environment – that you can adapt or oppose to gain momentum.
- Find a personal vehicle that you alone can ride.
- Ensure that you are ready to drive the vehicle to success.
- Even if there are several founders, only one person can drive the vehicle. Choose wisely, and if it doesn't work out, change the driver.
- Expect disagreements and don't be fazed by them.
- Don't surrender or sell your vehicle too early or easily.
- When you exit your vehicle, acquire another.
- A new vehicle may emerge by applying your expertise to a new area that is similar in some way to your old field, yet distinctly different from it in other ways.

19

Thrive on Setbacks

As I mentioned before, my most traumatic setback came at twenty-nine, when I had to part company from the Boston Consulting Group. For three years, I had loved working there – I relished the intellectual challenge, the exposure to our clients' triumphs and guilty secrets, the chance to gain the confidence and ear of top people, and the thrill of working with some of the brightest people on the planet.

But in my fourth and final year, I was failing – failing to win the confidence of BCG's leaders or do the heavy-duty analysis that impressed them, failing to get promoted, failing to explain why most of my clients really liked me for reasons unrelated to the analysis, failing to come to terms with failure itself.

Until then, I had never really failed. I didn't expect it and I felt I didn't deserve it. One of my bosses said that I was like a volcano, working away constructively, but then exploding when least expected. He also said I made my bosses nervous because they never knew what I would say at client meetings.

I reframed that as being fit for a top position at BCG, but not for a lower one.

> The first lesson is that failure can and often should be reframed – seen in a new light. Without diminishing the feedback you've received, which may cause you to change tack, reframing can boost your self-esteem by telling you that failure can be honourable.

I was never made to be a loyal, obedient employee. Even a rather forgiving and free-wheeling outfit such as BCG had its hierarchy and its limits.

The way to get ahead in any organisation is to please your bosses, not terrorise them or make them anxious. Be predictable, deliver exactly what they want (not what you think they should want), and when you can't agree with them, keep your mouth shut.

I am reminded of the boss who said, 'I don't want yes-men around me – I want them to speak their mind, even if it costs them their job.'

If I wanted to stay in strategy consulting, I had to behave differently.

> The second lesson is that after any failure you can choose to interpret it negatively, positively or neutrally; and you can decide either to change your actions and perhaps even part of your personality, or to change the context in which you deploy them.

I hedged my bets and interviewed with two firms in my existing strategy-consulting territory, together with one outside it, in the lucrative and then-fast-growing field of executive search – also known as head-hunting.

At the boardroom consulting blue-chip Firm of McKinsey – it always has a capital F, because Marvin Bower, its real founder, thought it should behave with the professional ethics of a law firm, at a time when consultants were cowboys and lawyers were honest and genuinely served their clients' interests rather than their own – I came across an engaging character called the Brigadier, an ex-army man who handled senior recruitment. He got the measure of me, telling me that I could go far, but was not suited to consulting. 'You don't want to advise,' he said, 'you want to do, to make decisions for yourself. You should become an entrepreneur, or, failing that, a venture capitalist.'

Next, I flew to Zurich to interview with Egon Zehnder, head of the eponymous firm of head-hunters. I liked him, and he liked me, and offered me a job. I nearly accepted on the spot. After all, head-hunting is all about decisions, and it was a great deal easier than strategy consulting.

But searching my heart, I realised that I wanted to stay in strategy consulting, work for another firm there, and then become a founder of a new business in the industry. My expectations remained very high, and I didn't want to settle for anything less. I was lucky to meet Bill Bain and join his team.

Much more than BCG, Bain & Company was a disciplined firm with a hidden but very real hierarchy, perhaps, I imagined, even Stalinist in terms of control. For the first time in my life, I decided to behave myself. At first it was a game, but then I really enjoyed playing it. I thought keeping my views to myself and joining the Bain cult would kill me, but it proved surprisingly easy and gratifying.

The third lesson is how easily one can sometimes adopt a different attitude and have it become second nature. If the motivation is great enough, you may be far more malleable than you might think. You may come to enjoy displaying a different side of yourself, just as I did.

When I left LEK, I started Strategy Ventures Plc, a small investment company, which was great fun but had limited capital and only made one (very successful) investment: Filofax. When we decided to cash in our chips at SVP, I didn't know what else to do: I took things easy, drifted a bit, and felt unfulfilled. It was stupid. I had lots of interests and should have pursued one of them, but I couldn't decide which. It would have been better to throw myself into any one of them.

After three years I decided to focus on writing and investing, which went well together. I became happier and more productive.

The fourth lesson is to keep happily busy after a setback or change of life, to resist drifting and dabbling, and to find one or two absorbing interests.

Over time, and particularly through writing this book, I've realised that success and failure are complements, not opposites. Failure gives us as much valuable feedback as success, sometimes a great deal more; and learning from failure is often the prelude and precondition for great success.

The final lesson is that to attain unreasonable success you must thrive on failure. Although setbacks will come, with the right mindset you can bounce back bigger and better. If you take intelligent risks, the universe will knock you down, but will also raise you up stronger than ever.

Summary

- Reframe failure in a new, more positive light.
- You can then change your behaviour or change the environment in which you act.
- Attitudes can be altered by wilfully changing your actions in a new context.
- Keep busy after a setback.
- Relishing failure leads to success.

20

Acquire Unique Intuition

My first key intuition was that it might be possible to start a new strategy consultancy based in London. This arose from my knowledge of a highly specialised area which I knew was relatively easy to operate and unreasonably lucrative.

> The first lesson is to build up expertise in a fast-growing but small, narrow area of expertise, where few people currently operate. Without deeply understanding a specialised and relatively unknown area, your intuition is unlikely to propel you forward decisively.

My second insight was that the incredibly powerful concepts of business strategy could be used to beat the odds investing in new and young companies. My starting capital was small, so this took a long time to have substantial impact. Still, my perception was right. I am encouraging other entrepreneurs and investors to follow suit so that the result affects the whole economy.

> The second lesson is the extraordinarily high value of rare knowledge about a sector or idea that is starting to spread like wildfire. If you have an unusually deep appreciation of a high-growth area, you are halfway to success.

Over the past three decades I have increasingly enjoyed fertilising my unconscious mind – setting it imaginative puzzles before I go for a walk or bike ride, exercise in the gym, or fall asleep.

> The third lesson is to increase your creativity and the power of your unconscious mind. Your unconscious mind is like a huge filing cabinet of everything you have learned in your life – everything! – with the ability to cross-reference anything from any file to another. It holds trillions of pieces of data which may be related to each other, thus generating an uncountable number of possible permutations, any one of which may be vital to your success. To change the metaphor, your unconscious mind is also like a bottomless well, from which, if you send the bucket down skilfully, you can dredge up endless buckets of gold. So, feed your unconscious mind every day, and learn how to tap it every day. I cannot over-emphasise how important this is, to help you generate unreasonable success.
>
> See the Further Reading section (page 287) to learn more.

One thing which has built my personal fortune is my habit of guessing outcomes of investments and events. I think in terms of probabilities and 'expected value'. For example, if I think investing in Venture X has a 30 per cent chance of making 50 times my money, I would prefer that to Venture Y, if it has an 80 per cent chance of making 10 times. The expected value of Venture X is $.3 \times 50 = 15$, which is better than Venture Y, where $.8 \times 10 = 8$. Of course, we need to invest money we can afford to lose, and be willing to take high risks.

The final lesson is that, if you can afford it and can stomach the risk, you can benefit from guessing outcomes and tracking how often you are right. If the outcome is great enough, you only need to be right once in your life.

Summary

- Build expertise in a small niche that is growing fast.
- Tap your unconscious mind daily.
- Life is a book of bets. Make astute bets at long odds.

21

Distort Reality

My first three years as a junior executive, fresh out of university, were not very enjoyable or successful. So I decided to go away from England to business school in America – to make a new start. It was a deliberate ploy to develop breadth of experience and a new and improved personality – more extrovert, open, friendly, can-do; less pedantic, gloomy and critical. I acquired remarkably little useful knowledge at Wharton, but as a finishing school it could hardly have been better.

The first lesson is that it is possible to change your current reality by changing yourself. This is probably best done when your personality is more angular, plastic, undefined – certainly in your twenties, though I have seen people change for the better at any age. To reinvent yourself, you need to go away – away from home, away from friends, away from co-workers, away from your job, away from your state or region and from your country.

> Personality reinvention is the ultimate in reality distortion – changing yourself is both easier and more likely to change your prospects than changing the world around you. It's not a good idea to take personality change too far, but self-improvement is always possible, and easier if you move to a more positive, outgoing, dynamic place.

I learned something valuable when I was commuting to South Africa for a long project at LEK. I loved the country, the flora and fauna, the sunshine, the vineyards, the mountains, the zest for life manifested by many South Africans, the hikes, the sport, and just about everything else.

Of course I wanted the project to be a great success, but I wanted to enjoy my time there as well. My team and I had a terrific time – talking, playing, going on trips, drinking, gambling and soaking up the sun, while also coming up with exceptional results. My plan was that we should only work on the few vital issues, get to grips with them in a deep way, and have plenty of time for leisure and team-building.

I believe we can always do this, if we have the right people on our side, and want a good time *and* high achievement. Life is generally not like this but making it so is the best way to distort reality.

> The second lesson is that it is not always necessary to work in the salt-mines to get ahead. Reality is often unpleasant, but you can distort and defeat the grim work ethic.

When we started LEK, we were clear about one reality we wanted to change. Up to then the only strategy firms that had made the big time were American. We were told that it was too late for a new firm to enter the select club of credible top-level consultants, and impossible for a European firm. The reality was that nobody had done it. We changed that reality.

> The third lesson is that if you want to defy reality – to shift it to something else – you must be very clear about what that reality is, and how to make it temporary.

What reality will you shift next?

Summary

- Reality is there to be challenged and distorted.
- Jump-start progress by making yourself better and more useful.
- Work can be hugely enjoyed while changing the world

CONCLUSION

Positioning Yourself for Unreasonable Success

'God plays dice with the universe. But they're loaded dice. And the main objective is to find out by what rules they were loaded and how we can use them for our own ends.'

—JOSEPH FORD

We have reached the end of our rollercoaster ride. We've seen that success does not require genius, consistency, all-round ability, a safe pair of hands or even basic competence. If it did, most of the players in this book would not have impacted the world as they did.

What the players all exhibited is a set of unusual and strongly effective attitudes and strategies – super-charged self-belief, elevated expectations of themselves and their collaborators, an experience that gave them rare knowledge, a single objective that would change their lives and those of myriad other people, the cussedness to carve out their own path through life, a personal vehicle that augmented their powers prodigiously, the ability to learn from failure and relish it, finely tuned intuition that they fed rather than throttled, and the confidence that they could make their own rules and defy the realities and obstacles that normal people accept as facts of life. They were unreasonable in a highly creative way, and hence unreasonably successful.

We can boil down what we have learned into two points.

1. **It's all about positioning yourself for success, not improving your performance**

   The players we've met had unreasonable success because they 'visited' the nine landmarks, not, in most cases, because their performance was outstanding in other respects – indeed, in many cases, it wasn't outstanding at all.

   This is very good news. If you can get the positioning right, your chances of high success rocket. You could spend enormous energy trying to become better at what you do – and still fail anyway. It takes much less effort to get your positioning right, and the results will be much more impressive.

2. **It's not all about your abilities – it's about having the right attitude and success strategies**

   The nine landmarks can be reduced to two mega-attributes – attitude and strategies.

   Attitude is my shorthand for the following qualities: self-belief, Olympian expectations, thriving on setbacks and distorting reality. These are not conventional ways of thinking and acting. Few people see the world through this lens and behave in the way that our players did. What these four attitude-based landmarks have in common, however, is that they greatly increase the chances of success.

Learning to see the world in these terms and acting this way is initially not easy – it comes naturally to a few people but not to most of us. Yet, if you truly want to win, it is far from impossible to learn these traits and make them habits.

These attitudes are a form of intelligent determination. More than determination alone, they train you to have the kind of impact on the world that you want.

The world works this way – it responds to people who possess huge self-belief geared towards an important goal. It responds to the very highest expectations. It responds to the belief that failure is functional and will help you succeed. It responds to the belief that reality is malleable and that you can inspire other people to see it that way.

Attitudes such as these are far more important than ability. To compete on ability is to enter a race where the prizes are small and there are many competitors. To compete on these kinds of attitude is to enter a race where the prize is huge and there are few people competing against you.

The **success strategies** are transforming experiences, making your own trail, finding and driving your personal vehicle, acquiring unique intuition and, above all, making one breakthrough achievement.

A transforming experience will make you hugely more effective because you will learn something rare and valuable. The way to find this experience is to join a company or group which is growing very fast and knows something unique.

Your own trail must be original, different, and *profitably* different.

Your personal vehicle must leverage your time and abilities to a far, far greater degree than they are leveraged now.

Unique intuition depends on knowing more in a narrow field than anyone else.

Most vital of all – and based on all the other strategies and attitudes – is one breakthrough achievement where you invent something which profoundly changes the world, or your part of it.

Positioning yourself for unreasonable success

		Attitude	Strategy
1	Self-belief	✓	
2	Olympian expectations	✓	
3	Transforming experiences		✓
4	One breakthrough achievement		✓
5	Make your own trail		✓
6	Drive your personal vehicle		✓
7	Thrive on setbacks	✓	
8	Acquire unique intuition		✓
9	Distort reality	✓	

Now you know that success isn't primarily about performance, but about positioning – that is, your attitudes and strategies – you are fully equipped for the journey to unreasonable success.

Luck always plays a huge part in success, but where there's life, luck can change. We can't control everything in life, but success is not mysterious either. With the right attitudes and strategies, anyone can realistically hope to be successful, even unreasonably so. You are playing with loaded dice, but now you know how they are loaded, and can adjust your actions accordingly.

The lack of fairness in the game of success is a cause for rejoicing rather than regret. If you understand how the odds are rigged, and play intelligently, cheerfully and often, who knows how high and wild you may win?

It's time for you to draw your own map. Bon voyage!

Further Reading

I have consulted many hundreds of books and multiple other sources in writing this book. Here I include only books (and the occasional article) that I consider highly relevant or pleasurable. I commend them all to you for the areas in which you are particularly interested. If there is more than one book under a particular heading, they are presented in the order of interest. Happy reading!

The players

Bill Bain

The Lords of Strategy by Walter Kiechel III. I cannot recommend this too highly: it is brilliant and spot-on regarding both Bill Bain and Bruce Henderon and their impact on the corporate world.

'Counselor to the King' by Liz Roman Gallese, *The New York Times Magazine*, September 24, 1989, Section 6, page 18. Terrific interview with Bill Bain.

Jeff Bezos

The Everything Store by Brad Stone. Fantastic research
and insight.
Jeff Bezos by J. R. MacGregor. Quirky and short, but not
without interest.

Otto von Bismarck

Bismarck by Volker Ullrich. Excellent. Now available in a very
good English translation by Timothy Beech.
Bismarck by A. J. P. Taylor. First published in 1955, but has aged
very well. Like all Alan Taylor's books, it is provocative,
perceptive, and a joy to read.

Marie Curie

Marie Curie: A Biography by Marilyn Bailey Ogilvie is excellent.
Madame Curie: A Biography by Marie Curie's youngest daughter
is very good, even though perhaps too detailed for anyone
other than enthusiasts or researchers. It's also rather old-
fashioned in style. But a valuable record.

Winston Churchill

Churchill by Andrew Roberts. Definitive.
Churchill by Roy Jenkins. If you are interested in Churchill,
you must read this biography as well as that by Roberts.
Wonderful.
My Early Life by Winston Churchill. Fascinating and
beautifully written.
In Churchill's Shadow by David Cannadine. A marvellous
collection of essays, not just about Churchill.

The English & Their History by Robert Tombs. A brilliant and
   witty book traversing English history from the Anglo-
   Saxons to the recent past. Insightful on Churchill – see
   especially pages 668–756.
The War Lords by A. J. P. Taylor. Chapter on Churchill is
   very good.
The Origins of the Second World War by A. J. P. Taylor.
   Unconventional thesis and I am not convinced, but
   definitely worth reading: exciting, fast-paced, and will
   make you think.
Winston Churchill by Martin Gilbert. About Churchill's
   wilderness years in the 1930s. Good.
Churchill by Martin Gilbert. About his whole life. Exhaustive.

Leonardo da Vinci

Leonardo da Vinci by Walter Isaacson. Very good. Be sure to buy
   the print edition, with its beautiful illustrations.

Walt Disney

Walt Disney by Neal Gabler. Scholarly, with access to the Disney
   archives, but lively and very well written too. Highly
   recommended.
The Ultimate Book of Business Breakthroughs by Tom Cannon. The
   chapter on Disneyland is a real gem. The rest of the book
   is a bonus.
The Magic Kingdom by Steven Watts. Subtitled *Walt Disney and
   the American Way of Life*, this is a very good cultural analysis
   of Disney's impact, as well as adding a lot of biographical
   details, especially about his private life.
The Real Walt Disney by Leonard Mosley. Gabler's biography is
   better in my view, but this is worth reading too.

Bob Dylan

Once Upon A Time: The Lives of Bob Dylan by Ian Bell. Superb
 biography. Not to be confused with *Time Out of Mind:
 The Lives of Bob Dylan* by the same author, which is about
 Dylan's later career.
Chronicles by Bob Dylan. Poignant and poetic, if unreliable, and
 highly revealing even when one suspects Dylan is being
 creative with the facts.

Albert Einstein

Einstein by Walter Isaacson. Authoritative. Very strong on
 the science, but also captures the elusive and paradoxical
 character of the man.
The Structure of Scientific Revolutions by Thomas S. Kuhn. This
 is one of the most brilliant and important books about
 science I have ever read, and it is fun to read too. It's about
 how science moves from one paradigm to another, and
 it highlights two themes. One is that a new paradigm
 'emerges all at once, sometimes in the middle of the night,
 in the mind of a man deeply immersed in crisis'. New
 paradigms emerge because new facts are noticed that are
 anomalies; they do not fit the existing paradigm. There is
 a strong suggestion that they emerge from the unconscious
 mind of creative scientists. The second theme is that the
 originators of new paradigms are nearly always 'very
 young or very new to the field' they transform – they
 are not dominated and blinded by the existing paradigm.
 Einstein clearly fits this template, and many passages in
 the book use Einstein as an example of how a new way
 of viewing the world emerges. If you want to understand
 Einstein's breakthroughs, this book is a marvellous

complement to Isaacson's biography. Use the index to
follow the passages.

Viktor Frankl

Man's Search for Meaning by Viktor E. Frankl. Both
    autobiographical and analytical, this moving book is a work
    of art and science.

Bruce Henderson

Perspectives on Strategy from The Boston Consulting Group edited by
    Carl W. Stern and George Stalk, Jr.
See also *The Lords of Strategy* – listed under Bill Bain above – for
    a great profile of Bruce Henderson.

Steve Jobs

Steve Jobs by Walter Isaacson. Possibly the best business
    biography ever. Detailed and meticulous, yet also sees the
    big picture.

John Maynard Keynes

*John Maynard Keynes: Volume Two, The Economist as Saviour,
    1920–1937* by Robert Skidelsky. Intellectual and personal
    history at its most elegant and lucid. This is the more
    relevant volume for my book.
John Maynard Keynes: Volume One, Hopes Betrayed, 1883–1920 by
    Robert Skidelsky.

Lenin

Lenin the Dictator by Victor Sebestyen. Excellent.
What Is To Be Done? by V. I. Lenin. Hard work reading this, but
 it does illuminate Lenin's ruthlessness.

Madonna

Madonna by J. Randy Taraborrelli. Breathless, gossipy,
 comprehensive, based on exhaustive research. If you are
 a Madonna fan, you will love this book. If not, here are
 three others I like, which are far better than the mass of
 Madonna books:
Life With My Sister Madonna by Christopher Ciccone. Amusing,
 bitter, but has the ring of truth.
Madonna by Lucy O'Brien. A bit tart, but all the better for that.
Madonna as Postmodern Myth by Georges-Claude Guilbert.
 I'm not sure why I enjoyed this academic book so much.
 Perhaps it is because it lays bare how she deliberately
 constructs and reconstructs herself. In the end it made me
 respect her despite my preconceptions.

Nelson Mandela

Long Walk to Freedom by Nelson Mandela. A very long
 autobiography but gripping and essential reading if you
 want to understand the South African Revolution of
 1994 and the evolution of a saintly terrorist – and, just
 as important, how and why the men running South
 Africa before Mandela took over engineered a deal with
 him. It's a fantastic, uplifting book, and extraordinarily
 well written.
Mandela by Peter Hain. A short guide to Mandela, from a

friend, sympathiser and under-rated statesman. I love
this book too.

Nelson Mandela by Richard Stengel. The journalist who
collaborated with Mandela on his autobiography gives the
best account of Mandela's personality, charm and blind spots.

Nelson Mandela by Mary Benson. Another good biography, but
the best part is the brief but very important and moving
Foreword by Archbishop Desmond Tutu.

J. K. Rowling

J. K. Rowling by Sean Smith. The nearest thing to a proper
biography.

J. K. Rowling by Victoria Peterson-Hilleque. Glossy, picture-
book, American potted biography for students. Well
written and presented, with a clear timeline and sources.

Work it, Girl: Boss the Bestseller List like J. K. Rowling by Caroline
Moss. A rather charming and funkily illustrated self-help
book for children, though not totally accurate.

Helena Rubinstein

War Paint: Elizabeth Arden and Helena Rubinstein by Lindy
Woodhead. First-rate.

Helena Rubinstein by Michèle Fitoussi. Almost equally good.

Paul of Tarsus

Paul by A. N. Wilson. Urbane, scholarly, imaginative and hard
to praise too highly. Nothing else written about Paul comes
close to this. Except . . .

The Beginnings of Christianity by Andrew Welburn. Not
principally about Paul, but Welburn sets the scene and

provides a brilliant new interpretation of Paul. According
to Welburn, Paul has more in common with his Gnostic
contemporaries than with later Christian orthodoxy, and
his Gospel of Love presents 'an extraordinarily demanding
vision of the self'. Anyone who wants to think deeply
about Paul and the reason he was so successful should read
Welburn's chapter, 'An Unfamiliar Paul'.

The Gnostic Religion by Hans Jonas. Subtitled *The Message of
the Alien God and the Beginnings of Christianity*. For anyone
intrigued by the intellectual background to Paul and Jesus,
this is absolutely fascinating. Be sure to get the enlarged
1963 edition.

Marcion by Adolf von Harnack. An old book from 1923, but still
the best guide, alongside the book above, for a perspective
on Marcion, without whom Paul's version of Christianity
might not have become so influential.

Jesus by A. N. Wilson. Written before Wilson's biography
of Paul, the chapter in *Jesus* referring to Paul is a
masterpiece of concision and can be viewed as a first
study for the later book. If you want to delve a little
more into Paul but not to read a full-length biography,
this is the piece for you. Alternatively, if you want to see
how Wilson subtly changed his view of Paul, you could
compare and contrast the two books. Personally, I love
both works.

The Gnostic Paul by Elaine Pagels. Scholarly; not for the general
reader, but informative.

Margaret Thatcher

The Iron Lady by John Campbell. Get the single-volume edition
(2012). The best and most balanced of the dozens of
Thatcher biographies I have read.

Margaret Thatcher by David Cannadine is my runner-up in
the Thatcher stakes. At 136 pages of main text this is a
masterpiece of brevity. It hits all the right notes and is a
pleasure to read.

Margaret Thatcher by Charles Moore. The authorised biography,
but still very good!

The Downing Street Years by Margaret Thatcher. Some memoirs
sound manufactured, but this one sounds authentic
Thatcher. I enjoyed it very much and found it revealing
about her obsession to reverse Britain's national decline.

See also *In Churchill's Shadow* (listed under Winston Churchill
above) for a particularly perceptive essay on 'The
Haunting Fear of National Decline', comparing Churchill
and Thatcher.

Acquire unique intuition: The unconscious mind

The Creative Brain by Nancy C. Andreasen. An accomplished
psychiatrist with an interest in literary and scientific
geniuses extols the unconscious mind and tells us how to
be more creative. Enjoyable and most instructive.

Strangers to Ourselves by Timothy D. Wilson. Excellent – perhaps
the most useful single book by a neuroscientist on how to
use the power of the unconscious mind.

Subliminal by Leonard Mlodinow. Witty and wise – what the
new unconscious teaches us.

Incognito by David Eagleman. Also excellent.

The Brain by David Eagleman. A more popular version of the
book above, but does not appeal to me quite as much.

Gut Feelings by Gerd Gigerenzer. How to make decisions better
and more easily. A brilliant celebration of simplicity.

The Zurich Axioms by Max Gunther. Splendid section on
intuition. The rest of the book is fascinating too.

The Luck Factor by Max Gunther, pages 133–155. Some overlap
with the book above, but also excellent. The subtitle
encapsulates the message – *Why some people are luckier than
others and how you can become one of them.*

The Genie Within by Harry W. Carpenter. Not up to date
scientifically, but more useful than many of the books by
expert neuroscientists.

The Power of Your Subconscious Mind by Joseph Murphy. As
above – very useful.

The New Unconscious edited by Ran R. Hassin, James S.
Uleman, and John A. Bargh. A collection of academic
papers. In my opinion numbers 11, 12, 17, 18 and 19 are the
most interesting and useful.

Blink by Malcolm Gladwell. Very good stories and a few
excellent points.

Acknowledgements

This book would not have been written but for my friend Marx Acosta-Rubio, who bombarded me with suggestions that I read particular biographies of famous people. The subjects and authors were brilliantly chosen and I became intrigued as to why the former were so successful, when really many of them were huge failures throughout much of their career. They seemed unlikely to realise their dreams, and when they did, often didn't seem to deserve their achievements.

Increasingly over time I have been curious about the conundrum of success – why some people make it big when often their more talented and hard-working peers don't. This book has been my excuse to combine my two greatest curiosities in life – the odd, perverse yet *universal* rules that seem to govern exceptional attainment, plus a study of *individuals* who manage to defy the odds to do so many unexpected and ultra-important things. I might not have found the answer but for Marx's constant badgering to read a large collection of biographies. Since then he has been a great enthusiast for this book and has generously provided a terrific amount of advice, insight and encouragement.

Albert Einstein said that the secret of originality is to conceal your sources, but I want to pay tribute to some of my most important sources. So thanks for writing great books to (in no particular order) A. J. P. Taylor, Brad Stone, Andrew Roberts, Roy Jenkins, Winston Churchill (the author), David Cannadine, Robert Tombs, Walter Isaacson, Neal Gabler, Tom Cannon, Bob Dylan (the author), Ian Bell, Thomas Kuhn, Viktor Frankl, Robert Skidelsky, Victor Sebestyen, Nelson Mandela (the author), Peter Hain, Lindy Woodhead, A. N. Wilson, Andrew Welburn, John Campbell, Nancy Andreasen, Timothy Wilson and Max Gunther.

Beyond Marx, I'd like to thank my friends who read various drafts of the manuscript and made valuable suggestions – notably John Hewitt, Jamie Reeve, Jamie Sirrat, Matthew Grimsdale, Peter Cadwallader, Nicholas Ladd and Perry Marshall. Jamie Reeve also supplied the title and structure of Part Three – Lessons Learned – as well as unique perceptions on the life and character of Bob Dylan; and John Hewitt provided sage counsel and practical ideas on the structure of the book, and invaluable feedback throughout.

I must also pay tribute to my unsuspecting mentors, Bruce Henderson and Bill Bain, for being such marvellous models, men who achieved far, far more than almost anybody realises, and who were all the greater for their massive but curiously loveable flaws and foibles. Though he did not realise it, Bruce was endlessly comical; while Bill was genuinely and acerbically amusing.

My heartfelt gratitude goes, as always, to Sally Holloway, my wonderful agent. She usually throws not a bucket but a whole car wash of cold water over most of my book suggestions, so I was astounded and delighted that she was mad for this project right from the get-go. Michele Topham, Carole Robinson and the whole team at Felicity Bryan Associates are also a joy to work with.

My American publisher, Jennifer Dorsey, also was enthusiastic right at the start, and it is a pleasure to work with her. As for the people at Piatkus and Little, Brown, their work, as always, has been magnificent. Tim Whiting and Tom Asker have taken an extraordinary interest in the book, and I have been bowled over by their zest and the deep thought they have given to making it as good and successful as possible. I would also like to thank Clara Diaz, the publicist, Hannah Methuen and Hermione Ireland, the sales directors, and their teams, Aimee Kitson, my marketing guru, and the rights team, especially Andy Hine, Kate Hibbert and Helena Doree. My copy editor, Alison Griffiths, has also been excellent. Making a book have maximum impact involves many talented individuals and I have been in very good hands on all fronts.

My friends and assistants Ricardo Santos, Pedro Santos and David Rautenbach have helped me brilliantly in getting the manuscript ready, and Pedro and I worked together on the 'secret map', with Pedro drawing the draft illustrations with great creativity. I am very lucky to have David Andrassy as the illustrator.

Finally, enormous thanks are due to Matthew, Sooty and Nick, for keeping me sane and happy throughout the writing process.

Notes

Chapter 1: Can We Map Success?

1 Quoted in Malcolm Gladwell (2008) *Outliers: The Story of Success*, New York: Little, Brown, page 49.

Chapter 3: The Players

1 https://www.forbes.com/profile/jeff-bezos/#580859421b23
2 Walter Isaacson (2017) *Leonardo da Vinci*, London: Simon & Schuster.
3 Personal recollection.
4 Carl W. Stern and George Stalk, Jr. (editors) (1998) *Perspectives on Strategy from The Boston Consulting Group*, New York: John Wiley, page 3.
5 *The Sunday Times Rich List 2019*, page 63.

Chapter 4: Landmark 1 – Self-belief

1 Roy Jenkins (2001) *Churchill*, London: Macmillan, page 3.
2 Winston Churchill (1930, 2012) *My Early Life*, London: Thornton Butterworth, Eland Publishing (respectively), pages 30–31.
3 Ibid., pages 15–16.
4 Andrew Roberts (2018) *Churchill*, London: Viking, pages 22–23.
5 Robert Skidelsky (1992) *John Maynard Keynes, Volume Two, The Economist as Saviour 1920–1937*, London: Macmillan, page 422.
6 Bob Dylan (2004) *Chronicles*, New York: Simon & Schuster, page 22.
7 Ian Bell (2012) *Once Upon a Time: The Lives of Bob Dylan*, Edinburgh: Mainstream Publishing, page 40.
8 Ibid., page 100.

9   Dylan, op. cit., page 18.

10 Guthrie was as much a deliberate confection as Dylan. It is unclear whether Guthrie really knew who Dylan was or endorsed him personally, but this did not matter to Dylan. In his own mind, Dylan was Guthrie's anointed successor. See Bell, pages 57–60.

11 Quoted in Walter Isaacson (2007) *Einstein: His Life And Universe*, London: Simon & Schuster, page 31.

12 Ibid., page 65.

13 This was Professor Weber. Quoted ibid., page 34.

14 Neal Gabler (2006) *Walt Disney: The Biography*, New York: Alfred A. Knopf, page 44.

15 Gabler, op. cit., pages 76–77.

16 Ibid., page 115.

17 Ibid., pages 117–118.

18 Eddie Brummelman, 'The Praise Paradox', *Behavioral Scientist*, January 22, 2018.

19 Paul's letter to the Galatians 1: 11-17.

20 The number of disciples Jesus chose matched the twelve tribes of Israel and was probably politically motivated; two of them – Simon the Zealot and Judas Iscariot – had subversive 'form'. It was therefore natural for the high priest and his guards to hand Jesus over to the Romans for crucifixion, and to want to hunt down followers of Jesus remaining afterwards. See A. N. Wilson (1997) *Paul: The Mind of the Apostle,* London: Pimlico, especially pages 15, 58–60.

21 Isaacson (2011) *Steve Jobs*, London: Little, Brown, page 4.

22 Ibid., page 4.

23 Ibid., page 5. The friend was Greg Calhoun, a close friend immediately after college.

24 Ibid., page 5.

25 Ibid., page 119.

26 Ibid., page 121.

27 Ibid., pages 4–5.

28 See Jenkins, op. cit., especially pages 469–477 and 493–496. Churchill 'was quicker than almost anyone else in fastening on the menace of Hitler . . . already by 13 April 1933 [less than three months after Hitler became chancellor] he was speaking in the House of Commons of the "odious conditions" now ruling in Germany and of the threat of "persecution and pogrom of Jews" being extended to areas (notably Poland) to which Nazi influence or conquest spread.' (pages 469–470). 'Apart from a small coterie Churchill was very isolated.'(472).

Chapter 5: Landmark 2 – Olympian Expectations

1   Felix Dennis talks about this in respect of people who want to become rich, but it is true of success in any sphere: 'Somewhere in the invisible heart of all self-made men and women is a sliver of razored ice . . . If you do not wish it to grow, then quit any dreams . . . now.' Felix Dennis (2006) *How to Get Rich*, London: Random House.

2   Robert Rosenthal and Lenmore Jackson, 'Teachers' Expectations: Determinants of Pupils' IQ Gains', *Psychological Reports* 19 (August 1966), pages 115–118.

3   A. N. Wilson, op. cit., pages 77–78.

4   Paul's letter to the Galatians 5:17.

5   Gabler, op. cit., page 46.

6   Ibid., page 60.

7   Ibid., page 68.

8   Ibid., page 85.

9   Ibid., page 128.

10   Ibid., page 166.

11   Ibid., page 157.

12   Ibid., page 133.

13   Ibid., page 168.

14   Ibid., page 170.

15   Ibid., page 212.

16   Isaacson, *Steve Jobs*, op. cit., page 136.

17   Ibid., pages 172, 315, 497, 561.

18   Ibid., page 131.

19   Isaacson, *Steve Jobs*, op. cit., page 121.

20   Brad Stone (2013) *The Everything Store: Jeff Bezos and the Age of Amazon*, New York: Little, Brown, page 194.

21   Ibid., page 146.

22   Einstein to Pauline Winteler, May 1897, quoted in Isaacson, *Einstein*, op. cit., page 41.

23   Einstein to Mileva Maric, 13 September 1900, quoted ibid., page 46.

24   Quoted ibid., page 67.

25   Einstein to Marcel Grossmann, 6 September 1901.

26   Isaacson, *Leonardo da Vinci*, op. cit., pages 2–3.

27   Ibid., page 88.

28   Ibid., page 263.

29   Skidelsky, op. cit., page 410.

30   Ibid., pages 410–411.

31   Ibid., page 411.

32   Ibid., page 423.

33   Ibid., page 423.

34   Ibid., page 425.
35   Dylan, op. cit., page 28.
36   Ibid., page 30.
37   Ibid., page 34.
38   Ibid., pages 68–69.
39   Ibid., page 55.
40   Ibid., pages 96–97.
41   Ibid., page 272.
42   Ibid., page 123.

Chapter 6: Landmark 3 – Transforming Experiences

1   Nelson Mandela (1994) *Long Walk to Freedom: The Autobiography of Nelson Mandela*, London: Little Brown, page 3. The Transkei is part of South Africa.
2   Ibid., page 5.
3   Ibid., pages 15–16. Mandela does not tell us what his original Xhosa name was.
4   Ibid., pages 40–41.
5   Ibid., page 44.
6   Ibid., page 45.
7   Ibid., pages 49–50.
8   Ibid., pages 65–70.
9   Ibid., pages 97–98.
10   Ibid., page 109.
11   www.ft.com/content/9981c870-e79a-11e6-967b-c88452263daf
12   Stone, op. cit., pages 34–35.
13   Ibid., pages 36–37.
14   Ibid., pages 38–39.
15   Victor Sebestyen (2017) *Lenin the Dictator: An Intimate Portrait*, London: Weidenfeld & Nicolson, pages 47–8.
16   Ibid., page 58.
17   John Campbell (2009) *The Iron Lady: Margaret Thatcher: From Grocer's Daughter to Iron Lady*, abridgement into one volume by David Freeman, London: Vintage, page 11.
18   Margaret Thatcher (1995) *The Path to Power*, London: HarperCollins, page 66.
19   Ibid., page 22.
20   Ibid., page 23.
21   Jonathan Aitken (2013) *Margaret Thatcher: Power and Personality*, London: Bloomsbury, page 177.
22   Ibid., page 177.
23   Campbell, op. cit., page 78.

24   David Cannadine (2017) *Margaret Thatcher: A Life and Legacy*, Oxford: Oxford University Press, pages 23–25.

25   Ibid., pages 28–32, 39–40.

26   Aitken, op. cit., pages 314–317.

27   Charles Moore (2013) *Margaret Thatcher: The Authorized Biography: Volume One*, London: Penguin, page 638.

28   Lawrence Freedman (2005) *The Official History of the Falklands Campaign*, London: Routledge, Volume I, page 207.

29   Moore, op. cit., page 666.

30   Ibid., page 667.

31   Ibid., page 673.

32   Campbell, op. cit., page 194.

33   Moore, op. cit., especially pages 682–704.

34   Campbell, op. cit., page 195.

35   Moore, op. cit., pages 681–682.

36   Cannadine, op. cit., page 49.

37   Quoted in Moore, op. cit., page 753.

38   Ibid., pages 753–4.

39   Ibid., page 754.

40   Campbell, op. cit., page 203.

41   Walter Kiechel III (2010) *The Lords of Strategy: The Secret Intellectual History of the New Corporate World*, Boston: Harvard Business Press, page 76.

42   Ibid., page 78.

43   Ibid., pages 60–66.

44   The most reliable (although not infallible) source is Lindy Woodhead (2003) *War Paint: Miss Elizabeth Arden and Madame Helena Rubinstein*, London: Virago, who says that she opened in 1903 in a small suite of rooms at 138 Elizabeth Street, Melbourne, and moved the following year to 242 Collins Street – see pages 50–52. I have drawn more details from Michèle Fitoussi (2010, 2012) *Helena Rubinstein: The Woman who Invented Beauty*, Paris/London: Bernard Grasset/Gallic Books, and from other sources. Both are excellent books.

45   Kiechel, op. cit., page 20.

46   Ibid., pages 14–17.

47   Ibid., pages 19–20, and more particularly personal experience at BCG.

48   Isaacson, *Leonardo da Vinci*, op. cit., pages 48–49 – see the magnificent illustration of *Tobias and the Angel* by Verrocchio and Leonardo on page 49.

49   Sean Smith (2001) *J. K. Rowling: A Biography*, London: Michael O'Mara, pages 81–82.

50   See Isaacson, *Einstein*, op. cit., pages 107–133, especially 122–124.

51   Ibid., page 140.

52   Ruth Picardie, 'Here Comes the New Lass', *Arena*, Summer 1995.

53   See particularly the brilliant book by Georges-Claude Guilbert (2002)

Madonna as Postmodern Myth, Jefferson: North Carolina: McFarland & Company.

54   Douglas Thompson (1991) *Madonna Revealed*, London: Warner Books, page 54.

55   Though Erasure had made it before Madonna started producing them.

56   'The reasonable man adapts himself to the world: the unreasonable man persists in trying to adapt the world to himself. Therefore all progress depends upon the unreasonable man.'
https://www.goodreads.com/quotes/536961

Chapter 7: Landmark 4 – One Breakthrough Achievement

1   Stone, op. cit., pages 414–416.
2   Ibid., pages 565–567.
3   We only have a draft of the letter from Leonardo's notebooks. See Isaacson, *Leonardo da Vinci*, op. cit., page 1.
4   Viktor E. Frankl, Preface to 1984 edition of *Man's Search for Freedom*, New York: Touchstone.
5   Tom Butler-Bowden (2017) *50 Economics Classics*, London: Nicholas Brealey, page 131.
6   A. J. P. Taylor (1955) *Bismarck*, London: Hamish Hamilton, pages 64 and 53 respectively.
7   Ibid., pages 60 and 70.
8   Ibid., page 64.
9   'I was conscious of a profound sense of walking with destiny': Winston Churchill (1948, 2008) *The Gathering Storm – Volume I of The History of The Second World War*, London: Penguin, pages 526–527.
10   Quoted in Martin Gilbert (1981) *Winston Churchill: The Wilderness Years*, London: Book Club Associates/Macmillan, pages 54–55.
11   Ibid., page 60.
12   Ibid., page 62.
13   Margaret Thatcher (1993) *The Downing Street Years*, London: HarperCollins, page 10.
14   The phrase used by Thatcher about Mikhail Gorbachev in the late 1980s, before the collapse of the Soviet Union. She could have equally used the phrase about Mandela, and perhaps did. For all her hatred of socialism and communism (with which Mandela was allied) Thatcher was pragmatic about pragmatic people, and one of the first to realise that these two 'enemies' could become friends.
15   The first of these was a visit from a troika of judges in the middle of 1971 – see Mandela, op. cit., pages 547–549.
16   After all, both the ANC and the government had perpetrated appalling acts of violence already, and the rhetoric on both sides was that they were

justified and would continue the war until it was won. Most of us may think the ANC was justified and the Nationalists were not, but that does not alter the reality – there was no compromise envisaged on either side, and the potential human cost was horrendous. The battle was unequal, because, at least in the short term, the government held most of the cards. It was the huge achievement of Mandela and F. W. de Klerk to do a deal for peace, and believe it would be honoured by the other side. I hope they were right, not just for a few years, but for the long term. As I write, that is far from assured.

Chapter 8: Landmark 5 – Make Your Own Trail

1 Stone, op. cit., page 72.
2 Ibid., page 74.
3 Ibid., page 97.
4 Ibid., page 117.
5 Gabler, op. cit., page 415.
6 Ibid., page 481.
7 Tom Cannon (2000) *The Ultimate Book of Business Breakthroughs: Lessons from the 20 Greatest Business Decisions Ever Made*, Oxford: Capstone, pages 221–237.
8 Marilyn Bailey Ogilvie (2004) *Marie Curie: A Biography*, Westport CT: Greenwood Press, pages 3–4.
9 Eva Curie (1937, 1940) *Madame Curie: A Biography*, Garden City NY: Garden City Publishing, page 23.
10 Ibid., page 9.
11 Ibid., page 95.
12 Bailey Ogilvie, op. cit., page 24.
13 Eva Curie, op. cit., page 106.
14 Ibid., page 107.
15 Bailey Ogilvie, op. cit., page xiii.
16 Eva Curie, op. cit., pages 121–137.
17 Bailey Ogilvie, op. cit., pages 29–30.
18 Ibid., page 38. Some examples of married scientific teams of the period are Annie and Walter Maunder, and Margaret and William Huggins (both couples were British astronomers), Anne Botsford Comstock and John Henry Comstock (American naturalists), Cecile Mugnier Vogt and Oskar Vogt (French neurologists), and Hertha Marks Ayrton and W. E. Ayrton (British physicists).
19 Einstein's discovery process is brilliantly described in Isaacson, *Einstein*, op. cit., pages 94–101.
20 Bailey Ogilvie, op. cit., pages 43–48.
21 Marie Curie (1923) *Pierre Curie*, New York: Macmillan, page 180.

22   This is explained very well in Bailey Ogilvie, op. cit., pages 47–50.
23   Eva Curie, op. cit., page 157.
24   Marie Curie, op. cit., page 1.
25   Bailey Ogilvie, op. cit., pages 51–52.
26   Ibid., page 52.
27   *Marie Curie – Research Breakthroughs (1897–1904) Part 2n*, American Institute of Physics.
28   L. Pearce Williams (1986) *Curie, Pierre and Marie*, Encyclopedia Americana, Volume 8, Danbury CT: Grolier, page 332.
29   Eva Curie, op. cit., page 199.
30   Cannadine, op. cit., page 93.
31   Ibid., page 94.
32   Ibid., also page 94.
33   Ibid., page 106.
34   Ibid., page 629.
35   Richard Stengel (2010) *Nelson Mandela: Portrait of an Extraordinary Man*, New York: Crown, page 5.
36   Ibid., pages 7–8.
37   Mandela, op. cit., pages 625–6.
38   Ibid., page 627.
39   Ibid., page 630.
40   Ibid., pages 749 and 751.

Chapter 9: Landmark 6 – Find and Drive Your Personal Vehicle

1   Victoria Peterson-Hilleque (1971) *J. K. Rowling, Extraordinary Author*, Edina, Minnesota: ABDO Publishing Company, page 20.
2   Quotes are from ibid., also page 20.
3   Isaacson, *Steve Jobs*, op. cit., page 219.
4   Sebestyen, op. cit., page 136.
5   V. I. Lenin (1902, 1961, 2014) *What Is To Be Done? – Burning Questions of Our Movement*, New York: International Publishers.
6   Ibid., page 139.
7   Ibid., page 149.
8   Ibid., also page 149.
9   Ibid., page 139.
10   Stengel, op. cit., page 15.
11   Ibid., also page 15.
12   Ibid., page 16.
13   Frankl, op. cit., page 136.
14   Ibid., page 144.
15   Hans Jonas (1958, 1963) *The Gnostic Religion: The Message of the Alien God and the Beginnings of Christianity*, Boston: Beacon Press, page 145; Jason D

BeDuhn (2013) *The First New Testament: Marcion's Scriptural Canon*, Salem, Oregon: Polebridge Press, which reconstructs Marcion's entire canon.

16 The best introductions to Marcion are Jonas, op. cit., pages 137–146, Adolf Harnack (1923, 1924) *Marcion: The Gospel of the Alien God*, Eugene, Oregon: Wipf and Stock, and Robert Smith Wilson (1933) *Marcion: A Study of a Second-Century Heretic*, London: James Clarke. See also Elaine Pagels (1975, 1992) *The Gnostic Paul: Gnostic exegesis of the Pauline letters*, London: Continuum.

Chapter 10: Landmark 7 – Thrive on Setbacks

1   Jenkins, op. cit., page 249.
2   Ibid., pages 250–251.
3   Roberts, op. cit., pages 208, 228.
4   Jenkins, op. cit., page 277.
5   Ibid., page 293.
6   Cannadine, op. cit., page 103.
7   Jenkins, op. cit., page 466.
8   Quoted in Gilbert (1981), op. cit., page 267.
9   Roberts, op. cit., page 534.
10 Nassim Nicholas Taleb (2013) *Anti-fragile: Things That Gain from Disorder*, London: Penguin, page 3.
11 Ibid., page 185.
12 Ibid., footnote on page 181; see also text on pages 180–1.
13 Isaacson, *Steve Jobs*, op. cit., page 219.
14 Ibid., page 234.
15 Ibid., page 229.
16 Ibid., page 334.
17 Isaacson, *Leonardo da Vinci*, op. cit., page 68.
18 A. L. Rowse (1977) *Homosexuals in History: A Study of Ambivalence in Society, Literature and the Arts*, New York: Carroll & Graf, page 14. Rowse says two months, though no evidence for this is cited.
19 *Leonardo da Vinci Notebooks*, J. P. Richter, pages 132, 135, quoted in Isaacson, *Leonardo da Vinci*, op. cit., page 69.
20 A. L. Rowse, op. cit., page 14.
21 Ibid., pages 14–15; Isaacson, *Leonardo da Vinci*, pages 68–72.
22 Ibid., page 89. See also Greene, op. cit., page 23.
23 Isaacson, *Leonardo da Vinci*, op. cit., page 89.
24 Greene, op. cit., page 23.
25 Caroline Moss (2019) *Work it, Girl: J K Rowling*, London: Quarto, page 22.
26 Smith, op. cit., page 108.
27 Moss, op. cit., pages 28–29.
28 Cannon, op. cit., pages 220–226.

29 'Counselor to the King', *The New York Times Magazine*, September 24, 1989, Section 6, page 18.
30 Paul's letter to the Galatians 3:28.

Chapter 11: Landmark 8 – Acquire Unique Intuition

1 Isaacson, *Einstein*, op. cit., page 113.
2 Max Gunther (1985) *The Zurich Axioms*, London: Souvenir Press, pages 103–4.
3 Quoted in Robert Tombs (2014, 2015) *The English and Their History*, London: Allen Lane/Penguin, page 679.
4 Ibid., page 677.
5 Ibid., pages 677–8.
6 Ibid., page 680.
7 Roberts, *Churchill*, op. cit., page 397.
8 Churchill to the House of Commons, April 1936, quoted in ibid., page 397.
9 Ibid., page 399.
10 Ibid., page 426.
11 Tombs, op. cit., page 681.
12 Ibid., page 681.
13 Ibid., page 399.
14 Peter Hain (2018) *Mandela: His Essential Life*, London: Rowman & Littlefield, page 125.
15 Ibid., page 118.
16 Mandela, op. cit., page 611.
17 Hain, op. cit., pages 126–7.
18 Ibid., page 127.
19 Ibid., page 127.
20 Ibid., page 127.
21 Ibid., page 131.
22 Mandela, op. cit., pages 657–660.
23 Volker Ullrich (1998, 2008) *Bismarck: The Iron Chancellor*, London: Haus Publishing, page 88.
24 Ibid., page 116.
25 Isaacson, *Einstein*, op. cit., pages 122–124.
26 Ibid., page 127.
27 Greene, op. cit., page 257.
28 Bailey Ogilvie, op. cit., page 138.
29 See Smith, op. cit., pages 81–82; Peterson-Hilleque, op. cit., pages 38–40; Lindsay Fraser (2000) *Conversations with J. K. Rowling*, New York: Scholastic, pages 37–38.
30 Quoted in Nancy C. Andreasen (2005) *The Creative Brain*, New York: Plume, page 21.

31 Ibid., pages 40–41.
32 Ibid., pages 41–46. The Tchaikovsky extract is on page 42.

Chapter 12: Landmark 9 – Distort Reality

1   Isaacson, *Steve Jobs*, op. cit., pages 117–118.
2   Ibid., pages 160, 123.
3   Ibid., page 123.
4   Ibid., page 161.
5   Ibid., page 161.
6   Ibid., page 474.
7   Ibid., pages 471–472.
8   Matthew 25:29.
9   Jenkins, op. cit., page 588.
10 Winston Churchill (1948, 2005) *The Gathering Storm*, op. cit., pages 526–527.
11 *Churchill War Papers,* Volume II, page 22.
12 Hugh Dalton and Ben Pimlott (1986) *The Second World War Diary of Hugh Dalton 1940–45*, London: Jonathan Cape, page 28.
13 Jenkins, op. cit., pages 589–590.
14 Ibid., page 591.
15 Paul's letter to the Galatians 2:20.

Chapter 15: Transforming Experiences

1   Brainyquote.com

Chapter 16: One Breakthrough Achievement

1   The Bismarck reference is from A. J. P. Taylor, op. cit., page 70.

Index